Heritage, Nationhood, and Language

The notion of "heritage" has become one of the global tropes in recent years. At the heart of heritage politics are three questions: what heritage is, who decides what it is, and for whom is the decision made. However, existing work on heritage language has rarely tackled these questions, assuming that teaching children of migrants their "heritage language" empowers them. We challenge this assumption, situating the notion of heritage language in the host society's involvement in social justice, nation-building efforts, (superficial) celebration of diversity, and investment on global links the migrants offer as well as the migrants' fear of discrimination and desire for belonging, social status, and economic gain. Based on ethnographic research in Bolivia, Peru, the United States, and Japan, we illuminate the complexity and political nature of determining what constitutes heritage language for migrants with connections to Japan. The articles in this volume open up a new field of investigation in heritage language studies: the complex linkage between heritage language and social justice for migrants.

The articles in this book were published in two issues of *Critical Asian Studies* in 2010: Vol. 42, No. 1 (March) and Vol. 42, No. 2 (June).

Neriko Musha Doerr received a PhD in cultural anthropology from Cornell University. She currently teaches cultural anthropology at Ramapo College (Mahwah, N.J.). Her recent publications include *Meaningful Inconsistencies: Bicultural Nationhood, Free Market, and Schooling in Aotearoa/New Zealand* (Berghahn Books, 2009; *The Native Speaker Concept: Ethnographic Investigations of Native Speaker Effects* (Mouton de Gruyter 2009; (as the editor), "Global Structures of Common Difference, Cultural Objectification, and their Subversions: Cultural Politics in an Aotearoa/New Zealand School" (in the journal *Identities: Global Studies in Culture and Power*).

HERITAGE, NATIONHOOD, AND LANGUAGE

Migrants with Japan Connections

Edited by Neriko Musha Doerr

LONDON AND NEW YORK

First published 2011 by Routledge
2 Park Square, Milton Park, Abingdon, Oxfordshire OX14 4RN

Simultaneously published in the USA and Canada
by Routledge
711 Third Avenue, New York, NY 10017

First issued in paperback 2014

Routledge is an imprint of the Taylor and Francis Group, an informa business

© 2011 BCAS, Inc.

The articles in this book were published in two issues of *Critical Asian Studies* in 2010: Vol. 42, No. 1 (March) and Vol. 42, No. 2 (June). The Publisher requests to those authors who may be citing this book to state, also, the bibliographical details of the issues of *Critical Asian Studies* on which the book is based.

Typeset in Garamond in the USA by BCAS, Inc.

All rights reserved. No part of this book may be reprinted or reproduced or utilised in any form or by any electronic, mechanical, or other means, now known or hereafter invented, including photocopying and recording, or in any information storage or retrieval system, without permission in writing from the publishers.

British Library Cataloguing in Publication Data
A catalogue record for this book is available from the British Library

ISBN 978-0-415-61213-5 (hbk)
ISBN 978-1-138-88038-2 (pbk)

Disclaimer
The publisher would like to make readers aware that the chapters in this book are referred to as articles as they had been in their original form in *Critical Asian Studies*. The publisher accepts responsibility for any inconsistencies that may have arisen in the course of preparing this volume for print.

Contents

Abstracts — vii

Introduction. Heritage, Nationhood, and Language: Migrants with Japan Connections — 1
    Neriko Musha Doerr

1. Learning to Be Transnational: Japanese Language Education for Bolivia's Okinawan Diaspora — 7
    Taku Suzuki

2. Conflicted Attitudes toward Heritage: Heritage Language Learning of Returnee Adolescents from Japan at a Nikkei School in Lima, Peru — 25
    Yuri Yamasaki

3. Heritage: Owned or Assigned? The Cultural Politics of Teaching Heritage Language in Osaka, Japan — 43
    Yuko Okubo

4. Inheriting "Japanese-ness" Diversely: Heritage Practices at a Weekend Japanese Language School in the United States — 64
    Neriko Musha Doerr and Kiri Lee

5. Rethinking Japanese American "Heritage" in the Homeland — 85
    Ayako Takamori

6. Afterword: Japan-Related Linguistic Intervention — 103
    Laura Miller

7. Afterword: Cross-Cultural Implications of Japanese Heritage Language Policies and Practices — 109
    Krista E. Van Vleet

8. Afterword: Dreaming in…English? The Complexity and Unexpectedness of Japanese Being and Becoming through Language — 117
    Barbra A. Meek

Notes — 124
References — 141
Contributors — 161
Index — 163

Abstracts

Introduction. Heritage, Nationhood, and Language: Migrants with Japan Connections

Neriko Musha Doerr

The latter half of the twentieth century saw the notion of "heritage" become one of the critical global tropes, through which many have voiced their preoccupations and aspirations. At the heart of heritage politics are three questions: what heritage is, who decides what it is, and for whom is the decision made. Researchers on heritage language education have rarely asked these questions. Determining what constitutes one's "heritage language" is a complex effort; for migrants, claiming which language is their heritage language can also be a political statement. Based on ethnographic research in Bolivia, Peru, the United States, and Japan, the articles in this volume, "Heritage, Nationhood, and Language," investigate diverse subjectivities of migrants with connections to Japan and analyze the processes by which they negotiate, contest, support, and rupture the notion of heritage. The authors examine the disjunctures between the notion of social justice and the experiences of empowerment and marginalization among these migrants. This volume sheds light on the conditions, processes, and effects of a particular language becoming one's "heritage." Intersecting factors that influence the ways a language becomes one's "heritage" include a desire for belonging, a drive for social status, aspirations for economic gain, fear and guilt about discrimination, and an obligation and hope for social justice. This introduction outlines the historical and theoretical backgrounds to the subject and introduces the main arguments of the articles in this collection.

1. Learning to Be Transnational: Japanese Language Education for Bolivia's Okinawan Diaspora

Taku Suzuki

Scholars and practitioners of heritage language education commonly hold two assumptions about heritage language: first, that heritage language is an official national language of a nation-state from which group originally migrated; and second, that heritage language is a vulnerable language on the verge of being eliminated by the national language of the nation-state of a migrant's current residence. This article questions these two assumptions by examining

Japanese language education and speech practices among Okinawan-Bolivians in a rural agricultural community called Colonia Okinawa. Okinawan-Bolivians' heritage language education and speech practices suggest that immigrants who were marginalized in the nation-states of their migratory/ancestral origin, like Okinawans, consciously transform their linguistic heritage from a sub-national one to a national one in order to gain socioeconomic advantages in their migratory destination. Furthermore, when immigrant community leaders deem the international standing of the country of their migratory origin higher than their host country's status, such as Okinawan-Bolivian leaders in Colonia Okinawa, they regard heritage language education as a crucial means to maintain their community members' political, economic, and symbolic powers over other local residents. By ethnographically portraying the ways in which Japanese is taught and spoken in Colonia Okinawa, this article highlights the shifting scales and locations of the immigrant community's "ancestral homeland" and draws attention to the multiple meanings of the language the community designates as its "heritage."

2. Conflicted Attitudes toward Heritage: Heritage Language Learning of Returnee Adolescents from Japan at a Nikkei School in Lima, Peru

Yuri Yamasaki

During their more than 100-year-long presence in Peru, Japanese descendants (Nikkei) have been linguistically integrated into Peruvian society. The portion of the population that speaks Japanese in daily life has been decreasing dramatically, and the majority of younger Nikkei typically grow up speaking mainly Spanish, mixed with a specific Japanese lexicon that has been transmitted intergenerationally within families. To prevent the complete loss of ancestral language and cultural traits, private all-day elementary and secondary schools, founded and run by the Nikkei, have been offering additional Japanese language educational programs. Drawing from an ethnographic study at one such Nikkei-sponsored secondary school in Lima, this article portrays the students' inconsistent and ambiguous attitudes toward learning Japanese as their heritage. More specifically, the article focuses on returnee students from Japan, a recently emerged diaspora group of youngsters who have spent time in Japan as emigrants and then returned to resettle in Peru. The article examines the returnees' negotiations with the language teachers regarding what is considered to be "proper" or "standard" Japanese. Classroom observations and interviews with both teachers and students demonstrate how contested the "heritage" of heritage language education is — defined as it is through social, economic, and political positions and interests of participants in the educational process. The study also shows how the institutionalized heritage language education at school sometimes results in encouraging the students to "dis-inherit" what they have learned outside school: this may relate to their family's social status in their ancestral country.

3. Heritage: Owned or Assigned? The Cultural Politics of Teaching Heritage Language in Osaka, Japan

Yuko Okubo

Teaching heritage language is regarded as an act of social justice, but under what conditions and in what context? This article examines the educational practice of introducing heritage language to Chinese return-migrant children and Japan-born Vietnamese children. The language programs under investigation are conducted in a community education center and in an after-school setting in a public elementary school in a multiethnic neighborhood in Osaka, Japan. This study demonstrates how the local community's practice of heritage language learning dissolves the boundaries among ethnic minorities, bringing together all participants and cutting across ethnic lines. The result is empowering, but with a limited effect. At the same time, the institutionalized practice of heritage language learning at school becomes a marker for ethnic minorities and is used to maintain the boundary between ethnic minorities and Japanese, despite official discourses of minority education for empowerment. Ethnographic data show discrepancies between the views of teachers and communities about what ethnic minorities should be like and what they are hoping to find in Japan. The politics of heritage involves the legitimization of power and distinction, as well as the exclusion of those who do not have access to heritage. Situating each case within the politics of heritage, schooling, and Japan's multicultural initiatives, this article examines what is legitimized and what is excluded through teaching and learning heritage language in both cases and discusses the implications of heritage language teaching for immigrant children in Japan.

4. Inheriting "Japanese-Ness" Diversely: Heritage Practices at a Weekend Japanese Language School in the United States

Neriko Musha Doerr and Kiri Lee

The late twentieth century saw a rise of global discourse about heritage. Research on heritage politics, however, has shed little light on heritage practices in schools, especially regarding language, that is, how *heritage* language is constructed and how it is "inherited" by students of various backgrounds. Heritage language education is often viewed as a means to empower heritage language speakers or to address the diverse needs of students in language classes. In existing works, the individual's link to "heritage" is assumed as given and stable. More recent works show that the processes and effects of heritage language education are complex and nuanced due to diverse personal backgrounds and changing political economy and cultural politics. The role of schooling in the process of "inheriting" language, however, has not attracted much attention: how students are grouped or tracked into a particular class, for example. After ethnographically investigating various views and practices at a weekend Japanese language school in the northeastern United States throughout 2007 and 2008, the authors of this article argue that heritage language school is not merely a place to reproduce "heritage" by passing it on to students, but it is also a *productive* site where ways to imagine "heritage" and "inherit" it proliferate. The article analyzes the processes by which what would be considered as merely "speaking Japanese" and "being Japanese" outside heritage language school are differentiated into diverse ways of being Japanese. It suggests a need to investigate school as a site of heritage politics as well as a need for researchers and practitioners to view heritage language education not only as a way to teach language but also as a means to gain an understanding of heritage politics.

5. Rethinking Japanese American "Heritage" in the Homeland

Ayako Takamori

In the United States, where language is an important arena of struggle for cultural and political activists, heritage language education is seen as vital for empowering students with a sense of cultural identity as they face pressures to assimilate. This article attempts to rethink reclamations of "heritage" through language and, more generally, the relationship between heritage language and identity. Japanese American ethnic identity is developed outside the context of the imagined "ethnic homeland." Return-migration, however, reconstructs the relationship between language, place, and identity. For Japanese Americans residing in Japan, then, Japanese as a heritage language becomes a newly fraught site of cultural negotiation. Drawing on ethnographic case studies, this article makes three arguments about how expectations of communicative competence shape experiences of being Japanese American in Japan. First, the significance of speaking a heritage language is contextually specific, differing according to the historical experiences of particular ethnic communities and the national (or transnational) location where a heritage language is spoken. Second, while activists have made great strides in reforming U.S. curricula to be more inclusive, in the case of Japanese Americans, the multiculturalist assumption that ethnic minorities should learn heritage languages to maintain their ethnic affiliation unintentionally plays into Japanese nationalist language ideologies. That is, it reinforces the cultural distance and non-belonging of Japanese American heritage language speakers in Japanese society. Finally, this article suggests that Japanese Americans residing in Japan are construed as uncanny contradictions of "Japanese-ness," destabilizing assumptions about the inalienability of language and identity through everyday speech acts and practices.

6. Afterword. Japan-Related Linguistic Intervention

Laura Miller

In this commentary on articles published in *Heritage, Nationhood, and Language: Japanese Connections,* the author observes that languages we speak are "often the product of historical, sociopolitical, and socioeconomic trends, accidents, and forces. They are insufficient to completely define or enclose our identities." Thus, the author wonders, can any language be said to be "the best, most perfect one for any of us?"

7. Afterward. Cross-Cultural Implications of Japanese Heritage Language

Krista E. Van Vleet

Scholars of regions where multiple languages are spoken have much to gain by considering heritage language education, individual identity, and state power through these ethnographic and historical cases that focus on Japan and the Japanese diaspora. The articles in this volume offer insights into the interrelationships of linguistic hierarchies and political economy, the navigation of ethnic and racial subjectivities, and the ways children and adolescents claim belonging to various communities through their linguistic practices. The articles interrogate not only heritage but remembrance and the ways individuals may produce identity through language in everyday interactions and institutional settings.

8. Afterword. Dreaming in…English? The Complexity and Unexpectedness of Japanese Being and Becoming through Language

Barbra A. Meek

Focusing on the articles in this issue by Doerr and Lee and by Takamori, this commentary asks what it means to identify some languages as heritage languages and others as not, and considers the various social processes, contexts, and ideologies that mediate the ways in which we go about doing so. The goal is to further draw out the complexities and the contradictions embedded in such processes of identification, both of and through language, as illustrated by these authors.

❏

Introduction

Heritage, Nationhood, and Language: Migrants with Japan Connections

Neriko Musha Doerr

THE LATTER HALF OF THE TWENTIETH CENTURY saw the notion of "heritage" become one of the critical global tropes through which many have voiced their preoccupations and aspirations.[1] Three developments regarding heritage have influenced the relationships between groups within and across nation-states: (1) Unesco's "world heritage" designation, which raises the status of those who have been awarded its designation (the social status of outcaste religious practitioners [shamans], for instance, was elevated once they were given the "world heritage" designation); (2) the emergence and growth of "heritage tourism" as a local industry; and (3) the development of heritage language educational programs for linguistically minority groups. At the heart of heritage politics are three questions that have rarely been asked: What is heritage? Who decides what it is? And for whom is the decision made.[2] The articles in this book address these questions through ethnographic investigations of the politics of heritage language education, education grounded in a concern for social justice for linguistically minority groups. The articles examine the disjunctures between the notion of social justice and the experiences of empowerment and marginalization among migrants with connections to Japan in the context of Japan's changing cultural politics as well as its position in the world.

Earlier studies of heritage typically focused on issues related to the representation of heritage in museum exhibitions[3] and in so-called heritage tourism.[4] Relationships between heritage and nationalism were also analyzed.[5] In these contexts, heritage was often objectified: those involved in the heritage industry, such as museum curators and tourist industry personnel, took aspects of the social world such as cuisine and religious practices and interpreted these as typifying the totality. These they represented as detached, object-like "traits" that the bearers of a particular heritage were believed to possess.[6] In recent studies, heritage has been understood as an assemblage of multivocal processes that involve various social actors and institutions, all making claims on ownership, custodianship, and cultural inheritance of the heritage. These claims involve contestations regarding land tenure and property ownership, social codes of behavior for locals and visitors, archaeological science, and ideologies of nationalism, ethnicity, and development.[7] At stake in heritage-related practices is the government of values and meanings associated with a particular "heritage," so that the memories and knowledge of the "holders" of the heritage are (re)shaped to make sense of the present.[8]

Heritage has been defined as a collection of practices that transform the relationship between individuals and what they do, awakening in them a metacultural awareness about their daily lives. Discussing the processes and effects of Unesco's World Heritage designation, Barbara Kirshenblatt-Gimblett argues that when heritage professionals bring cultural phenomena and practitioners into the heritage sphere by valorizing, regulating, and instrumentalizing them, they transform the relationships between the cultural phenomena and their practitioners such as performers, ritual specialists, and artisans. Such heritage interventions change how people understand their culture and themselves, and they alter the fundamental conditions for cultural production and reproduction.[9]

Similarly, naming a language one's "heritage" changes an individual's relationship with his/her linguistic practices, other individuals, and an imagined ancestral homeland. Determining what constitutes one's "native language," "mother tongue," or "heritage language" is a complex process. Tove Skutnabb-Kangas and Robert Phillipson suggest four possible definitions of "mother tongue": (1) the language(s) one learns first; (2) the language(s) one knows best; (3) the language(s) one uses most; and (4) the language(s) one identifies with most. Thus, one person may have different languages as one's mother tongues, depending on which definition is used.[10]

Recent scholarship also challenges the stable and taken-for-granted relationship of an individual to a homogeneous language inherent in the notion of "native speaker."[11] Articles in this book show that, for migrants, claiming which language is their "mother tongue" or "heritage language" is often a political statement. For example, Taku Suzuki vividly illustrates in his article that for Okinawan immigrants in Bolivia to identify with the Japanese language as their "heritage language" allows them to capitalize on the position of Japan on the global stage.[12] Ayako Takamori's article shows that for Japanese Americans in Japan to claim Japanese as their mother tongue (by speaking it well) serves to make them responsible for their actions as "Japanese" rather than as foreign visitors or migrants.[13] Yuko Okubo's article in this issue illustrates how some minority groups in Japan fear being openly assigned minority status and associated with marginalized languages as their "heritage language" because this marks them as different and makes them targets of discriminatory actions.[14]

The complex links between an individual and his/her "heritage language" (hereafter with no quotation marks) are not addressed in the existing studies of heritage language education. Emerging in the late 1970s as a new label for minority language education,[15] heritage language education[16] challenges the power relations between speakers of the dominant language and those of minority languages.[17] Joshua Fishman argues that "promoting heritage language proficiency...will not only give us more individuals proficient in these languages, it will also dignify our country's heritage language communities and the cultural and religious values that their languages represent."[18]

Research on heritage language education with minority language students has assumed that teaching heritage language constitutes an antihegemonic act of social justice.[19] But the articles in this book question this assumption that heritage language education is in itself an antihegemonic process. More specifically, we are interested in who decides what heritage is, whose heritage it is, for whom it is considered heritage, and in what contexts.

What are the implications of calling a certain language a "heritage"? Does the act of "inheriting" language produce the heritage itself? What are the different consequences when a language taught to immigrant children is called their heritage language and when it is called their mother tongue? What are the effects of teaching a heritage language to children of racially and/or nationally mixed descent? What gives rise to a people's urge to inculcate a heritage language in the younger generation? What kind of cultural politics does the idea of heritage language give rise to? What conditions spawn the view that teaching heritage language to immigrants' children is an act of social justice? Based on ethnographic research in various contexts — Bolivia, Peru, the United States, and Japan — articles in this book explore these questions and investigate contextual and contested practices of "inheriting" language by migrants who are, in various ways, "connected" to Japan.

Language and Nation-States

In the modern world, made up of a jigsaw puzzle of nation-states, a nation is imagined as a linguistically and culturally homogeneous unit that is defined in relation to other nations.[20] In late-eighteenth-century Germany, Johann Gottfried von Herder argued that each nation was set off by the "natural" characteristics of language and the intangible quality of a specific *Volkgeist*. The possession of its own distinctive language constitutes the touchstone of a people, or *Volk*, what is essential to its "national identity and spirit." Herder argued that a Volk, a nation, a culture, and a polity must be homogeneous and that cultural and linguistic diversity within a nation is unnatural and potentially destructive. However, Herder was in fact not so much describing the contemporary situation as contributing to the *creation* of the Volk. His idea was a model *for* the nation rather than model *of* the nation, creating a myth of one-nation, one-language in the nation-state. Herder's view also influenced the study of linguistics, such as Ferdinand de Saussure's structural linguistics.[21] Researchers of nation-states also note the importance of language as a metaphor for "nation." Etienne Balibar argues that language can provide a group of people with a meaning for their continued existence, and a shared language makes it possible for "people" to be represented as an autonomous unit.[22]

Linguistic diversity, if recognized, was supposed to disappear through the standardization processes within a nation-state. Pierre Bourdieu argues that a hierarchy among linguistic varieties emerges as the state imposes on its citizens an official language as the only legitimate one. This standardization establishes a "linguistic community," in which the common recognition of the legitimacy of the standard occurs while access to that language remains uneven. The language chosen as the standard gains symbolic capital through a unified education system that teaches it as the only legitimate language, a unified labor market that receives a labor force differentiated by the education system, and a perceived connection between the standard language and social qualities such as moral rectitude, civilization, and education.[23]

Language ideologies facilitate such a process of standardization by underpinning linguistic forms and uses as well as the very notion of personhood and social groups.[24] The language ideology of standardization organizes regional variation in language into hierarchical standard–dialect relationships and discourages the maintenance of minority languages.[25] Political authorities tend to be suspicious of multilingualism as they view multiple languages as multiple loyalties and thus a temperamental flaw, a lack of trustworthiness.[26]

As the modern nation-state of Japan emerged in the late nineteenth century, standardization of the Japanese language became an issue. With the rise of nationalism in the post–Sino-Japan War (1894–1895) era, language standardization began to be carried out mainly through *kokugo* (national language; language arts) education. This process began in 1900, using Standard Japanese based on a linguistic variety used by educated people in Tokyo, Japan's capital city.[27]

In the latter half of the twentieth century, however, the notion of "one nation, one language" began to give way to new forms of nation-states in many parts of the world. Resurgences of minority groups within nation-states and the postcolonial movements in the 1960s introduced the politics of difference, pushing for political orders that recognize cultural and linguistic differences of minority groups rather than suppress them.[28] Globalization processes in various domains changed the shape and meaning of nation-states, making it difficult to assume territorially bounded and stable nation-states.[29] The reconfiguration of world alliances after the cold war, especially the emergence of new nation-states, also encouraged nation-states to allow minority groups to express their cultural differences rather than risk potential political secession.[30]

In the domain of language, calls to reverse the language shift of a marginalized minority language are viewed as more than a language issue: they are a matter of self-determination.[31] Maintaining minority languages, which results in bi/multilingualism, came to be viewed as an asset and/or a right rather than a problem[32] and the cognitive benefits of bi/multilingualism for the bi/multilingual speakers became evident.[33] Some linguistic human rights advocates insisted that individuals have a right to identify positively with their mother tongue and to have others respect that identification. In addition, advocates argue, linguistic groups have the right to develop an autonomous education in their own language.[34]

Heritage Practices of Migrants with Connections to Japan

Although the global shift in discourse from monolingualism to an increased support for multilingualism suggests that heritage language education is by nature an antihegemonic practice that empowers minority students, articles in this book present more complex, multifaceted, and contextually shifting effects of "inheriting language," situated in the language politics of particular national and local arenas. Suzuki's article illustrates the transformation of the conceptualization of ancestral homeland through standardization processes in the education of heritage language — Japanese — in an Okinawan settlement in Bolivia, in spite of decades of Okinawa's struggle against the cultural and political domination by mainland Japanese but in tune with the current position of Japan in Bolivia.[35] Yamasaki's article examines the contestation over what is considered to be "proper" Japanese between Japanese Peruvian students who have returned from Japan and teachers at a school that teaches Japanese as one subject in the regular curriculum in Peru.[36] Neriko Musha Doerr and Kiri Lee's article investigates the role of heritage language schooling in proliferating the imagining of the "heritage" — Japanese language — and ways of inheriting it in the United States.[37] These three articles show that maintenance of minority language can replicate standardizing processes, marginalizing the peripheral variety of the minority language. Okubo's article in this issue examines how, in the context of the monocultural language ideology in Japan, the multiculturalist discourse of nurturing heritage through teaching a heritage language results ironically in marking and marginalizing Chinese and Vietnamese immigrants in Japan.[38] Okubo's article, along with Suzuki's, shows how acquiring standard language and developing code-switching skills between the standard and minority language allows the minority group access to the "culture of power" and education and career opportunities in mainstream society.[39] Takamori's article illustrates the complex ways in which Japanese Americans who moved to Japan manipulate, are constrained by, and go along with the boundaries of heritage and alterity contextually.[40]

This book closes with Afterwords by Laura Miller, Krista Van Vleet, and Barbra Meek. Miller connects all of the chapters and situates them in the current understanding of language and the sense of self, linguistic diversity and standardization, and political economy and cultural politics. She points out the underlying complexity behind the migrants' act of forging relationships to "their language." Van Vleet situates the chapters on cross-cultural scholarship on language, such as Quechua speakers in the Andean region, in terms of (1) state power and language ideologies in the language hierarchy in multilingual situations, (2) expressions of "identity" through the use of language, and (3) the agency of children and the issue of socialization for migrants. Meek focuses on the latter half of the book — Takamori's and Doerr and Lee's chapters — and discusses them regarding language shift, language socialization, and sociolinguistic disjuncture. Meek situates these chapters' ethnographic attention in the "complications and the contradictions that arise in practices of choosing, labeling, and performing a singular heritage (and language)"[41] in existing research on heritage language, and points to further questions that need to be explored and more globally comparative works. These articles urge us to examine the conditions, processes, and effects of certain languages becoming one's "heritage" at the intersections of desires, fears, goodwill, guilt, and hopes.

The articles in this book investigate the complex ways in which heritage politics manifests itself through the learning of "heritage" languages, which involves personal investment of time, money, and effort as well as one's past personal connections, present interests, and future aspirations.[42] The complex ways in which heritage politics manifests itself are situated nonetheless in wider contexts of political economy, changing forms and meanings of nation-states, and global flows[43] and frictions[44] in various domains. The authors of these articles question and disrupt the assumption that nurturing heritage is an act of social justice. They do so through their ethnographic investigations of the diverse subjectivities of migrants and through their analyses of the processes by which the migrants negotiate, contest, support, and rupture the notion of heritage against the backdrop of the standardization of the Japanese language. Thus, the authors open up discussions of heritage politics and social justice among migrants with connections to Japan and beyond.

ACKNOWLEDGMENTS: This collection of works evolved from a session I and Michiyo Takato co-organized at the annual meeting of the American Anthropological Association in Washington, D.C., in November 2007. (The articles were guest-edited for *Critical Asian Studies* and for this book by myself alone.) I would like to express my appreciation to Michiyo Takato, with whom I developed the idea for this project and who commented on earlier drafts of this introduction. I also thank Taku Suzuki, Ayako Takamori, Yuko Okubo, and Laura Miller for their insightful comments on earlier drafts. I thank Christopher Doerr for proofreading and Tom Fenton for copy-editing, proofreading, and production. Any deficiency in this introduction is my responsibility.

❑

1. Learning to Be Transnational

Japanese Language Education for Bolivia's Okinawan Diaspora

Taku Suzuki

VARIOUS DEFINITIONS OF "HERITAGE LANGUAGE" and heritage language education notwithstanding, within the context of the United States and Canada, where the concepts were developed, heritage languages are typically defined as "the languages of immigrant, refugee, and indigenous groups… other than English."[1] Heritage language, encompassing both immigrant and indigenous languages, is the language "spoken in a community where that language is being replaced by a language of wider communication."[2] Heritage language education, its advocates argue, helps children and youth in non-majority-language–speaking minority groups within a state "feel connected to their roots, or…to participate more fully in the life of their [heritage linguistic and heritage cultural] community and contribute to the preservation of its beliefs and practices."[3] The concept of heritage language has gained acceptance among linguists and educators in Europe and Australia. In these regions, in which linguistic diversity is increasing due to the influx of new immigrant groups, the preservation and/or revitalization of distinct regional and indigenous languages that differ from the official national language has long been a crucial issue. (Examples include Corsican in France, Sámi in Norway, and aboriginal languages in Australia.)[4]

In these studies of heritage language and heritage language education, linguists typically understand heritage language education to be a defensive strategy that immigrant minority groups adopt in order to retain the "culture" and tradition of their ancestral homeland against the overwhelming pressure of linguistic, cultural, and identity assimilation in their host society. Heritage language education, it is expected, thus facilitates the formation of a strong sense of solidarity among these vulnerable communities; hence, the terms "community language" and "minoritized/minority language" are often used interchangeably for heritage language.[5] Along with other contributors in this volume, I challenge the underlying assumptions of heritage language scholars and practitioners that have shaped the definitions and significances of heritage language education.

Specifically, this article calls into question two popular assumptions regarding heritage language and heritage language education: First, that immigrant and refugee groups consider heritage language as an official language in the nation-state from which they emigrated. This belief collapses the "heritage" of heritage language into *national* heritage. Second, heritage language is a vulnerable language on the verge of getting swept away by the national language of the nation-state of their current residence. Joining the recent critiques of the North American– and English language–centered conceptualizations of heritage language and heritage language education,[6] this article challenges these assumptions in two ways. First, I contend that, while immigrant minority groups commonly choose the national language of their ancestral nation-state as their heritage language, this choice is far from an inevitable or "natural" one for the members of immigrant groups who were marginalized in the nation-states of their migratory/ancestral origin. The designation of heritage language for the immigrant groups and their native-born offspring could involve a transformation in their conceptualization of ancestral homeland from a sub-national territory to a national one. Heritage language education, in other words, involves a process of "nationalization" of the immigrant group's ancestral homeland, which takes place in the nation-state of their current residence. Second, I argue that heritage language education is not always a defensive strategy for immigrants and their offspring in the face of the host society's assimilating forces, since in certain circumstances heritage language can function as an effective means to symbolically express their power vis-à-vis the majority of the nation-state of their residence. In a host nation-state where possessing (real or imagined) transnational connections outside of its state borders is highly valued, teaching and learning the language of their ancestral origin constitutes a process of making and maintaining the boundary between the majority of the host nation-state and themselves by not only actively embodying and displaying their difference as being of foreign origin, but also by their economic and symbolic power implied by their (real or imagined) transnational connections to the nation-state of their origin.[7]

Drawing upon my field research on Japanese language education in an Okinawan immigrant settlement in rural Bolivia, this article explores the locally specific considerations behind the immigrants' heritage language education, in which the standardized Japanese language, the "national" heritage language of Okinawans, rather than the Okinawan language, or Uchināguchi,[8] which the majority of the immigrant generation had spoken most comfortably before and after the immigration to Bolivia, became their group's heritage language in Bolivia. Moreover, for affluent large-scale farm owners in rural Bolivia, who employ working-class Bolivians with no Japanese or Okinawan ancestry ("non-Nikkei Bolivians," hereafter) as farm laborers, their acts of learning and using standardized Japanese constitute what sociologist Pei-Chia Lan calls "boundary work," everyday practices that "weave institutional divisions and cognitive classification" between groups.[9] Their linguistic practices in Colonia Okinawa, whether within educational settings or in the community at large, were, consciously or not, an engagement in boundary work, a way they aligned themselves with or distinguished themselves from other groups.

My field research in Colonia Okinawa lasted from 1997 to 2001, but the bulk of information used in this essay comes from the eleven-month-long research I conducted from 2000 to 2001. During the course of my research, I was a volunteer teacher of Japanese language in two Colonia Okinawa schools, which nearly all Okinawan-Bolivian students attended. As a Japanese national, who was born and raised near Tokyo in mainland Japan and had lived much of his adult life in the United States, I was asked by the community leaders to teach third-grade and fourth-grade Japanese classes, and, during the winter break, to conduct English lessons for middle school students. As a school staff member, I not only observed the daily activities of the students in and outside of the classroom, but I was also actively involved in extracurricular activities both within and outside the school. I lived with three different Okinawan-Bolivian families during my research. During my stays with these families, I observed how Okinawan-Bolivian family members communicated with their non-Nikkei Bolivian employees (farm laborers or domestic workers), as well as among themselves.

I begin by outlining the history of Okinawans' tenuous relationship with the Japanese nation-state, and contextualizing Okinawan immigration to Bolivia and the foundation of Colonia Okinawa within this relationship. I then describe Japanese language education in Colonia Okinawa, its foundation and transformations. The process has been shaped as much by the immigrant community's desire for maintaining "national" cultural heritage as by its need to mark the ethnic/class boundary between themselves and their local Others. Finally, by providing a few ethnographic "snapshots" of Okinawan-Bolivians' language use in Colonia Okinawa, I will illuminate the linguistic boundary work in which Okinawan-Bolivians engage in their lives.

Modern Okinawan Diaspora and Colonia Okinawa

Emigration from Okinawa in modern times began in 1899, when Tōyama Kyūzō, a democratic rights activist, led a group of Okinawans to Hawai'i to work on sugarcane plantations.[10] While the dispersal of Okinawans overseas in the twentieth century proceeded, as Robert Arakaki argues, in the form of an "apolitical labor diaspora," the Okinawan diaspora's history and subjectivity are profoundly political, shaped by Okinawans' struggles under Imperial Japan and, later, under U.S. military occupation.[11]

Despite numerous political and military intrusions by China and Japan since the seventeenth century, and even after becoming a tributary state to both China and Japan in the seventeenth century, the Ryūkyū Kingdom flourished as an international trade hub in East Asia and Okinawans enjoyed economic and cultural prosperity. Under Ryūkyū Kingdom rule, Okinawans developed a distinct culture and language by creatively blending cultural and linguistic elements from Southeast China, Korea, and Indochina.[12] It is commonly believed that the Japanese and Okinawan languages sprang from a common parent language, although Japanese absorbed far more Chinese into its older

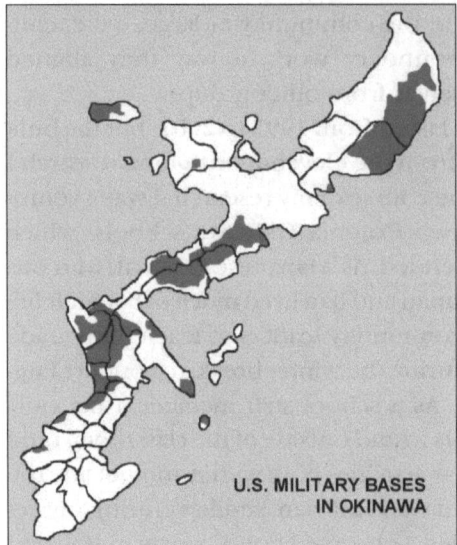

"The Prefecture of Okinawa remains home to 75 percent of U.S. bases and the majority of U.S. military forces in Japan. (The bases occupy 20 percent of the Okinawa Hontō Island.)" (Credit: Wikimedia Commons)

language forms than did the Okinawan language. As a result of a long process of cultural and linguistic mixture, the Okinawan language, while philologically similar, remained distinctively different from the standardized mainland Japanese language. After the Meiji government's annexation of Okinawa in 1879, known as the Ryūkyū Shobun (Ryūkyū Disposition), the kingdom became a prefecture of Japan and Okinawa became the Japanese empire's laboratory for colonial policies in culture and economy. The Meiji government rigorously instituted linguistic and cultural "Japanization" through school education in order to "produce" Japanese national subjects, an agenda that was later applied to the peoples of Taiwan, Micronesia, and the Korean peninsula.[13] After the annexation, enormous economic obligations to the central government were imposed on Okinawans in the form of newly instituted land tax laws, and Okinawa's economy became unstable as Tokyo promoted sugar production as the prefecture's sole economic backbone. To rescue the nearly bankrupt Okinawan economy and to cope with the increasing population pressure, the prefectural and national governments promoted overseas emigration. Emigration had two effects: it reduced the population and it generated income through remittances from émigrés.[14] By 1927, an estimated 15 percent of the prefecture's population lived outside of Okinawa: more than 32,000 Okinawans were working in industrial areas in Japan proper and another 26,500 had migrated to foreign countries.[15] In the 1920s, as the U.S. government gradually curtailed, and later prohibited, Japanese immigration, more Okinawans were encouraged by the Japanese government to migrate to the Philippines, Micronesia, Taiwan, and, from the late 1930s to 1940s, Manchuria (northeast province of China). Between 1899 and 1941, the number of emigrants from Okinawa Prefecture totaled 72,789, or 11 percent of all emigrants from Japan, second only to Hiroshima Prefecture.[16]

Okinawans in Okinawa and Okinawan émigrés abroad both lived in a precarious subject position vis-à-vis the Japanese nation-state and Japanese mainlanders, or Naichi-jin.[17] Historian Eiji Oguma argues that Imperial Japan sought to absorb Okinawans into the Japanese nation-state as "children" of the "multiethnic Japanese family," which was imagined as a mixture of heterogeneous Asian peoples.[18] Imperial Japan promoted itself as a harmonious and benevolent "family state," or *kazoku kokka*, that embraced diverse ethnic groups within the empire, uniting them as a family with a common ancestry.

Within Imperial Japan's multiethnic family state ideology, colonial expansion was justified not only as repatriation of the "original" Japanese peoples, but also as the paternalistic adoption of other Asians, who were perceived as wrongly raised, and therefore underdeveloped, "children" of the Japanese nation.[19] As adopted "children," colonized subjects, including Okinawans, were expected not only to abandon their previous customs, beliefs, and language in order to become indistinguishable members of the Japanese nation, but also to "naturally" obey the household head, the Japanese government, and the elder sibling, the majority Naichi-jin population.[20] Under this logic, Okinawans, as young "children" of the family state, did not deserve the equal rights as the Naichi-jin; although the Meiji government enforced educational policies to facilitate Okinawans' cultural and linguistic assimilation, it took decades of advocacy campaigns by Okinawan intellectuals before Okinawans were given the same legal rights as Naichi-jin's.[21]

Their ambiguous subject-position within the Japanese "family state" left Okinawans with a psychological trauma when they faced Japanese Naichi-jin in Japan or in overseas migratory locales.[22] Naichi-jin émigrés frowned upon Okinawans overseas as "the other Japanese," who were "almost, but not quite" the same as Naichi-jin, and frequently discriminated against them.[23] In response, Okinawan émigrés in Brazil, Peru, and Micronesia, who daily faced prejudice from the Naichi-jin migrants, tried to evade humiliation and discrimination by self-inspection and self-acculturation. Okinawan immigrant community leaders in Micronesia, for instance, organized a Lifestyle Reform Movement (*seikatsu kaizen undō*) that prohibited community members from using their native language and practicing their traditional customs, and sometimes, in an effort to highlight their identity as "Japanese" nationals, blatantly discriminated against locals in their migratory destinations.[24]

The struggle of Okinawans and the Okinawan diaspora continued even after the end of the tragic Battle of Okinawa in 1945, which resulted in the deaths of more than one-fourth of the entire local population of the Okinawa Hontō Island, the largest and most populous island within Okinawa Prefecture.[25] Japan's surrender to the Allies on 15 August 1945 marked not simply the emancipation of Okinawans from a form of colonial oppression, but also the beginning of Okinawa's transformation into the largest U.S. military stronghold in East Asia against the perceived communist threat in the region. In December 1950, the U.S. military administration was renamed the U.S. Civil Administration of the Ryukyu Islands (Uscar). Two years later the Government of Ryūkyū Islands (hereafter GRI) was founded.[26] Uscar invested billions of dollars in developing Okinawa's public service and educational systems, while it maintained the power to veto decisions made by the administrative, legislative, and judicial branches of GRI, which consisted of popularly elected local Okinawan officials.[27]

Under such circumstances, Okinawans working at U.S. military installations were not allowed collective bargaining, which the GRI's labor laws guaranteed, but the Uscar failed to enforce. Local Okinawan workers at U.S. military bases, the only major employer in Okinawa at the time, earned wages substantially below legal minimum wage, while Okinawans who protested or disobeyed

Uscar's orders were accused of being communists and were often arrested and charged with civil disturbance.[28] Okinawans' frustration grew as the U.S. military began to expand bases on the island after the outbreak of the Korean War in June 1950. In April 1953, Uscar released the Compulsory Land Expropriation order, which permitted the U.S. military to remove Okinawan residents and to seize their land regardless of the landowners' will.[29]

Many Okinawans, who became dissatisfied with their second-class citizenship status at home, looked for hope in overseas migration.[30] Uscar and GRI were acutely aware of Okinawans' growing resentment, so they began to promote overseas emigration as a way to ease social unrest in Okinawa. In 1951, Uscar and GRI sent James L. Tigner of the Hoover Institute and Library at Stanford University to Latin America, in search of possible destinations for Okinawan emigration. In September 1952, Uscar accepted Tigner's proposal for a migration and settlement program in Bolivia's Santa Cruz region. The Okinawan settlement plan was finalized in June 1953, when the Bolivian government permitted the entrance of 3,000 families, or 10,000 persons, over a ten-year period. The immigrants were granted 9,400 hectares in a fertile but heavily wooded area. In August 1954 the first group of 406 settlers arrived in their allocated settlement. After two relocations within the area, they settled in the current location of Colonia Okinawa Uno and began the arduous task of clearing the tropical jungle.[31] In 1959 and 1961, respectively, the Colonia Dos and Colonia Trés settlements were opened in order to accommodate the growing population. By 1964, the population of Colonia Okinawa reached over 3,200, or more than five hundred households.

Due to the small size of the Naichi-jin immigrant population in Bolivia and minimal intervention by the Japanese government throughout the 1950s and 1960s, the Okinawan settlers in Colonia Okinawa maintained strong autonomy in a remote area of the Santa Cruz region in the early years. When the reversion of Okinawa to Japan became imminent in the mid 1960s a discussion began concerning the ways in which the Japanese government would assume the role of an overseer of the Colonia Okinawa affairs. In 1967, the Japanese government agency Kaigai Ijū Jigyōdan (KIJ, Overseas Migration Agency), a predecessor of the Japan International Cooperation Agency (JICA), opened an office with permanent Japanese staff in Colonia Okinawa. Additionally, the U.S. and Japanese governments declared that Okinawan settlers in Bolivia would legally become Japanese citizens five years before Okinawa's reversion to Japan in 1972.

More than two-thirds of the settlers left Colonia Okinawa as a result of frequent floods and droughts in Bolivia's Santa Cruz region (see map), as well as the nation's political and economic instabilities. They moved to the nearby metropolis of Santa Cruz de la Sierra or emigrated to São Paulo, Brazil, or Buenos Aires, Argentina. Some settlers returned to Okinawa. Those who stayed and persevered in Colonia Okinawa eventually prospered in the 1980s. The assistance the Japanese government provided for Colonia Okinawa, mainly through JICA loans for Okinawans' farming operations, transformed the settlers into a ruling socioeconomic class in the village by the late 1980s.[32] Taking advantage of an area with one of the most fertile soils in the South American continent, the Okinawan-Bolivian farm owners had become some of the most prominent producers of soybeans, wheat, and sorghum in the country by the 1990s. In the early 2000s, approximately 820 people, or 210 households, mostly headed by second-generation Okinawan-Bolivians, belonged to Okinawa Nihon Boribia Kyōkai (Japan-Bolivia Association of Okinawa), or Nichibo Kyōkai, an Okinawan community organization. Nichibo Kyōkai estimated that the average landholding of Okinawan-Bolivian farmers was more than four hundred hectares, whereas the estimated average size of non-Nikkei Bolivians' farmland in Santa Cruz region is only thirty hectares. As *patrones* (farm owners), these Okinawan-Bolivians did not work in their vast farm fields themselves; each farmer typically employed from five to ten laborers to operate farming machines and weed fields, taking advantage of the abundant and inexpensive labor pool of non-Nikkei Bolivians in the area, who vastly outnumbered the ethnic Okinawan population.[33] In Colonia Okinawa, where local non-Nikkei Bolivians did not distinguish Japan from Okinawa and Naichi-jin from Okinawans, Okinawan-Bolivians came to be referred to simply as *patrones Japonesas* (Japanese farm owners) locally. Unlike the urban Nikkei ethnic communities in Lima, portrayed by Yamasaki,[34] where Nikkei ethnicity carries no strong socioeconomic class implication, the ethnic difference between the two groups in Colonia Okinawa came to be equated with the class difference between affluent farm owners and poor farm laborers.[35]

Japanese Language Education in Colonia Okinawa

Given the ethnic/class polarization in Colonia Okinawa, heritage language education for second- and third-generation Okinawan-Bolivians became crucial for the ethnic Okinawan community members as a way to preserve their ancestral culture and as a means to maintain and bolster their upper-class status within the rural Bolivian society, which was marked by their "Japanese" (not Okinawan) heritage.

After the informal education immigrant parents had provided their children in the early years, Okinawan community leaders in 1958 built a K-6 grade school that followed the Bolivian national curriculum. During the 1960s, Catholic and Protestant churches operated Colonia Okinawa's formal educational system, including Japanese language instruction. In 1964, four Japanese nuns from Miyazaki Karitasu Shūdōjo-kai (Caritas Sisters of Miyazaki), a Catholic organization in Miyazaki Prefecture, who possessed teacher's licenses, began to teach Japanese to the settlers' children.[36] In the 1970s and early 1980s, the ratio between Okinawan-Bolivians and non-Nikkei Bolivian students in Colonia schools, which had turned public during the late 1960s, changed dramatically due to two factors: the domestic migration of Bolivians from western to eastern Bolivia and the exodus of a large number of Okinawan settlers who had failed to establish successful farming operations. The changing demographics worried the Okinawan parents. They feared that incorporating non-Nikkei Bolivian students into the integrated learning environment in their children's schools would lower their children's "learning ability" (*gakuryoku*).[37] In addition, due to the lack of public funding and often-unmotivated teachers, who were disappointed in being assigned to under-equipped and understaffed rural schools, Okinawan settlers had difficulty attracting and retaining qualified teachers in their schools.[38] The situation compounded during the nationwide hyperinflation in the 1980s, as teachers' labor conditions and salaries worsened, prompting frequent teacher strikes that paralyzed the schools in Colonia Okinawa.

These conditions generated heated debates among the Okinawan settlers regarding the future of school education in Colonia Okinawa in the mid 1980s, especially after they learned of a test result involving their children. The results of the test, which was conducted by a group of Japanese scholars in schools in Colonia Okinawa and elite private schools in the city of Santa Cruz de la Sierra, revealed that Okinawan-Bolivian students performed considerably worse than wealthy non-Nikkei Bolivian students in private schools in Santa Cruz de la Sierra.[39] This finding validated the settlers' fear that the ethnically mixed educational environment was facilitating their children's cultural assimilation into the rural, working-class, non-Nikkei Bolivian population.

The immigrant parents' concern was alleviated in 1987 by the founding of a new private school, funded and constructed by the settlers themselves:[40] Okinawa Uno Japanese-Bolivian school (Colegio Particular Mixto Centro Boliviano Japones Okinawa Numero Uno: CBJ school hereafter) for elementary (five years) and intermediate (three years) education. The new school accepted both Okinawan-Bolivian and non-Nikkei Bolivian children, but set its tuition high.[41] By charging high tuition and fees, Okinawan settlers were able to make the new school a de facto single ethnic school for their children, keeping their children from studying with lower-class non-Nikkei Bolivian children in the village. Of the few non-Nikkei Bolivian students in the CBJ school most were children of middle-class Nichibo Kyōkai employees or of school teachers, or were the stepchildren of intermarried Okinawan-Bolivians, all of whom were integrated into the Okinawan-Bolivian community through marriage and/or employment and were able to afford the tuition.[42]

In the 2001 school year, the CBJ school had seventy-six students, sixty-five Okinawan-Bolivians and eleven non-Nikkei Bolivians. All Okinawan-Bolivian students voluntarily paid extra tuition to attend the afternoon Japanese language classes, which are not mandatory. Only three among the eleven non-Nikkei Bolivian students stayed for Japanese classes in the afternoon. The school's five educational objectives indicate that the institution focuses on the instruction of "Japanese" culture and characters to the students via Japanese language education, in addition to fulfilling the Bolivian national curriculum's requirements. The school brochure lists the following objectives: (1) We pursue the coverage of educational requirements set by the Ministry of Education of Bolivia, and provide the education for non-Nikkei Bolivian population. (2) We pursue an education that instills the students with pride and the intellect to live as Bolivians of Japanese descent (Boribia Nikkeijin). (3) We foster the students' ability to understand and express proper Japanese. (4) Through the learning of the Japanese language, we enable the students to learn Japanese culture, learn and embody (*taitoku suru*) the good characters that Japanese have, and develop as unique human beings with rich personalities. (5) We pursue co-living (*kyōsei*), cooperation, and coexistence with non-Nikkei Bolivians.[43] The emphasis here is on cultivating and affirming Okinawan-Bolivian children's subjectivity as Nikkei, Bolivians of Japanese descent, by learning and embodying what they viewed as the "good" characteristics of their Japanese, rather than their Okinawan, heritage and culture.[44] Establishment of the private CBJ community school, with weekday afternoons set aside for Japanese language instruction, was intended to counter what the immigrant community leaders perceived as the degenerative influence of local Bolivians by instilling idealized Japanese national moral character and mannerisms into their Bolivian-born children.

In the after-school Japanese language classes the sixty-eight students were divided into nine levels, from the "Special Class," for those with little Japanese proficiency, to Classes 1 through 8, for students with more advanced language skills. As with other community affairs in Colonia Okinawa, JICA has been the most influential Japanese state institution in educational affairs, providing approximately 20 percent of the school's revenue.[45] JICA's Japanese Language Teaching Materials Donation Program also provided the school with Japanese language teaching materials. The textbooks the JICA supplied were the same national language (*kokugo*) textbooks used in Japanese elementary schools. Other JICA donations included writing and grammar workbooks, a Japanese language teaching manual, and Japanese dictionaries and encyclopedias.[46]

Three types of instructors taught in the school's afternoon Japanese language classes: (1) Second-generation Okinawan-Bolivian adults, mostly wives of the second-generation farm owners. These instructors had little formal training in teaching, let alone in Japanese language teaching; (2) Japanese Naichi-jin from Japan, such as teachers assigned to the school for a two-year term through JICA programs that assist overseas ethnic Japanese communities ("JICA teachers," hereafter), and Japanese residents who came to Colonia Okinawa on a short-term basis, such as those who came to help the Methodist Church, originally founded by a Japanese Naichi-jin pastor; (3) Okinawan teachers from Okinawa Prefecture ("Okinawa Prefecture teachers," hereafter). Like JICA teachers, Okinawa Prefecture teachers spend two years in the Colonia schools through the prefectural government's teacher placement program for the overseas settlements of Okinawans, which the Okinawa Prefectural government administers. Two JICA teachers and one Okinawa Prefecture teacher had been permanent fixtures in the CBJ school since the 1990s, but school administrators struggled to fill other Japanese language teaching positions with local second-generation Okinawan-Bolivians. Aging first-generation settlers were more comfortable with Uchināguchi (or its regional variant) than with Japanese. Meanwhile, the Colonia-born second-generations were not confident enough in their command of "standard" Japanese (hereafter without quotation marks) to teach in the classroom, especially writing and reading. For most in these generations the formal Japanese language education they had received in Colonia Okinawa, if any at all, extended only through middle school. During the

2000–2001 school year the teaching staff included three Colonia-born or -raised Japanese teachers, all wives of Okinawan-Bolivian farm owners.

Among the three groups of teachers, the Japanese Naichi-jin teachers, especially the JICA teachers, assumed the leadership role in Japanese language education and were expected to bring a sense of authenticity to the school's Japanese linguistic and cultural education.

The authority Okinawan Bolivians gave to Japanese Naichi-jin in Japanese language educational matters was apparent when I first visited the school in the beginning of my fieldwork. When I asked the Japanese class department principal, a second-generation Okinawan-Bolivian woman, about the possibility of volunteering at the school, I was surprised at how easily she allowed me to start teaching Japanese classes, without asking me if I had teaching experience. In her eyes, it appeared, the fact that I was born and raised in Japan and had a college education was enough to qualify me to teach the language to the school's Okinawan-Bolivian students.

One of the two JICA teachers stationed in Colonia Okinawa in 2001 had been a public school principal in Japan. In addition to teaching regular Japanese classes this teacher offered a weekly training session for other teachers, especially for the second-generation Okinawan-Bolivians, to improve their instruction skills. During one of these sessions I observed, the teacher discussed the new *Instruction and Advising Guidelines (Kyōiku Shidō Yōryō)* for elementary education in Japan. As he detailed the newly released guidelines, the second-generation Okinawan-Bolivian teachers took notes diligently, showing their willingness to keep up with the latest educational trends in Japan, even though the enforcement of these guidelines in Japanese language schools overseas was not mandatory. Japanese Naichi-jin teachers, such as the JICA teachers were, in short, expected not only to teach the Colonia-born Okinawan-Bolivian children "proper" heritage language, standardized Japanese, but also to transmit an institutional framework of "national language" instruction from the Japanese state to the diasporic community in Colonia Okinawa.

The Okinawa Prefecture teachers in the CBJ school filled the same roles as the JICA teachers, but they were also expected to introduce Okinawan traditional arts, such as *eisa* dance, *shimedaiko* drums, and *sanshin* (a stringed musical instrument) to the CBJ students and Okinawan-Bolivian community members at large during their tenure in Colonia Okinawa. Although they taught these Okinawan traditional arts, they were not expected to teach Uchināguchi in the Japanese language classes even if they spoke the language fluently. Mr. Gushiken,[47] an Okinawa Prefecture teacher in the CBJ school in 2000–2001, told me that he was surprised by how few Okinawan-Bolivians other than first-generation settlers spoke Uchināguchi. In hopes of helping second- and third-generation students realize their linguistic and cultural heritages, as distinct from the Japanese Naichi-jin's, Gushiken frequently used Uchināguchi terms and expressions during his Japanese language classes, even if only a few students could understand him. When his students were preparing a play for a school festival, a third-generation student came into Gushiken's office to ask him how to say certain standard Japanese expressions in Okinawan "dialect" (*hōgen*). Gushiken told him the corresponding Uchināguchi terms, then added, "Well, [the language] is not a [mere Japanese] dialect, it is Uchināguchi," reminding the student that Uchināguchi is not a regional subordinate of standard Japanese, but a unique and autonomous language.

Despite the efforts of some Okinawan teachers in the CBJ school, second- and third-generation students did not speak Uchināguchi fluently and understood very little. By contrast, first-generation settlers and the majority of older second-generations who grew up in a relatively isolated and insulated ethnic community claimed to speak Uchināguchi "very" or "reasonably" well.[48] During my field research in Colonia Okinawa, I found that Uchināguchi was the main language spoken among the first-generation elders and between them and their middle-aged children (who had been born either in Bolivia or in Okinawa, but had moved to Bolivia as young children). The majority of younger Colonia-born generations could understand the elders' speech in Uchināguchi, but rarely, if ever, used it among themselves.

It appears, therefore, that Okinawan-Bolivians in Colonia Okinawa encouraged their Colonia-born offspring to locate their linguistic heritage in the Japanese nation-state, rather than in Okinawa, and focused on standard Japanese language education, while trying to preserve Okinawan heritage in non-linguistic aspects, such as art, music, and dance.

Heritage Language Education as Negotiation of Boundaries

Why was Japanese, not Uchināguchi, taught as the heritage language in Colonia Okinawa, despite Okinawa's tenuous relationship with the Japanese nation-state throughout the modern era and the community's historical origin as an Okinawan, not Japanese, immigrant settlement? One obvious reason was the fact that the standard Japanese has become a primary language used in Okinawa Prefecture itself and in many ethnic Okinawan communities abroad;[49] Uchināguchi is actively spoken only in rural areas of Okinawa Hontō island and smaller peripheral islands, and few young people today speak it in urban cen-

An Okinawan-Bolivian farm owner (*patron*) checking his field and his non-Nikkei Bolivian worker, who is operating a bulldozer in the background, in Colonia Okinawa. "As *patrones*...Okinawan-Bolivians did not work in their vast farm fields themselves; each farmer typically employed from five to ten laborers to operate farming machines and weed fields, taking advantage of the abundant and inexpensive labor pool of non-Nikkei Bolivians in the area, who vastly outnumbered the ethnic Okinawan population. (Credit: author)

ters of Okinawa. There are two other, and, in my view, more important, reasons behind the "nationalization" of heritage language among Okinawan-Bolivians in Colonia Okinawa. First, self-identifying as "Japanese" diasporic subjects and learning primarily standard Japanese language as their heritage language has brought tangible material benefits to the Okinawan-Bolivian community from the Japanese state; and second, the practice of commanding Japanese language itself functioned as a means of symbolically embodying ethnic and class differences vis-à-vis the local non-Nikkei Bolivians. Japanese heritage language education and speech practices in Colonia Okinawa served, in short, as acts of boundary work on two fronts: vis-à-vis Japanese Naichi-jin's governmental institutions and local non-Nikkei Bolivians in Colonia Okinawa.

"Nationalizing" Self: Boundary Work with the Japanese State

The tremendous effort that the Okinawan settlers have made in the undeveloped tropical forest in the Santa Cruz region of Bolivia notwithstanding, the immigrant community's economic prosperity since the 1990s is undeniably due to the financial support the Japanese government provided. In addition to the low-interest loans made widely available for Okinawan-Bolivian farm owners, funding for many key community facilities in Colonia Okinawa, such as schools, hospitals, and gymnasiums, has come from the Japanese national government. Even in the late 1990s, for instance, JICA, a Japanese governmental agency, provided 30 percent of the entire annual revenue of Nichibo Kyōkai and the same percentage of the operating budget for Colonia Okinawa hospital.[50]

Okinawan-Bolivian community leaders have also relied on the Japanese government for recovery from local natural disasters and for political leveraging with the Bolivian government in legal disputes with non-Nikkei Bolivians. When a flood hit Colonia Okinawa in 1992, for instance, Nichibo Kyōkai promptly reported its damage to the regional office of JICA and the Japanese Consulate General in Santa Cruz de la Sierra to ask for emergency help to repair roads and to drain farmland. In early 1992, flood waters in the Rio Pailón, which runs through the west end of Colonia Okinawa, severely damaged Okinawan-Bolivians' farms and ranches. In addition, a bridge collapsed on the only major road between Colonia Okinawa and Montero, a gateway city for Colonia

Japanese language speech contest (*Ohanashi taikai*), hosted by a Japanese language education council in Bolivia, held at Colonia Okinawa. (Credit: author)

Okinawa and surrounding area, leaving the Colonia completely isolated. After Nichibo Kyōkai's repeated requests, in March 1993, the Japanese government granted JICA to provide approximately US$220,000 for the reconstruction of the roads. After the initial road repairs were completed, the Japanese government decided to fund the construction of seven concrete bridges between Okinawa Uno and Montero as part of Overseas Development Aid for the Bolivian government. The construction of the bridges was completed in May 1997, with a festive inauguration ceremony that was attended by the Bolivian president and the Japanese ambassador.

The Japanese government's protection of Okinawan-Bolivians' economic assets extended to land ownership. Since the 1960s, Okinawan-Bolivians have struggled with what they call "land invasion" by non-Nikkei Bolivians in the area. The problem began as early as 1963, when several non-Nikkei Bolivian landowners claimed ownership of part of the Okinawan-Bolivians' farmland, which the Bolivian government had owned originally and then gave to the Okinawan settlers under an agreement with the GRI. With complicated practices of land entitlement in Bolivia, particularly after a series of agrarian reforms in the 1950s, it was not uncommon for one land lot to have multiple legal title holders.[51] Article 77 of the Agrarian Reform Law of 1953 made matters worse, as it granted unused land to any individual who had cultivated, or intended to cultivate, the land into farmland, even if the grantee possessed no legal title. In 1994, a non-Nikkei Bolivian man claimed five hundred hectares of an Okinawan-Bolivian man's property in Colonia Okinawa. Both men appeared to have a legal land title to the disputed lot. The president of Nichibo Kyōkai sent a letter to the Japanese Embassy in La Paz in which he wrote, "This [land title] problem jeopardizes not only the property of [the Okinawan-Bolivian farm owner in dispute], but also the social rights of all Japanese residents in Bolivia."[52] After two years of Nichibo Kyōkai's pleading to the Japanese Embassy, the Japanese ambassador to Bolivia engaged the help of the Japanese minister of foreign affairs, who raised the issue during Bolivian president Sanchez de Lozada's official visit to Japan in October 1996. The Okinawan-Bolivian farm owner whose land ownership had been legally challenged told me that the Japanese minister had subtly warned of a possible cut of Japan's ODA [official development assistance] for Bolivia. Immediately, the Bolivian president agreed to resolve the issue with "administrative rather than legal means." Soon thereafter in March 1997, the president signed an executive order giving the land title to the Okinawan-Bolivian farmer.

The Okinawan-Bolivian community's dependence on the Japanese state in Colonia Okinawa made it imperative to learn standard Japanese in order to communicate with Naichi-jin officials in JICA's regional office and with officials in the Japanese General Consulate in Santa Cruz de la Sierra and the Japanese Embassy in La Paz. This was true even for the Colonia-born second-generations, who were gradually taking over the community leadership from the late 1990s. Being able to communicate in standard Japanese would help the Okinawan-Bolivian community receive Japanese government assistance for and protection of its economic interests in Bolivia. Against this backdrop, heritage language education in Colonia Okinawa can be viewed as the community's effort to make the boundary between Naichi-jin's Japanese state and the Okinawan diasporic community more porous and ambiguous in pursuit of tangible benefits.

From the mid 1980s to mid 1990s, approximately four hundred second-generation Okinawan-Bolivians left Colonia Okinawa for mainland Japanese cities to find jobs, a phenomenon widely known as *dekasegi*, or sojourning.[53] In the mid 1980s, lured by the booming manufacturing and construction industries in Japan and discouraged by the unstable Bolivian economy, the first group of Okinawans in Colonia Okinawa moved to Yokohama, Osaka, and other cities in Japan in search of work. In the early 1990s, many second-generation youngsters followed this first wave of migration. These formed what Okinawan-Bolivians in Colonia Okinawa today call the "*dekasegi būmu*" (dekasegi fad). Many of these young people had quit high school in order to go to Japan. When first-generation Okinawan-Bolivian settlers retired from managing their farms, their eldest sons typically took over the business; this meant that siblings had to find a means of living outside of Colonia Okinawa. Many Okinawan-Bolivian children who were not the eldest sons of the families found it difficult to find stable professional jobs in Bolivia, given the country's weak economy and highly competitive labor market. Okinawan-Bolivian men left for Japan and became construction workers, electricians, or factory workers, while women often worked in retail or manufacturing industries.[54]

With the migration of Colonia-born youth to Japan, Japanese-language education in Colonia Okinawa became a way to prepare Okinawan-Bolivian children for dekasegi migration. Several JICA teachers and Okinawa Prefecture teachers I worked with at the CBJ school could not help but find their service in Colonia Okinawa ironic. One Okinawa Prefecture teacher told me, "Sometimes it makes me wonder why we are teaching Japanese to these kids. An official reason is to maintain Japanese culture and tradition in the community, but it seems like all we are doing is getting them ready for dekasegi in the future."

In addition to preparing for dekasegi, second- and third-generation Okinawan-Bolivians could also take advantage of various scholarships and technical training programs offered through Japanese, Okinawan, and other prefectural or municipal governments and nongovernmental organizations, if they could prove they were fluent in standard Japanese. An older second-generation Okinawan-Bolivian teacher at the CBJ school told me that it was the school's unofficial goal that Japanese language students would be able to pass the grade 2 test of the Japanese Language Proficiency Examination (Nihon-go Nōryoku Kentei Shiken), administered by the Japan Foundation (a governmental foundation that promotes Japan studies overseas), before graduating from the middle school.[55] This would enable them to pass the language proficiency requirement for most training programs offered by Japanese (national, prefectural, and municipal) state institutions.

Even though access to future financial benefits was never an official objective of Japanese language education for Okinawan-Bolivian youth in Colonia Okinawa, CBJ school's strong emphasis on teaching standard Japanese, instead of Uchināguchi, appeared to have steered the Colonia-born second- and third-generation children toward migration to mainland Japanese cities, where jobs were more plentiful than in Okinawa Prefecture and earning potential was greater.[56] Heritage language education in Colonia Okinawa, then, eased the transition of Colonia-born Okinawan-Bolivians into the Japanese labor market by enabling them to overcome the linguistic and cultural boundaries between the Okinawan diasporic subjects in Bolivia and mainland Japan's Naichi-jin society.

Embodying "Foreignness": Boundary Work with Local Non-Nikkei Bolivians

In addition to the material benefits that heritage language education afforded, a command of Japanese also enabled the ethnic Okinawan community to mark and highlight the ethnic/class boundary between Okinawan-Bolivians and local non-Nikkei Bolivians in Colonia Okinawa.

This linguistic boundary work was most evident in the switching of languages between Spanish and Japanese. During my stay in the house of Mr. Yamakawa, one of the wealthiest Okinawan-Bolivians in Colonia Okinawa, I encountered numerous awkward situations in which Mr. Yamakawa gave work-related instructions in Spanish to his non-Nikkei Bolivian employees in my presence. After rudely grunting to his employees in Spanish about mending the barbwire fences surrounding his property, he turned around to me and openly criticized them in Japanese: "You have to give them strict directions, or they won't do it right." In another period of my fieldwork, I lived with the Yaras, another Okinawan-Bolivian family, who employed Julia, a non-Nikkei Bolivian high school girl, as a domestic helper. Mrs. Yara used Spanish to give instructions to Julia, but then switched to Japanese to express her lack of trust in the girl. On one occasion Mrs. Yara gave Julia brief instructions in Spanish about cleaning the house. When she saw her daughter leave the living room that Julia was about to clean, she yelled at her in Japanese: "Don't let [Julia] stay there

Youth (including CBJ students) present a drum performance (*shimedaiko*) at a community festival in Colonia Okinawa. (Credit: author)

alone! She might steal something." Using Japanese to create a secure communication space, Okinawan-Bolivians, including those Colonia-born generations who were comfortable communicating in Spanish, established a boundary between the two ethnic/class groups in the village.[57]

Mr. Kawabata, formerly Nichibo Kyōkai's secretary general and a Japanese language teacher in the CBJ school, acknowledged and defended the Okinawan-Bolivians' boundary maintenance practices:

> Some [outsiders] criticize that [Okinawan-Bolivian] residents here unfairly discriminate against [non-Nikkei] Bolivians. But [such criticism] is missing the point. If the two groups want to coexist smoothly without problems, it is necessary to have some separation between them. If differences between the two groups' cultures result in a crime, like theft, a simplistic egalitarian ideal is not a solution.

Given the underlying ethnic/class division existing already in Colonia Okinawa at large, speaking Japanese was but one practice that contributed to, and affirmed, the stratified socioeconomic relationship between the two groups. Heritage language education in Colonia Okinawa schools was, in this sense, a process of both educating second- and third-generation Okinawan-Bolivian children about the need to maintain social boundaries vis-à-vis local non-Nikkei Bolivians, and passing the (nationalized) cultural traditions of the ancestral homeland to the Bolivia-born generations.

The symbolic value of the Japanese language[58] taught and spoken in Colonia Okinawa lies in a unique socioeconomic situation in which Okinawan-Bolivians are the dominant *patrones Japonesas*, but their rigorous pursuit of heritage language education in Colonia Okinawa has to be understood within the larger socio-cultural and ideological context of Bolivian society. From the Spanish colonial era to today, Bolivian society has placed more value on embodied "foreign-ness" than on "native-ness" of individuals and groups. Historian Marcia Stephenson points out that Bolivian ethnic/class formations have revolved around the dichotomy between white Europeans and indigenous peoples in the popular imaginary: *blancos* represent power, modernity, and the capitalist market, represented by their Spanish heritage, while *indios* are stigmatized as embodying economic impoverishment and cultural backwardness.[59] In this sociocultural context of modern Bolivia, historian Marc Osterweil argues, immigrants with no Spanish heritage, such as Arabs and Jews who moved to Bolivia in the late nineteenth and early twentieth century, have had to demonstrate their values in society in different manners. Arabs and Jews are identified not as indios or blancos, but instead as *extranjeros*, or foreigners. The category of extranjeros implies the group's integration into the industrial capitalist economy and transnational networks, and thereby signifies them as "the upper-level social group who are urban and worldly," in contrast with Bolivianos, who are viewed as being located in the peripheries of the global economy.[60] In the Bolivian ethnic/class ideological contexts, therefore, one may embody (real or imagined) "foreignness" to be recognized as "the upper-level social group." Considering the relatively weak global standing of Bolivia in international politics and economy, then, the effort to teach Japanese to their children could be interpreted as a way for Okinawan-Bolivians to distance themselves from the "native" population (Bolivianos) and their culture, and to portray themselves as "foreign" Others (extranjeros) — with their "different" cultural and linguistic practices — in order to gain respectability within Bolivian society.

Combined with the tangible benefits the ability to speak standard Japanese holds out for them, such as obtaining various assistances for the community affairs from the Japanese state institutions, qualifying themselves for Japanese state–sponsored training or scholarship programs, or finding jobs in mainland Japanese cities to earn more than they could in Bolivia, it made much sense for the community to maintain standard Japanese as its heritage language rather than Uchināguchi. Through heritage language education at community schools, and through daily communication practices in Colonia Okinawa, Okinawan-Bolivians effectively executed linguistic boundary work to approximate themselves to the Japanese nation-state and distance themselves from the local non-Nikkei Bolivians in Colonia Okinawa.

Conclusion

The concept of heritage in heritage language has too often been unexamined in the studies of heritage language education, which are to this date largely drawn from case studies in the foreign language education in English-speaking states, such as the United States, Canada, and Australia. My case study of the Okinawan diasporic community in Bolivia complicates the notion of heritage by revealing that a cultural and linguistic heritage is informed and even shaped by the particular local socioeconomic and political contexts of the host society. Anthropologist Brian Axel has argued that a fixed and historical "homeland" for diasporic groups does not exist a priori, but is imagined and articulated by those in diaspora. Following Axel, I suggest that we scrutinize the very concept of heritage in heritage language and heritage language education. Diasporic communities, like the Okinawan-Bolivians' Colonia Okinawa, choose and deploy a particular heritage language for different reasons and objectives.[61] The

Nichibo Kyōkai (community organization) HQ building in Colonia Okinawa. "In the early 2000s, approximately 820 people, or 210 households, mostly headed by second-generation Okinawan-Bolivians, belonged to Okinawa Nihon Boribia Kyōkai (Japan-Bolivia Association of Okinawa), or Nichibo Kyōkai, an Okinawan community organization." (Credit: author)

ways in which standard Japanese is taught, learned, and used in the ethnic Okinawan community in Bolivia illuminate the ambiguous and complex definitions of ancestral "homeland," especially when a transmigrant group is a marginalized ethnic, regional, and/or linguistic group within the nation-state of its migratory origin. Rather than being conceived as purely sentimental, and potentially nostalgic, the notion of the homeland nation-state can be strategically chosen by those in diaspora as a way to better their living conditions in their new "home," the nation-state of their current residence.

The ways Okinawan-Bolivians learn and speak Japanese in Colonia Okinawa show why the heritage in heritage language needs to be understood not in purely cultural and psychological terms, but in its material and symbolic values within the host society at local and national levels. If the language that the diasporic group designates as a carrier of its ancestral heritage brings material benefits and becomes a marker of privilege in the society in which a group currently lives, then heritage language education takes on far more significance than cultural and linguistic inheritance. As my case study has shown, heritage language education can help keep the immigrant groups from being culturally and psychologically immersed into the host society while buttressing their socioeconomic and symbolic powers within it. The objectives, means, and actual functioning of heritage language and heritage language education, then, must be understood against the backdrop of local socioeconomic relations and global political economies, for these both shape the material and symbolic values of a heritage language.

❏

2. Conflicted Attitudes toward Heritage

Heritage Language Learning of Returnee Adolescents from Japan at a Nikkei School in Lima, Peru

Yuri Yamasaki

IN MODERN-DAY PERU, many Japanese descendants commonly use the term *Nikkei* (meaning "non-Japanese nationals of Japanese descent") to identify themselves. The emergence of the Nikkei population in Peru — now estimated to number 90,000[1] — is rooted in the migration of Japanese nationals to Peru as indentured immigrants to work on sugarcane plantations, beginning at the end of the nineteenth century. Although 80 percent of the Nikkei population is concentrated in Lima and its outskirts, the Japanese immigrants no longer form a coherent group, due to their socioeconomic differentiation and the mixing of races and their assimilation into local cultures.[2] Nevertheless, the Nikkei have created a set of institutions in Lima, Peru, that exhibit "a clear identification with Japan and its culture."[3] These institutions include a variety of associations (prefectural clubs, village clubs, cooperatives, foundations), entertainment venues (athletics stadiums, a museum, a theater), financial institutions, health-care facilities, and newspapers. According to Ayumi Takenaka,[4] these institutions play an important role in reinforcing the Nikkei's mutual solidarity and collective identity. Therefore, although there is no exclusively Japanese neighborhood in present-day Lima, the Nikkei are still seen by the non-Nikkei Peruvian majority as a major ethnic group forming a closely tied and coherent community based on this set of institutions.[5]

The younger generations of Nikkei Peruvians typically grow up speaking mainly Spanish, mixed with a specific Japanese lexicon that has been transmitted intergenerationally within families. To prevent the complete loss of ancestral language and cultural traits, private all-day elementary and secondary schools, founded and run by the Nikkei, offer additional Japanese language education. At these Nikkei schools, Japanese is taught in all grades as a mandatory subject, in addition to the curriculum followed in the local Peruvian schools. In other words, the most distinguishing characteristic of the Nikkei schools is their Japanese language education.

In 1990, stimulated by a labor shortage in Japan, the Japanese government amended its Immigration Control Law to permit Japanese descendants from overseas to live and work in Japan. As a result, large numbers of Nikkei left Peru to become migrant laborers in Japan, the majority of them employed in unskilled jobs in the manufacturing and construction industries, regardless of their skills or prior qualifications.[6] The migration pattern of Nikkei Peruvians is characterized as recurrent migration, since many of them have repeatedly returned to Peru and re-emigrated to Japan. This transmigration trend has resulted in the emergence of a new type of youth group in Peru's Nikkei community: returnees from Japan. In the past decade, an increasing number of children and teenagers, who were born or received schooling in Japan, have returned to Peru to resettle. Enrolling in Nikkei schools, these returnee students bring new experiences from outside that enrich the cultural and linguistic diversification of the student body. Unlike adult returnees, school-age youngsters need to relearn or improve their Spanish language skills when they return to Peru, but their fluency in Japanese and familiarity with Japanese culture distinguishes them in the Nikkei schools.

Does their fluency in Japanese give the returnees an advantage in Japanese language education in the Nikkei schools? The answer is not clear. First, many have no interest in learning Japanese. Some believe that they are already fluent enough in Japanese, while others may not find this language necessary to live in Peru. Second, and more interestingly, the returnees' language usage may be judged "incorrect" or "inappropriate" in the classroom. In a heritage language classroom, which brings together learners with different linguistic backgrounds and experiences, their vernacular speech varieties or personal forms of expression are sometimes marginalized when measured against the "standard" language planners and teachers aim to convey.[7] For example, in the study of a heritage language class for Korean American students at the University of Illinois, Hye-young Jo found that the "standard" Korean language taught in the classroom conflicted with students' previous experiences with the Korean language, particularly language habits and expressions used in informal environments.[8] When linguistic variations exist within the group, one of these tends to be favored as a legitimate language over others, based on the ideological orientations that the group members have about certain language repertoires and style, based on social, economic, and political positions and interests that these variations imply.[9]

Heritage language[10] for individual speakers or learners often becomes ambiguous, since the same ideas and beliefs about a given language are not necessarily shared. As Paul Kroskrity's studies have shown,[11] even within the same language group the multiplicity of the members' subject positions in terms of class, gender, and generation creates multiple language ideologies as well as different degrees of awareness of these. (Michael Silverstein defines language ideology as "a set of beliefs about language articulated by users as a rationalization or justification of perceived language structure and use."[12]) According to ethnographic studies on indigenous language maintenance and revitalization movements, language ideologies often play an important role in the outcome of school or community-based bilingual and heritage language education.[13] These studies argue that there are often ideological inconsistencies and tensions among those involved in heritage language education regarding the designation of their heritage language, which often affect the individuals' attitudes about their language maintenance and language learning. In other words, the teachers and learners may not necessarily share the same ideas about the language they teach or learn as their heritage language, or the same attitudes toward it.

To illuminate the inconsistent and ambiguous attitudes of heritage language learners toward what constitutes heritage language and how to learn it, this article examines school-based Japanese language education among younger generations of Nikkei in Peru. Particularly, I focus on the returnee students from Japan, a newly emerged young diaspora who shuttle between one space in which Japanese is shared as a communicative tool and another in which the Japanese language can become a symbol of their heritage and ethnic identity. Drawing from an ethnographic study on a small, private secondary school in Peru's capital city, Lima, this article portrays the returnee Nikkei students' diverse attitudes towards (re)learning Japanese as their "heritage," and more specifically, their conflict with what the language teachers consider to be "proper" or "standard" Japanese. By paying critical attention to the students' contestation regarding what constitutes proper Japanese language learning, this article demonstrates the ideological inconsistencies in institutional heritage language education involving diverse participants who have different experiences and relationships with the language, and therefore different level of awareness of the language as heritage. In doing so, the study shows how the school-based heritage language education sometimes encourages students to "dis-inherit" what they have learned outside school: this may relate to their family's social status in their ancestral country.

Through the analysis of the process of negotiation regarding what is considered proper heritage language and who gets to decide what it is, the article ultimately attempts to challenge the concept of "heritage" per se, by showing how contested the "heritage" of heritage language education is, and how it is subjectively defined through the participants' social, economic, and political positions and interests.

My data come from a three-month-long ethnographic study of Japanese language education and returnee youth's experiences in one of the Nikkei schools in Lima, Colegio El Agustino (hereafter CEA; all names of the students and staff are pseudonyms). The findings and interpretations presented here are based mainly on analysis of classroom discourses, as well as ethnographic interviews and many informal conversations with teachers and students, both in and out of the classroom setting. I will examine the interaction and negotiation that takes place between those who have acquired current Japanese vernaculars and the teachers engaged in heritage language education, which fosters formal and polite forms of Japanese. Finally, I will consider what constitutes a heritage language and what school-based heritage language education means for the younger generations of immigrants in this particular school — youngsters who are experiencing the tension between modernity and tradition that is a byproduct of globalization.

Nikkei Schools in Lima

The first Japanese-owned elementary school in Lima was established by immigrant parents in 1908, ten years after the arrival of the first group of emigrants. Many other schools were founded later by Japanese emigrants throughout Peru before World War II. Since most Japanese initially intended to return to Japan after several years, educating their children in the Japanese way was one of their most important concerns. Thus, in these schools, all subjects were taught in Japanese, using the same curricula and textbooks as in Japan. During World War II, however, the Peruvian government, a U.S. ally, froze the assets of the Japanese and disbanded all the community institutions, including the schools. Using and teaching the Japanese language was officially prohibited until the war ended.

Shortly after the Peruvian government lifted its ban on Japanese use in 1947, CEA was established in Lima at the request of many Japanese parents, as the first postwar Nikkei educational institution. CEA provided an eleven-year curriculum for elementary and secondary schooling in one institution. Unlike in the prewar schools, however, CEA students were taught in Spanish in all subjects except the Japanese language class. The school set this language policy in order to assimilate young generations into Peruvian society, rather than to maintain the Japanese language and value system. Their reasoning was that due to the loss of their property during the war and Japan's military defeat, most Japanese had given up on returning to their home country and had decided to settle permanently in Peru.

By the mid 1970s, the Nikkei had established several preschools and elementary schools, both in Lima and in its suburbs. Initially the curriculum emphasized the teaching of Japanese language and culture, but because of growing aspirations for higher education among the Nikkei, as well as the decrease in their younger population in the suburbs, these schools gradually ceased emphasizing Japanese, and began to focus on teaching English. Parents of the students had demanded this change.[14] While the policy of language education has changed over time, these Nikkei schools continue to sponsor a curriculum that includes Japanese language education along with opportunities for students to practice Japanese school customs on a daily basis. For example, all students and teachers practice *radio taisō* (warm-up exercises conventionally practiced in the morning and at sports events in Japan) on the playground every morning. The Japanese flag is displayed alongside the Peruvian flag, and the Japanese national anthem is sung along with the Peruvian anthem at many school-sponsored events. The schools connect closely with other Nikkei institutions, and community-based newspapers report on all school events. The biggest event each year is *undōkai*, an athletic meet to which many guests from other Nikkei institutions are invited.[15]

Table 1: School System at CEA	
Grade	**Typical age**
Preschool	
	3–5
Elementary school	
1st Grade	5–7
2nd Grade	7–8
3rd Grade	8–9
4th Grade	9–10
5th Grade	10–11
6th Grade	11–12
Secondary school	
7th Grade	12–13
8th Grade	13–14
9th Grade	14–15
10th Grade	15–16
11th Grade	16–17

This ethnographic study took place at CEA in 2005, from 30 May to 25 August. CEA is a comprehensive educational institution consisting of preschool, elementary school, and secondary school, housed in one four-story building. The school is fairly small in size and number of students, and thus each grade has only one class of seven to fifteen students. Table 1 illustrates the school system and students' typical ages.

When the school was built, about sixty years ago, the neighborhood was a prosperous center of commerce in Lima. The area was densely populated with Japanese immigrants whose businesses were centered there. Some parents want their children educated in the Nikkei school in hopes of maintaining their family's Nikkei identity; other parents choose CEA simply because they live in the neighborhood. Over the past twenty years, however, the neighborhood has declined and become notorious as one of the most dangerous areas in Lima, with a high incidence of robbery. The decision made by many Nikkei families to move to other areas of Lima has resulted in a dramatic decline in the Nikkei student enrollment. The massive emigration of the Nikkei to Japan in the beginning of 1990s also had a direct impact on school enrollment. When adults emigrated to Japan, they usually took their young children with them, or invited children to join them once they were settled in Japan. Furthermore, in recent years, an increasing number of middle-class Nikkei families have begun sending their children to private American, or other bilingual schools, which are viewed as more prestigious in Peru.[16] Likewise, Nikkei who belong to the lower classes, economically and socially speaking, tend to enroll their children in local public schools. As a consequence of all of the above-cited factors, the number of CEA students had dropped from a high of 700 to half that number by the late 1990s. In addition, since the 1990s, the student body has diversified with the admission of students of non-Japanese descent from the neighborhood. Unlike the Bolivian Nikkei school in Taku Suzuki's article[17] in which most non-Nikkei students were integrated with the Okinawan-Bolivian community, the non-Nikkei students in CEA are not necessarily connected to the Nikkei community in Lima.[18] During the 1990s CEA faced the loss of Japanese heritage students, just as other Nikkei schools in the provinces did.[19] Meanwhile, Nikkei youngsters returning from Japan began to appear at the school in the mid 1990s.

Over time, the student body of CEA has consisted predominantly of Japanese descendants. In 2005, 76 percent of the 121 elementary and secondary school students were Japanese descendants, and most of them fourth or fifth generation. At the time of my research, CEA employed four Japanese language teachers, all of them women: one was Japanese-born, another was bilingual second-generation. Both of these women had been teaching at CEA for nearly thirty years, but had little training in teaching when they were hired. The remaining two teachers, both third-generation Nikkei, had trained as language instructors. CEA employed no specially dispatched teachers from Japan.[20] With the exception of the principal, the four Japanese language teachers, and a few others, the majority of the school's thirty teachers were non-Nikkei Peruvians who had little facility with Japanese.

In this study, which is based principally on direct observation of classroom interactions among the returnees and other participants, I focus on the returnee teenagers in secondary school, most of whom have been in CEA for several years.[21] Since one of the focuses of the study was on interaction and negotiation between the language teachers and the returnee students, direct observation of the Japanese language classroom was the best way to understand these phenomena and the nature of the Japanese language education. The research also included observations and many informal conversations with teachers and students carried out during lunchtime, recesses, after school, and at school-sponsored activities, not only in the classrooms but also on the playground, in hallways, and away from the school site. I also had frequent interactions with returnees and the Japanese language teachers outside the school, mostly at other Nikkei institutions. Audio-taped, semi-structured interviews were conducted with five secondary school returnees outside the school, in addition to informal interviews guided by a flexible set of questions with eight secondary school returnee students at the school site, either in or outside of the classrooms. The five key informants for the semi-structured interviews were selected from each grade of secondary school except the seventh grade. These interviews were conducted to supplement the observation data and aimed at understanding the returning migrants' experiences and their opinions about Japanese language education. I did not determine the interview language but left it to each respondent to decide which language to use.[22] In addition, I was able to have informal conversations with six parents of returnees, taking advantage of after-school and school events, which helped me to gain a better understanding of the returnees' backgrounds.

Japanese Language Education and Japanese Usage at CEA

As briefly mentioned above, in recent years more and more Nikkei parents have opted for high-quality education over heritage education and prefer English language education that they hope will help their children achieve socioeconomic success in mainstream society.[23] In another prominent Nikkei school in Lima, Japanese is currently taught as a foreign language subject only twice a

Secondary school girls performing a traditional Japanese dance on the CEA playground at undōkai. (Credit: author)

week, while English language classes are held every day, in both elementary and secondary schools years.[24] Unlike this latter school, CEA continues to emphasize Japanese language teaching as the school's heritage, in addition to following the Peruvian national curriculum. At CEA Japanese class is a compulsory subject, taught every day in all grades from preschool to secondary school, while English is taught only once a week as a foreign language at the elementary and secondary levels.

Advocates of heritage language teaching generally stress the value of bilingual and multilingual skills for the individual and society as a whole.[25] In the 1950s and 1960s, CEA educated students in Spanish and Japanese, hoping they would become fluent in both languages. As later generations of Japanese descendants became linguistically integrated into Peruvian society after the war, however, they opted for Spanish as their first language. (By contrast, second-generation immigrants who were educated at Japanese-owned schools before World War II continued to favor Japanese over Spanish.) Most of the students at CEA are now fourth- and fifth-generation. With few opportunities to learn Japanese systematically outside school, the students' prospects for improving their conversational ability or becoming proficient Japanese speakers are slim — and their parents appear not to have high expectations in this regard. CEA's Japanese language education program aims simply to expose students to their ancestral language, making them aware of some Japanese expressions, but with no expectations that they will learn to speak more than a few easy phrases or be able to construct sentences with any facility.[26]

CEA secondary school students doing radio taisō at undōkai. (Credit: author)

Nevertheless, students do pick up a range of Japanese terms and everyday expressions outside the classroom, in rather informal settings. In their daily conversations in Spanish, the students share and use an inventory of specific Japanese vocabularies and expressions, most of which refer to family relationships, customs, numbers, and greetings. This particular code of speech, Spanish mixed with selected Japanese words, is in fact characteristic of the Nikkei community. This inventory of terms has been passed down from generation to generation through the schools as well as families.[27] Raúl Araki explains that by using words and expressions from this inventory, Nikkei transmit and understand values that are important in shaping their identities as Nikkei.[28] In addition to a certain range of Japanese vocabulary, the students also draw terms from regional Okinawan dialects in their day-to-day conversation at school.[29] Moreover, students playfully use certain words that are now obsolete in Japan, including some considered derogatory, such as *ki-chigai* (crazy), *do-jin* (indigenous inhabitant), and *ai-no-ko* (half-breed). Such words were common in the early and mid twentieth century when the first-generation Japanese people immigrated to Peru and have been handed down through the generations and are still in use among Nikkei.

The students have even created new words by taking elements of both languages. One example, for instance, is "*hontōte*," a word meaning "absolutely true." The word is a combination of the Japanese word *hontō* (true) and the Spanish suffix "ote/a," which is used to augment the original meaning (*grandote*, for example, means "huge," amplifying the adjective *grande* meaning big).

Some of the language terms students use are highly conventional and have been adopted by non-Nikkei students and teachers as well. Furthermore, in school, the students have their own rules about Japanese language usage. Elementary school children, for example, do not use the word *sensei* (teacher) when addressing all of their teachers. Generally, only classroom teachers and the Japanese teachers are called sensei; those who teach special subjects, such as gym or music, are addressed with the colloquial Spanish expression, *Profe*. Moreover, the students playfully change the word order so that they mix Japanese and Spanish language elements. In standard Japanese, for example, Señora (Sra.) Nora would be called "Nora Sensei," but the children instead employ the Spanish word order and call her "Sensei Nora" just like *"Profesora Nora."*

While CEA has played an important role in preserving and transmitting some Japanese heritage it is important to note that many Japanese expressions and vocabulary terms are not learned and shared in institutionalized heritage language education, but rather in more informal settings such as in daily conversation at home. In what follows, I will show that teachers challenge the informal and vernacular forms of Japanese that returnees acquire and share outside the classroom and emphasize instead "formal" Japanese forms. First, however, I will describe how the returnees respond to the school's Japanese language education curriculum and to the task of relearning Japanese as their heritage language.

The Returnees in Japanese Language Classrooms

During the period of my fieldwork, the returnee students from Japan accounted for 30 percent of CEA's total student body.[30] Of the twenty-three secondary school returnees, nearly all had returned to Peru several years earlier. From my observations, they had no trouble communicating in Spanish, and they looked to be fairly well assimilated with the other students. Nevertheless, the Japanese language teachers often categorized them as *nihon-gaeri*, a colloquial Japanese term that literally means "those who returned from Japan," to distinguish them from the non-returnee students. There were also institutional practices in which the returnees were positioned as a distinct population, who were expected to have greater Japanese proficiency in Japanese language classes and related activities. In the secondary school, students were placed in different groups, such as A, B, and C, according to their Japanese language abilities, and the classes were held separately. Students with a better knowledge of Japanese were placed in Group A. Although the returnee students' level varied widely depending on the condition of migration and length of time since they had left Japan, most of the returnee students were placed in the most advanced class, regardless of their actual language capabilities. Moreover, the returnees were strongly encouraged to take the Japanese Language Proficiency Test (JLPT, *nihon-go nōryoku shiken*)[31] and to participate in the annual Japanese speech contest in Lima. In the speech contest the returnees were placed in a special category in order to distinguish them from the general Japanese learners. In this category, the participants had to memorize the contents of their compositions and recite them by heart, while participants in other categories could read their compositions. Through this institutional practice, the returnees were officially and visibly positioned as those who should be good at the Japanese language, an ostensibly important subject at the Japanese heritage school.

The Japanese language classroom should have been a place where the returnees were in a superior position to other students. Instead, however, the returnees had to (re)learn Japanese as a means of everyday conversation and not simply as an academic subject and their "heritage" language. In the elementary school, where class placement was not a practice, the Japanese language lessons centered on the memorization of a fixed range of vocabulary terms using a set of word cards. Most of the texts and teaching materials had been donated by the Japanese Embassy or brought by visiting Japanese teachers from Japan. Most of them were not up-to-date. The lessons generally stuck to a fixed sequence, and the students were expected to carry out routine practices. The class usually started by singing four or five Japanese children's songs, and then the lesson moved to the activities using flashcards with pictures and another activity that used the students' own set of word cards. Typically the teacher had few opportunities to incorporate the returnees' knowledge and experience into the class.

Similar situations were observed at the secondary school level. Lessons generally centered on learning grammar and some expressions from the textbooks. No active interactions between the teachers and the students took place. In each grade, a few returnees evidenced a high level of Japanese proficiency, irrespective of their age upon return. These students in particular were not happy about having to relearn the basic rules of grammar and elementary vocabulary terms.

Advanced returnee students sometimes questioned their teachers based on their own experience and sense of proper word choice. The following are excerpts taken from a Group A lesson at the tenth-grade level, which occurred soon after the teacher gave the students examples of the Japanese expression *de nakereba ikemasen* (I have to). The interaction took place between Claudia, one of the returnee girls, and Sra. Masako, a Japanese teacher, who was born in Japan, migrated to Peru in the 1960s, and had been teaching at CEA for twenty-five years.[32]

Sra. Masako: "Seifuku wo kinakereba ikemasen."
(I have to wear uniform.)
"Nihon-go de hanasanakereba ikemasen."
(I have to speak Japanese.)
Claudia: Sensei, "nakereba narimasen" wa?
(Teacher, what about "I need to"?)
Sra. Masako: Confunde surukara koko de wa "nakereba ikemasen" dake. Claudia wa nihon-go ga wakaru kara iikeredo, ryōhō oshieruto sensei mo confunde, seito mo confunde.
(I only teach "have to" here, otherwise other students will get <u>confused</u>. You will be fine because you understand Japanese, but if I teach both expressions I get <u>confused</u>, and the students get <u>confused</u>, too.)

Schedule for second graders, showing that they have Japanese class everyday. (Credit: author)

In this way, the teachers would avoid answering a returnee's question on the grounds that a proposed alternative would confuse the other students. Several returnees complained that the Japanese classes were tedious. Claudia had returned from Japan nine years earlier, when she was seven years old. She had not lost her fluency in Japanese, because her third-generation Nikkei mother had maintained her daughter's language ability by exposing her to Japanese as much as possible outside the school. In an interview, Claudia complained about the Japanese class as follows (translated from Japanese):

> Well, the Japanese class at school is boring. The other students' Japanese doesn't progress at all, even if they have been learning it since preschool. Well, 'cause they're not interested in Japanese. What for [they have to learn it]? They learn some words, and then soon forget, you know. When the teacher asks a question, like "Ok, Javier, read the next sentence," he turns to me, like "what, what [did she say]?" Then I tell him the answer. You know, it's boring! Absolutely boring! I want the teachers to do something about it. They order us to speak in Japanese, but well...I don't know what to say. If I speak to my classmates in Japanese, how can they understand me? You know, it's boring.

In the classroom, some returnee students would translate the teacher's instructions into Spanish, and even, unknown to the teacher, give the correct answers to students who understood little Japanese. Even when called upon by the teacher, some students would turn to a returnee student to check the meaning of the question and to ask for the correct answers before responding.

As mentioned above, according to the Japanese language teachers, a student's language ability was the primary criterion for class placement. Some returnees, however, had been placed in Group A in spite of their limited Japanese ability. In class, these students would also ask other returnees the meaning of some Japanese words while they were doing their exercises. They conversed with me for the most part in Spanish, borrowing some Japanese words and phrases. To me, they seemed to speak Japanese no better than the other students in the lower-level groups. Class placement was supposed to be based on the Japanese teachers' evaluation of the students' language level, but this criterion seemed to be rather ambiguous.

The returnees with little Japanese knowledge tended to express negative feelings toward the Japanese class. For example, a tenth-grade girl in Group A, Yuriko, had lived in Japan from age one to six and was enrolled in the CEA preschool as soon as she returned to Peru. In the Japanese class, she overtly showed indifference toward the teacher's instructions. Yuriko was always chatting with the other students and did not listen to the teacher. When I first met her in the classroom, I asked her whether she liked the Japanese language. She said that she had never liked Japanese and in fact she hated Japan. Sra. Masako, who overheard our conversation, asked Yuriko why she did not like Japan:

Sra. Masako: Dōshite?
  (*Why?*)
Yuriko: Peru to chigau kara.
  (*Because it's different from Peru.*)
Sra. Masako: Dō chigauno?
  (*How is it different?*)
Yuriko: Es que aqui es feo pero chevere.
  (<u>*This place is horrible but cool*</u>.)
Sra. Masako: Dō chevere nano?
  (*How is it <u>cool</u>?*)
Yuriko: (laughs) Kokoni wa tomodachi ga irukara.
  (*Because here I have friends.*)

As this interaction shows, Yuriko made no effort to hide her negative attitude toward the Japanese class from the teacher.[33] In a later interview, Yuriko said that she did not understand why she had to keep studying Japanese since she had no intention of going back to Japan. One day, I saw Yuriko's mother speaking to Sra. Masako at the entrance of school. She was asking the teacher to transfer Yuriko to Group B. According to Yuriko's mother, Group A was too difficult for Yuriko, and if they kept her in Group A, she would hate Japanese even more. Sra. Masako turned this request down, however, because she believed Yuriko just wanted to move to Group B in order to be with her best friends. A few days later, however, Sra. Masako was finally convinced to transfer Yuriko to Group B, when Yuriko scored the lowest mark in a quiz. After switching to Group B, Yuriko seemed happy to be with her friends, but did not appear more motivated to learn Japanese.

Noriko, another tenth-grade girl in Group A, who had lived in Japan from age one to age nine, failed to get a passing grade in the finals before the winter break. The segment below describes the interaction between Noriko and Sra.

Masako in the first class after the break. This group included three female returnees (Noriko, Claudia, and Susan) and one non-Nikkei Peruvian boy, Javier, who had been in CEA since preschool.

As the class started, Sra. Masako announced that, overall, the students' grades had slipped in the finals. When she noticed four students whispering to each other she told them to speak in Japanese while they were in Japanese class.

Sra. Masako: Claudia to Javier no seiseki wa mae wa agatteta kedo ima wa sagatteru.
>(*Claudia and Javier used to have good marks, but now their grades have been slipping.*)

Las dos atras peor, ya. Fukumoto [Noriko's last name], especialmente.
>(<u>*The two sitting in the back row are even worse. Fukumoto, especially.*</u>)

Noriko: (distracted) ¿Qué cosa?
>(<u>*What?*</u>)

Claudia: Nihon-go.
>(*Japanese*).

Noriko: Es que yo no sé nihon-go.
>(<u>*Because I don't know</u> Japanese.*)

Sra. Masako: Nani ga "yo no sé"!
>(*What do you mean by "<u>I don't know</u>"!?*)

Nōryoku shiken san-kyū motterun dayo.
>(*You own a Level 3 certificate of Japanese Language Proficiency Test.*)

Noriko: Pero yo no sé!
>(<u>*But, I don't know!*</u>)

Sra. Masako: Nani itteruno! Nihon ni ita kuseni!
>(*How can you possibly say that? I know you were in Japan!*)

After the class, Sra. Masako complained to me about Noriko's low motivation. Noriko would always sit in the back of class with Susan, another returnee girl, conspicuously showing cutouts of Japanese teenagers' magazines to each other, and paying no attention to the teacher's instructions.

Some returnees were rather reluctant to demonstrate their Japanese communicative ability, even though they had a decent command of the language. For example, Diana, a ninth-grader, had a high level of comprehension of Japanese and always had good marks in written exams; she was therefore placed in Group A. She and Jessica were the only students in Group A from the ninth grade, but in the classroom, she rarely spoke in full sentences in Japanese. Outside school, however, she talked with me only in Japanese. Her peer returnee, Jessica, also told me that she sometimes talked with Diana in Japanese outside the classroom. When I asked Diana why she did not want to speak Japanese in the class, she said to me, "Yadayo, datte hazukashii yo" (I don't want to, 'cause I feel embarrassed). Since Diana did not speak Japanese properly in the classroom, the Japanese teachers believed that, although she had good marks in written exams, her command of spoken Japanese was not good.

Overall, the Japanese class was not very popular among the secondary students at CEA. Some reasons for their lack of enthusiasm were understandable. First, unlike English, Japanese would not prove useful in the labor market after graduation. Second, as Claudia had noted, some returnees did not seem to be satisfied with the teachers' traditional method of teaching. While I did not observe any overtly rebellious behavior among the students, the students' reluctance and low-key level of participation in class, such as silent or mumbling responses to the teacher, indicated their dissatisfaction with the instruction style. Negative attitudes were especially obvious among the upper-grade students. Some spent the language class hour chatting with other students or doing unrelated activities. This tendency was not evident only among the returnees, but also among most of the students in the tenth and eleventh grades.

In short, the gap between the level of Japanese taught by the teacher in the class and the competence of certain returnees was large. Clearly, CEA's Japanese language education program in both the elementary and secondary schools was not appropriate for the returnees who had a high level of proficiency in Japanese. More importantly, the distance between the teachers' enthusiasm and the students' motivation was considerable. Despite the teachers' expectations, the students were ambivalent about Japanese as their heritage and as a mandatory subject.[34]

Returnees' Challenges to the Classroom Japanese

Hye-young Jo's observations of the participation of second-generation Korean American students in heritage language classes have shown that individual language repertoire and usage are related to diverse social worlds and locations, such as the time of immigration, place of residence, and relationship to the homeland. Through these diverse social worlds and locations the transnational lived histories of the students had been constituted.[35] Similarly, the Japanese used in the CEA school has been influenced by the particular language habits and expressions of the Japanese immigrants: students bring in informal Japanese expressions and dialects that they learn at home and from watching Japanese TV programs and integrate these words into their daily conversations in Spanish.

As Korean American students demonstrated in the heritage language classes Jo describes, the Nikkei returnee students' personal forms of language expression conflicted with the "standard" or "authentic" language expressions shown in textbooks and taught by the teachers.[36] Hisako, an eighth-grader, told me that the form of Japanese she now spoke had changed. When she first enrolled in CEA, she explained, she spoke Japanese fluently in the Kansai (Western part of Japan) dialect, which has an accent distinct from standard Japanese. Her teachers told her, however, that her Japanese sounded strange and she had to correct it. Likewise, the returnees often brought informal expressions into the Japanese classroom, but the teachers did not regard them as standard Japanese, and tried to correct them. The older-generation teachers, in particular, constantly criticized what they saw as the returnees' excessively informal Japanese speech and urged them to speak more formally. For example, Diana, the ninth-grader who was reluctant to show her Japanese ability in the classroom (see above), often answered the teacher's questions in a rather impolite way.

(The students were practicing some expressions.)
Sra. Masako: Ima kazoku wa nani wo shite imasuka?
(*What is your family doing now?*)
Diana: Shiraaan.
(*Dunno*).
Sra. Masako: Shiraaan jya nai! Shirimasen to iuno!
(*Don't say "dunno," you should say "I don't know" properly!*)

Interestingly, one of the teachers complained that the students were imitating their parents' style of speech, using informal and impolite forms of Japanese the parents had learned at their workplaces, such as factories or construction sites, in Japan. Sra. Masako criticized this tendency, saying "the students would use only informal Japanese because they believe it's 'cool.'" According to the old-generation teachers, if the students used only informal forms of Japanese, they would be disdained in Japan, particularly if they went to Japan to study, not to work. Japan's national and local governments offer a variety of scholarships for students to go to Japan for college education and vocational training programs, particularly for the Nikkei. Students with advanced levels of Japanese can win these scholarships since the qualifying examination includes Japanese language aptitude tests. In other words, Japanese language proficiency offers the Nikkei students a way to take a path different from the one their parents followed, going to Japan as migrant laborers. The teachers believe strongly that learning formal Japanese is important if students want to go to Japan as students or trainees.

In contrast, there appeared to be an ongoing attempt by the returnees to disrupt the "boring" Japanese class. It is noteworthy that no matter what their level of Japanese, many returnee teenagers, particularly girls, were infatuated with Japanese popular culture, such as pop music and comic books (*manga*). These artifacts, and information about them, were obtained either through the internet, or from family members or friends in Japan, and were often exchanged among the returnees across the grades. Therefore, they were familiar with the latest Japanese trends, regardless of the length of time since they had left Japan. In the Japanese classes I observed I often noticed returnee girls showing one another clippings from Japanese magazines of pop stars or drawing Japanese animation characters behind the teacher's back.

Returnee students seemed to share their lived experiences with one another — their time in Japan — through talking about Japanese youth culture and exchanging cultural products. These products, such as comic books or lyrics of pop songs, were another source from which the students learned the informal Japanese expressions and catchphrases that young people used. So just as the

Nikkei students had learned and developed particular Japanese (or Nikkei) vernaculars outside the institutionalized heritage language education program, the returnee students also acquired and shared an inventory of modern and informal Japanese language and culture that differed from what they were taught in the classroom.

These "un-institutionalized" heritage language learning practices did not always take place outside the class. I observed the returnees skillfully attempting to take control of a Japanese class from the teachers, using their own cultural resources. One day, for example, a tenth-grade returnee named Susan brought a copy of a Japanese TV talk show program that her grandmother had videotaped in Japan. The other returnees in the advanced group banded together to ask the teacher if they could watch the video in class, on the grounds that learning Japanese youth culture would be useful. The teacher finally gave in to their persistent requests, and in the end, they spent the whole class hour watching the video. The students were very excited about the program, which had recently aired in Japan, and seemed familiar with most of the popular TV personalities who appeared in it. They constantly pointed at the TV screen, yelling the name of the pop stars and comedians, and discussing which one they favored. A few days later, Susan brought another videotape of a Japanese variety show, videotaped while she was in Japan approximately fifteen years earlier. The show, which was very popular at that time, was a rather raunchy comedy program and completely devoid of educational value from the teacher's point of view. Nevertheless, the students succeeded once again in convincing the teacher to let them watch it during the class. This incident illustrated the returnee students' cooperative strategies for changing a "boring" Japanese class into a more entertaining class of their own taste. Their behavior can be interpreted as a challenge to the Japanese language as a "heritage" and an academic subject, and also as resistance to the Japanese teaching style, which they regarded as overly rigid.

A wide range of Japanese popular culture practices also took place during school-sponsored events. The dance show that all the secondary school students performed during the undōkai athletic event, for example, used to be the full responsibility of the Japanese language teachers, who had choreographed it with traditional Japanese music. In 2005, however, when I was researching at CEA, the eleventh-grade returnee students began taking charge of dance performance and they selected a song by a Japanese pop group that was very popular among Japanese young girls. A returnee girl in the tenth grade drew a popular Japanese manga character for posters and fliers promoting the undōkai event. These were distributed to school members and guests. In this way, the returnees' knowledge of current Japanese trends appeared to be having an impact on the CEA's conventional heritage practices.

The incorporation of popular culture into classes and school events have been for the purely subjective pleasure of the returnee students, but as John Fiske points out, it could also be a sign of their resistance to, or evasion of, the attempt by a dominant group to regulate and control them, in this case by imposing the proper "heritage" language defined and regulated by the teachers.[37] By bringing their own Japanese usage and pop culture to the classroom and to the school's heritage practices, the returnees appeared to be trying to change their roles from passive and sullen recipients to active participants in heritage language education.

Conclusion

This ethnographic study on heritage language education at a small private school in Lima has illustrated two types of heritage practice, one institutionalized within the school, and the other, un-institutionalized outside school. Although most of the Nikkei students speak very little Japanese (except for the returnees from Japan), they grow up familiar with informal Japanese expressions and the regional dialect, in addition to Spanish, through exposure at home and through their Nikkei friends.[38] The students' familiarity with a certain amount of their heritage language suggests that heritage is learned more effectively by students in informal, un-institutionalized settings such as at home and with peers, than in the school that claims to teach them their "heritage." That is, the students' sense of heritage has more to do with home and peer relations than with schooling.

Moreover, the massive emigration of the Nikkei to Japan, and the return migration of some Nikkei to Peru, have added complexities in the Japanese language education program in Nikkei schools. The returnee students' personal experiences and knowledge of Japanese raises questions about school-based heritage language education itself. The returnee students' Japanese language ability does not fully function to their advantage at CEA, since the school's heritage language education values polite and standard Japanese, and does not recognize language practices related to individuals' diverse social worlds and experience. In heritage language education at CEA, based on an ideology that favors a formal style of Japanese, the returnees' informal language habits and expressions tend to be stigmatized. Unless the returnees (re)learn formal and academic Japanese at the school, and prove their language ability by means of the official language test for nonnative speakers, they are told by the school's teachers that they may not be able to go back to Japan as college students or trainees, but like their parents and many other Nikkei youth, only as unskilled migrant laborers.

These learnings suggest that the school-based heritage education philosophy may sometimes end up encouraging the students to "dis-inherit" cultural practices they have learned outside school, practices that may reflect their family's class status in their ancestral country. Pierre Bourdieu contends that schools often privilege particular forms of cultural and linguistic competence based on the dominant class's criteria for the most valued cultural capital, marginalizing other varieties.[39] Heritage language education has tried to counter this tendency by fostering marginalized, minority groups' languages.[40] However, the forms of language selected in teaching at CEA appear to create a new linguistic hierarchy by valuing formal and academic language and discouraging the returnees' personal language practices.

After all, the nature of institutionalized heritage language education, emphasizing standard and "authentic" language, may support intergenerational transmission of Japanese linguistic and cultural traits in some sense, but it does not benefit speakers of a variable and diverse Japanese language. Thus, CEA's long-standing educational effort to pass on the Japanese language and culture are unlikely to appeal to those who have acquired modern-day Japanese vernaculars, since they neither recognize Japanese taught at school as their heritage language, nor do they find the mandatory relearning of Japanese to be useful for living in Peru. Therefore, despite teachers' expectations, returnee teenagers try to distance themselves from the Japanese language class through reluctant participation in the classroom. In contrast, however, returnees seemed eager to learn the Japanese language and culture from a variety of informal sources outside the classroom. In doing so, they also appeared to challenge and resist the imposition of an exclusive use of a polite and respectful form of language, which the teachers considered proper Japanese.

The study at CEA has shown that diverse actors, with different attitudes and awareness toward inheriting Japanese and also different definitions of what it means to be of Japanese heritage, are involved in diverse heritage practices. Ideological inconsistencies among those involved in heritage language learning about what is a "proper" heritage language complicate the premise of language as heritage, and call into question the notion of "heritage" in heritage language itself, meaning who gets to decide what counts as proper or authentic heritage, under what circumstances and authority, and for whom. In her analysis of efforts to protect cultural heritage, Barbara Kirshenblatt-Gimblett points out that people are not only passive cultural transmitters but also conscious, reflexive agents in the heritage enterprise itself.[41] The conflict between the returnee students and the Japanese teachers at CEA reminds us that what constitutes heritage is not static but alive, and is constantly being changed by its "conscious, reflexive" users, so that what is considered to be a heritage language is also continuously transformed according to individual users' language ideologies and practices.

ACKNOWLEDGMENTS: I would like to express my gratitude to all the students and staff in the CEA for accepting me as a researcher and helping me during the research. I would also like to thank Neriko Doerr, Yuko Okubo, Taku Suzuki, Michiyo Takato, and two anonymous reviewers for their feedback and *CAS* editor Tom Fenton for his copy-editing assistance in completing this article.

❑

3. Heritage: Owned or Assigned?

The Cultural Politics of Teaching Heritage Language in Osaka, Japan

Yuko Okubo

CULTURAL POLITICS IS AN APPROACH that treats culture itself as a site of political struggle, as an analytic that emphasizes power, process, and practice, and as an approach that bears political effects such as forging communities, reproducing inequalities, and legitimizing exclusions. At the same time, these political effects provide the means by which the effects themselves are challenged.[1] Accordingly, these effects contribute to both the cultural production and reproduction of the hegemonic structure, which may unexpectedly result in sustaining the dominant-minority relations based on ethnicity in contemporary Japan. In this article I intend to capture the political meanings of the cultural differences created in everyday life by focusing on such phenomena.

Heritage is understood as "an approach to the past" that enables us to recognize and attempt to preserve important disappearing cultural and natural practices.[2] Heritage is multifariously defined as products, resources, knowledge, and rights to material and symbolic estate connected to the past. Scholars on heritage contend that heritage is legally and ethically "owned,"[3] a cultural product and political resource[4] that is considered to be a "rightful legacy of distinct people."[5] Heritage also constitutes a large part of personal identity[6] and collective ethnic and national identity.[7] In order to grasp the reality of heritage, one must ask, "What is heritage? Why, and for whom, is heritage created?"[8] Since the 1960s, anthropologists have begun to emphasize power, difference, and contestation over consensus in examining the meanings of the past.[9] The understanding has become prevalent that contestation lies within heritage itself, which even makes "discordance or lack of agreement and consistency" a meaning of heritage.[10] This approach generates further questions such as, "Who is contesting what, and with whom?"[11] or "Can the past be 'owned' and, if so, who 'owns' it? What do we mean by 'own' and who reconciles conflicting claims to such ownership?"[12]

Within this framework of the politics of heritage, I specifically focus on the issues associated with teaching a heritage language in a school and community for immigrant children with Chinese and Vietnamese backgrounds in Osaka, Japan. Heritage language in the U.S. context is defined as "a language of personal relevance other than English"[13] — or otherwise, as a language that cannot be regarded as foreign because it is your parents' language, even though it is a language that you do not use every day.[14] Since meanings and values attached to heritage language depend on the power relationships between the language of the host society as well as on generational differences,[15] Nelleke van Deusen-Scholl argues that the political and historical forces that create the language environment for heritage language learners, the sociocultural factors that form the subjectivities of heritage language learners, as well as their individual ties to their heritage all need to be understood when examining the practice of heritage language learning.[16]

This article demonstrates how heritage language teaching institutionalized in school settings becomes a marker for ethnic minorities and is used to manage the boundary between ethnic minorities and the Japanese. In contrast, the boundary among ethnic minority participants is dissolved to include all participants across ethnic lines in the case of a local community's practice of heritage language learning. The result is empowering, but with limited effect. I argue that the effect is limited due to the nature of Japan's multiculturalism.

The ethnographic data I present in this article show discrepancies between teachers' and communities' beliefs about what ethnic minorities should be like, as well as about what immigrants are hoping to find in Japanese society.[17] The politics of heritage involves the legitimization of power and distinction,[18] as well as practices that exclude those who do not have access to heritage.[19] Therefore, by illuminating who decides what heritage is in this specific space where heritage language teaching unfolds in Osaka, Japan, I hope to examine what this practice legitimizes or excludes.

Changing Japan's Demography and Multiculturalism

Beginning in the 1970s Japan saw an influx of immigrants of various cultural backgrounds who came to Japan mainly as laborers. The immigrants included war-displaced Japanese orphans and their families from China in the 1970s, refugees from Indochina in the 1980s, and migrant workers of Japanese descent (*Nikkei*) from South America in the 1990s. According to Ministry of Justice statistics, registered foreigners in Japan in December 2008 numbered 2.2 million. The proportion of registered foreigners in the national population in 2008 was 1.74 percent, an increase of more than 64,000 (3.0 percent) from 2007.[20] In accordance with these numbers, the Ministry of Education, Culture, Sports, Science and Technology (hereafter, Ministry of Education) reported that 28,575 foreign children and students were enrolled in primary and senior high schools and schools for the physically and mentally challenged in 2008. Approximately 68 percent of these children were in primary schools. Speakers of Portuguese, Chinese, and Spanish totaled more than 70 percent of the 28,575.[21] Despite this increasing linguistic and cultural diversity in the educational arena, as Haruo Ota argues, the Ministry of Education recognizes foreign children as solely

Brazilian immigrant children in an elementary school classroom in Gunma Prefecture, Japan, 2008. "According to Ministry of Justice statistics, registered foreigners in Japan in December 2008 numbered 2.2 million. The proportion of registered foreigners in the national population in 2008 was 1.74 percent, an increase of more than 64,000 (3.0 percent) from 2007." (Credit: Apichai Shipper)

"those who need assistance with language," and only sets national guidelines for supporting these children's linguistic ability.[22]

In Japan, the ratio of foreign residents to the rest of the population is relatively low compared with that of other immigrant-accepting countries; nonetheless, as Stephen Castles and Mark Miller report in their discussion of immigration policies, scholars have considered multiculturalism and pluralism as the ideal form for the integration for immigrants.[23] In a multicultural or pluralistic structure, immigrants are not expected to give up their own cultural traditions, although it is anticipated that they will conform to certain key values while being granted equal rights in all spheres of society. The state's involvement (whether active or passive) in realizing this ideal is significant. In the case of Japan, the notion of multiculturalism and coexistence (*tabunka kyōsei*) is now the agenda of researchers, policy-makers, and teachers. Hiroshi Komai defines *tabunka kyōsei shakai,* a society for multiculturalism and coexistence, as one based on the ideal of respect for the cultures of ethnic groups composed of multiple immigrant and indigenous populations.[24] This is in contrast to mono-ethnicism (*tannitsu minzoku shugi*).[25]

In reality, however, there have not been any nationwide guidelines for promoting social integration until recently, when the government began to deal with a low birthrate and an aging society. In March 2006, the Ministry of Internal Affairs and Communications (MIC) published a report recommending programs for promoting tabunka kyōsei. This was the result of a year-long discussion by a study group launched by the Ministry in June 2005 on promoting multiculturalism and coexistence, the Study Group on Promoting Tabunka Kyōsei, composed of members of the learned class.[26] The MIC report recommends that the state request local governments to set multiculturalism and coexistence as their third goal following international exchange (*kokusai kōryū*) and international cooperation (*kokusai kyōryoku*), which have been in place since the latter half of the 1980s.²⁷ The impact of this report remains questionable, since my research in the summer of 2008 showed that not many people working with foreign residents and immigrants in Osaka were even aware of the report.

Since tabunka kyōsei is still a recent phenomenon in Japan, it is difficult to evaluate the effects of this discourse and the state's initiatives to promote multiculturalism. My ethnographic research and the literature on this issue shows, however, that Japan's multiculturalism manifests itself as "difference" multiculturalism, one that conceptualizes culture as homogeneous and reduces it to a means to an end, namely, as a badge for ethnic and national identity, despite the notion's grassroots origin as "critical" or "transformative" multiculturalism, which challenges the dominant norms and values to create a more democratic society.²⁸ Analyzing the discourses of tabunka kyōsei, scholars argue that Japan's multiculturalism attempts to "manage diversity by the strategic inclusion of difference,"²⁹ or even resonates with "assimilation" of foreigners under the discourse of "support" (*shien*),³⁰ instead of promoting diversity. In a sense, Japan's multiculturalism is similar to what Elizabeth Povinelli describes as "liberal multiculturalism" in Australia, which functions as an ideology and practice of governance and as a form of domination based on the dominant society's moral obligations toward minority subaltern subjects; the distinction is just that a different sense of moral obligation is at play.³¹ This twisting of the meaning of multiculturalism for "assimilation" and domination, despite its grassroots origin as "critical" or "transformative" happens despite the fact that the local minority education, which I argue is a forerunner of the localized multicultural education, shares a "transformative" goal of encouraging student empowerment and social action.³² The discrepancy occurs because approaches and modalities of multicultural education are numerous and may be inconsistently practiced, as Lotty Eldering argues in regards to multiculturalism in North America, Europe, and

"It Is Fun to Be Multiethnic," reads the cover of this booklet published to mark the thirtieth anniversary of Takatsuki Mukugenokai, a community-based education and activist group established by Korean teenagers in Osaka Prefecture. (Credit: Eika Tai/*Critical Asian Studies* 36:3 [2004])

Australia.³³ Despite its goal to involve everyone, in reality not all pupils are incorporated into multicultural education. Multicultural education that enables the participation of all is limited to an ideological discourse, for it exists merely as an addition to or a minor adaptation of the regular curriculum and tends to lean toward assimilation rather than cultural pluralism.³⁴ Although ethnic education in the local community began as an anti-hegemonic practice, the Japanese case presented below reveals that multicultural education in Japan, as Eldering explains, is practiced merely as an addition to or a minor adaptation of the regular curriculum, does not incorporate all students, and thus, leans toward assimilation rather than cultural pluralism.

In contrast to the slow pace of those issued by the national government, guidelines regarding foreigners/foreign residents were proposed at the prefectural and municipal levels as far back as the late 1970s. For example, in Aoyama City (pseudonym) in Osaka, the prefecture with the second largest population located in the western part of Japan, the guidelines for the education of foreign residents (*zainichi gaikokujin kyōiku shishin*) were announced in 1990. These stated that the goal of such education was to "retain and enhance ethnic identity" (*minzokuteki aidentiti no hoji shinchō*) of foreign children and to educate Japanese children about foreign histories and cultures. More recently, the city issued the guidelines for promoting internationalization (2003) and the plan for internationalization (2004) in order to advance understanding between foreigners and the Japanese; these were based on the goal of raising awareness about human rights.³⁵ Internationalization founded on the concept of human rights in the city was a result of the history of social movements of the former outcast people, Buraku (*burakumin*), and resident Koreans (as explained in the next section). Accordingly, while the Buraku and resident Koreans laid the foundation of this work, the focus of this article will be on Chinese and Vietnamese new immigrants.

Multiethnic Miyako

Scholars have drawn attention to the fact that Japan has been multiethnic since the late nineteenth century, and that the homogeneity of Japan is a myth that became prevalent in the postwar period.³⁶ Miyako (pseudonym), located in Aoyama City, is one of the neighborhoods that can be portrayed as being multiethnic. Koreans, Chinese, and Vietnamese entered the Miyako Buraku area, along with working-class non-Buraku Japanese, creating a neighborhood consisting of people with various social and cultural backgrounds. The Buraku are the descendants of the outcastes of the Tokugawa period (1603–1867) who were prone to discrimination due to their outcaste status, which was itself based on their occupation.³⁷ Koreans include those who migrated to Japan during Japan's annexation of Korea from 1910 to 1945 and their descendants, i.e., resident Koreans. The Chinese here are the returned migrants: war-displaced Japanese and their families left in China after World War II and who have returned to Japan.³⁸ The Vietnamese are refugees and their families whom the Japanese government has allowed to immigrate since the late 1970s, prior to the government's ratification of an international treaty.³⁹

Facing discrimination and poverty similar to that experienced by the Buraku, Koreans began residing in Miyako in the 1920s, and are said to have moved into Miyako from other cities in Osaka Prefecture and outside Osaka after World War II.[40] The Vietnamese arrived in Miyako in the late 1980s, while the Chinese have resided there since the mid 1990s. In June 2008, in Aoyama City, Koreans numbered 4,248; Chinese numbered 1,473; and Vietnamese numbered 833.[41] These figures only include nationals of each country, those who have formal membership in each state, excluding those who were originally from these countries but who have become naturalized Japanese. In the 2000 survey of Buraku communities conducted by Osaka Prefecture the population of the government-assigned Dowa district[42] of Miyako was 2,297. Only 30 percent of the residents claimed to be members of the Buraku; approximately 60 percent claimed to be non-Burakumin; and the rest (approximately 10 percent) were reported as "unknown." Among all the residents in the Dowa district of Miyako, 90 percent were Japanese (including the Buraku), 9 percent were Koreans, and almost 2 percent were other nationals, i.e., the "newcomer" Chinese and Vietnamese immigrants.[43]

In 2003 I argued that examining the situation of the older minority groups (i.e., resident Koreans and the Buraku) is essential to the understanding of the situation of recently arrived immigrants in my field site.[44] The city's internationalization initiatives have been of the "human rights" type, following Keizo Yamawaki's classification,[45] due to the earlier social movements of the Buraku and resident Koreans. Whether under the name of either "multicultural education" or "education for international understanding" for immigrant children, newer programs and the philosophy behind them can be traced back to the educational programs previously developed as Dowa education for the Buraku and ethnic education for resident Koreans. For this reason, in the following section I briefly review the situation of resident Koreans in relation to the Buraku community.

During my initial fieldwork between 1998 and 2000, I lived in Miyako and conducted participant observations of everyday practices. In particular, I examined the educational practices directed toward 1.5-generation Chinese and second-generation Vietnamese children in school and within their local community, where minority groups with different historical, cultural, and political locations reside. The public elementary school in Miyako was my main field site. I conducted participant observations of class activities, as well as formal[46] and informal interviews with teachers, children, parents, and other residents both in and out of school. I especially focused on Chinese and Vietnamese children participating in extracurricular ethnic club activities, such as heritage language teaching (*bogo shidō*) in the elementary school. Following these children over eighteen months, I spent one semester each observing a second-grade homeroom class and a fifth-grade homeroom class where Chinese and Vietnamese children were in attendance. I helped students as a teacher's aide upon request, but other teachers, children, and parents all called me "teacher" (*sensei*). I also participated in school events as a "teacher," had school lunch with other non-homeroom teachers in the teachers' office, and attended teacher's meetings. Outside the school, I visited community centers — including Tomoni (pseudonym), the community education center that I discuss in the next section. The follow-up to this research was conducted for one month per year in 2001, 2004, and 2008.

Heritage Language Education in the Local Community

In order to better understand the cultural politics of the local community and to contextualize the current situation of Miyako residents of different backgrounds, I first briefly present the history of Tomoni, a community education center in Miyako where ethnic education for resident Koreans in Aoyama originated. While Tomoni now provides activities for Chinese and Vietnamese immigrants, it originally offered activities for resident Koreans only.

Tomoni, intended for those of Korean ethnic and cultural background, was founded in 1974 as a Korean community protest against a junior high school in the neighborhood. Because the Korean community believed that their problems (such as underachievement and delinquency) could not be reduced to the fact that they were residing in the Buraku community or to social class issues, they realized the importance of starting an educational program of their own for Korean children. With the support of Japanese teachers, a second-generation Korean college student began a study group to tutor Korean junior high school students twice a week in a room in the Miyako branch office of the Buraku Liberation League (hereafter, BLL).[47] Although the coalition between the Buraku and

Table 1.

	Local Community	Public School
Locality	Heritage language classes (*rūtsu-go kyōshitsu*) for Chinese, Vietnamese, and Koreans (ended in 2004) at Tomoni.	Heritage language teaching (*bogo shidō*) for Vietnamese in the Vietnamese ethnic club at Miyako Elementary School.
When activities are offered	On Saturday since 2004.	Once a week during after-school ethnic club activities as an extracurricular activity, 1998 to 2000.
Participants	Children "with roots in foreign countries" such as those with Korean, Vietnamese, or Chinese background.	Children "whose parents were from Vietnam," including Japanese nationals and Japan-born.
Goals	International understanding and exchange; strengthening pride in ancestral backgrounds; improving Japanese language ability.	Maintaining Vietnamese language ability; improving Japanese language ability; nurturing identity as Vietnamese.
Tabunka kyōsei	Tabunka kyōsei among participants, i.e., those "with roots in foreign countries."	Participants were segregated from other students during ethnic club activities

Korean communities was not always free from tensions, the Miyako BLL branch office did support Tomoni as a subsection for an "ethnic group" (*minzoku bukai*), and together they formed a joint front against the Buraku discrimination.[48] In 1981, Tomoni's ethnic educational activities received official assistance from the city after many negotiations and the Tomoni center became an annex of Miyako's Youth Center. The involvement of some teachers in Tomoni's activities dates back to the 1980s; their long-standing interest in ethnic education led them to cooperate with school personnel to support ethnic club activities in public schools. Thus, Tomoni had a strong tie to the Miyako Buraku community, although Korean community activists were hesitant to depend on this community and wanted to seek their own path. But the fact that no city funds were available for Koreans, who were foreign nationals, hindered Tomoni from developing independently from the Miyako Buraku community.[49] Tomoni lasted for twenty-two years as an annex of the Youth Center — until March 2002, when the special measures for the Buraku officially ended. The Special Measures Legislation of 1969 was meant to allocate resources in such a way as to eliminate the disadvantaged status of and prejudice against the Buraku; it was to do so by providing a physical environment for the community, by providing grants to Buraku families, and by offering education that would change public attitudes.[50] In September 2002, Tomoni was split into a sort of city center for education for international understanding and a not-for-profit organization (NPO) of Osaka Prefecture, independent of the Miyako Buraku and the city,[51] for providing educational activities for ethnic minorities in Aoyama (especially Miyako).

In the mid 1990s Tomoni started providing cultural activities for immigrant children and adults as the city's center for international exchange (*kokusai kōryū*). In April 1999 it began offering after-school educational activities for Vietnamese and Chinese children on a regular basis in addition to those it already provided for Korean children. Tomoni staff members saw similarities between their own experience "as minorities with roots in foreign countries" and that of the Chinese and Vietnamese children, despite the differences in their ethnic and cultural origins. According to Tomoni, hardships for foreigners living in Japan (such as discrimination against those seeking employment or looking to rent an apartment) still persist today for resident Koreans and recent immigrants. Tomoni is working to raise citizens' awareness of human rights to promote understanding between the Japanese and those with different cultural roots and to create a multicultural society based on human rights, where all cultural and social backgrounds are equally respected.[52] Heritage language classes are one of the services Tomoni offers.

The origin of heritage language teaching in Miyako can be traced back to the fall of 1998, when a naturalized Japanese woman of Vietnamese descent began to teach Vietnamese to eight children from four families in the neighborhood. The language instruction, which began at the request of the students' mothers, took place in a rented apartment that became a "cultural center" (*bunka sentā*) for children and adults.[53] Unfortunately the Vietnamese class had to be canceled after three months due to the instructor's other commitments.

Multilingual signs in Miyako (left) and in the city hall in Aoyama City, Osaka, are everyday reminders of Japan's growing diversity. (Credit: author. All geographical names are pseudonyms.)

In June 2004, Tomoni began offering heritage language classes as "root languages" (*rūtsu-go*) classes to Koreans, Chinese, and Vietnamese.[54] These classes were part of a larger Tomoni cultural program for international exchange that came about due to an increase in the number of immigrant children from Vietnam and China in the neighborhood, as well as in response to a decline in resident Koreans' interests in ethnic club activities.[55] A Tomoni official quoted in a March 2008 *Asahi Shimbun* article observed that resident Korean children, who are now fourth generation, are becoming "invisible" in Miyako. Few children have Korean nationality, Korean culture is no longer passed down at home, and a decreasing number of children are gathering at Tomoni for their activities. Instead of educating students of Korean descent, Tomoni is now receiving consultation requests from Indochinese refugees and Chinese returnees, who are moving into the neighborhood's public housing. In the *Asahi Shimbun* article, a Tomoni official explains that Tomoni started heritage language classes for the Vietnamese and Chinese in 2004 because the "identity struggles [*yuragi*] that resident Koreans experienced earlier" are similar to those the Vietnamese and Chinese were facing. He continues, "Once you become 'invisible,' you need to make an extra effort to go back. Although the children of Korean descent believe that they are no different from the Japanese, they will come up against a brick wall being conscious of their identity." He adds, "I hope that 'invisible' Korean children can gain an opportunity to become conscious of their roots [by participating in Tomoni's activities with other more 'visible' Vietnamese and Chinese children])."[56]

Reflecting a practice of minority education that essentializes the idea of culture, identity here is collectively defined as one based on countries of origin, disregarding individual differences among the groups. This conceptualization will be problematized and discussed later on.

The Tomoni heritage language classes, which were offered once a week on Saturday mornings, started in June 2004 with the Vietnamese; three months later classes began for the Chinese and Koreans. During the academic year 2005–2006, participants included fifteen Vietnamese (reduced later to twelve), twelve Chinese (dropping later to eight), and four Koreans (up to fourth generation, introductory level). The classes were started at the request of community members who were worried that their children were becoming too dependent on the Japanese language in their everyday life. The specific reasons for requesting heritage language classes differed slightly from group to group. The Vietnamese parents were concerned about their communication with their children, who were forgetting their parents' language. Three or four Vietnamese parents especially requested that they teach "writing" (*moji*). Vietnamese children themselves also wanted to learn the language of their "roots," or of their cultural background. Since the same Chinese characters can have different meanings in Japanese, the Chinese children themselves requested heritage language classes in which they might learn the written language, which they thought they were lacking. A Korean heritage language class was offered in response to a demand by children of Korean descent; a Tomoni staff member explained, however, that the Korean heritage language class ended in the second semester of that year.[57]

The heritage language classes at Tomoni are envisioned as a way to keep children in touch with their root languages, and to strengthen their pride in their ancestral backgrounds as they gather together with peers who share the same backgrounds. The belief that speaking a language other than Japanese improves Japanese language skills inspired the creation of Tomoni's heritage language classes as well.[58] These views can also be observed in other institutional settings such as in school, for they have become a foundation for the value of the education for immigrants in Aoyama City.

Heritage Language Education in Public School

During my fieldwork in Miyako's elementary school, heritage language teaching (*bogo shidō*) was offered as an ethnic club activity and paired with Japanese language instruction in after-school Japanese language classes (*nihongo kyōshitsu*). Although ethnic club activities for Chinese children also included teaching some Chinese words and phrases, the emphasis on heritage language was stronger in the ethnic club activities for Vietnamese children despite the fact that many of them had been born in Japan. For this reason, in this section, I focus on the ethnic club activities provided between 1998 and 2000 for the Vietnamese children, which included heritage language instruction.

Heritage language teaching began in Miyako in April 1998 as an after-school ethnic club activity for Vietnamese elementary school children with the teaching of simple words and greetings. Other schools in Aoyama City sponsored Japanese language classes and heritage language teaching for foreign children, but their programs were irregular. Miyako was unique in offering heritage language learning activities on a regular weekly basis, with Vietnamese children particularly in mind. They introduced these activities early on in a Ministry of Education–designated Center School (*sentā-kō*) of the Area for the Promotion of Educating and Receiving Foreign Children (*gaikokujin shijo kyōiku ukeire suishin chiiki*). The Ministry of Education expected the Center School to play a leading role and propose innovative practices for the instruction of Vietnamese children. By the summer of 2008, however, the heritage language teaching programs in Miyako and its neighboring school were gone, reflecting the transient and unstructured nature of educational activities and programs for "children of foreign nationalities" in Japan. Decisions regarding which activities to provide for these children were left to the teachers at each school.

Table 2 shows the cultural backgrounds other than Japanese of the 418 students enrolled in the elementary school in 1998.

Table 2. Enrollment of children with cultural backgrounds other than Japanese

Vietnamese*	19
Chinese*	12
Ethnic Koreans§	59
Children with one Japanese parent†	2
Total (out of 418 total enrollment)	92

* Including one Japanese national.
§ Including thirty-three Japanese nationals.
† "Doubles" or half-Japanese.

In addition to the 92, 46 students were Buraku (although the official record reported 203, or 48.6 percent of the total).[59] This categorization of foreign children based on their cultural backgrounds does not match the legal classifications based on students' nationalities, for each group includes Japanese whose nationality is based on descent or was acquired through the naturalization process. Following the school's categorization schemes, I refer to the children whose parents are from China and Vietnam as "Chinese" and "Vietnamese," respectively, including in these categories students who were Japan-born or who became naturalized Japanese citizens.

In 1987, five years before the Ministry of Education promulgated national guidelines for assisting "foreign children who need Japanese language assistance," Miyako's elementary school had taken the initiative to begin providing Japanese language instruction for immigrant children. In 1991, the school expanded beyond simple language instruction and established a "Japanese language class," meaning a classroom with a teacher with responsibility for both language instruction and the weekly ethnic club activities.[60] As the number of immigrant children in Miyako increased — and with the 1992 national guidelines in mind — schools began registering students identified as Chinese or Vietnamese in language classes. The students were enrolled as soon as they entered school and took part in the classes — in addition to their regular homeroom assignments — regardless of the children's and their parents' pref-

Vietnamese (above) practicing a lion's dance for a New Year's Festival in the gymnasium of a school in Aoyama City, December 1998. (Left) A lion dance performed in a park in Miyako during the Vietnamese Mid-Autumn Moon Festival, October 2009. (Credit: author. All names are pseudonyms.)

erence or their backgrounds. In the 1998 academic year, all twelve Chinese children had been born in China; most of them had been in Japan for only two to three years and were still learning Japanese. As for the nineteen Vietnamese children, most had been born in Japan or had come to Japan as infants. They were thus technically second-generation Vietnamese. All had a functional command of conversational Japanese, except for one child who had come to Japan half a year earlier.

Weekly after-school ethnic club programs originated in the minority education services offered in local communities such as Miyako, i.e., the education for the Buraku and for resident Koreans run by Tomoni. Accordingly, national and local educational discourses and practices all combined to shape the Japanese language classes that Chinese and Vietnamese children participated in after school.[61] Elsewhere I have explained that the space where heritage language teaching was practiced in Japanese language classes in the Miyako school's multicultural education program was constituted by (1) discourses and practices of traditional minority education, i.e., ethnic education for resident Koreans and Dowa education for the Buraku, as well as the programs for "international exchange" and "international understanding" promoted as part of this education at the local level; and (2) the national government guidelines that established Japanese language classes for non-Japanese speaking children.[62] This intertwining of various discourses and practices made up a unique environment for immigrant children in Miyako.

The weekly ethnic club featured activities to help students learn about their own cultures, e.g., games, history lessons, and cooking classes. In addition, the teacher in charge of the Vietnamese children was particularly enthusiastic about introducing her students to the Vietnamese language in order to help them maintain their "mother tongue." A visiting Vietnamese college student, who was helping as an instructor in the Japanese language class, was asked to read stories aloud in Vietnamese, pronounce Vietnamese words, speak to the children in Vietnamese, and share her experience "as a Vietnamese living in Japan" — to be a role model for the children.

Japanese Teachers' Essentialism vs. Communities' Feelings and Practical Concerns

Heritage language teaching and other ethnic club activities in Miyako's elementary school aimed to help immigrant and ethnic minority children learn about their cultures and languages. The goal of these activities was to "retain and nurture ethnic identity" (*minzokuteki aidentiti no hoji shinchō*),[63] in keeping with the goal of local minority education, namely, education for the Buraku and for resident Koreans. The aim of this education was to raise and nurture self-awareness in members of these minority groups in society. The phrase "awareness of social location" (*shakaiteki tachiba no jikaku*) was used from the start in Burakumin educational programs; in educational programs involving resident Koreans the phrase used was "awareness of one's ethnic background" (*minzokuteki jikaku*). When the term "identity" was introduced to the teachers' community in Osaka in the mid 1990s, it came to be used interchangeably with the phrase "awareness of one's ethnic background" for resident Koreans. Thus, for teachers, the term "ethnic identity" (*aidentiti*) encompasses both "awareness of one's ethnic background [for resident Koreans] and social location" [for the Buraku].[64]

Aiming to "retain and nurture ethnic identity," heritage language teaching was offered to Vietnamese students in Miyako. Teachers regarded Vietnamese language instruction as important for three reasons: (1) it helped students maintain their Vietnamese language skills so they could communicate with their parents, who often did not speak much Japanese; (2) it improved their Japanese; and (3) it nurtured their identity as Vietnamese. The message imparted to the students was, "You should not speak only Japanese. You should speak both [Japanese and Vietnamese]. Be proud of yourself as Vietnamese in Japan." To a Vietnamese child who uses a Japanese name, the message was, "You should use your ethnically distinctive name."

A similarity between the goals of the old and new minority education was the essentializing practice of associating members of each group with the social categories of each particular group (the Buraku, Korean, Chinese, and Vietnamese), reducing them to their ancestral origins. As special programs for children of Buraku and Korean backgrounds became relatively inactive in the Miyako community, this identity association began to apply more and more to the "newcomer" Chinese and Vietnamese. As the social categories of "Chinese"

Pictured here is a heritage language class for Vietnamese organized by Tomoni, September 2009. Established in 1974, the Tomoni community education center in Miyako is the place where ethnic education for resident Koreans in Aoyama originated. While it now provides activities for Chinese and Vietnamese immigrants, the Tomoni community education center originally offered activities for resident Koreans only. (Credit: author. All names are pseudonyms.)

and "Vietnamese" illustrate, Chinese and Vietnamese referred to those who were from a foreign nation (Chinese) and those whose parents were originally from a foreign nation (Vietnamese) despite their nationalities or places of birth; naturalized Japanese nationals of Chinese or Vietnamese origins or those who were born in Japan were referred to as "Chinese" and "Vietnamese." This also reflected the limitation of Japan's multiculturalism, which manages differences based on ethnic backgrounds instead of promoting diversity.

In this section, I present ethnographic data that show discrepancies between teachers' beliefs regarding how ethnic minorities/immigrants should be educated and conduct themselves, and what immigrants and their descendants were hoping to find in Japanese society. Teachers in Miyako described Chinese and Vietnamese children as "not taken care of at home," "not disciplined as Japanese children," "having a difficult family background," or "without the ability to absorb complex and abstract ideas due to being 'semi-lingual,'" suggesting a preference for Japanese middle-class norms and cultural capital.[65] Convinced of the value of essentializing and strengthening the ethnic identities of their students, teachers encouraged them to take pride in their ethnic backgrounds. This effort reflected the teachers' own essentializing view that heritage and identity are linked to empower minority students, which was a counter-hegemonic move. Based on my ethnographic observations and interviews, however, I argue that these disagreements between the views of teachers and the community reveal that the essentializing practices become a way of marginalizing immigrants in the space constructed by the dominant Japanese culture. The first two cases below illustrate the immigrants' and ethnic minorities' responses

Heritage: Owned or Assigned?

to the way the dominant society tries to preserve heritage through language and cultural practices taught in schools. I follow with two cases that illustrate educational practices that encourage ethnic minorities and immigrants to retain their ethnic identities.

When I was talking with Kim (pseudonym), a second-grade Vietnamese girl (born in Japan), in her homeroom during a lunch break, Ms. Fukui came up to us and asked the girl how she was doing. Kim replied, "Yes, I am doing well." And then, the teacher said smilingly, "What is 'hello' in Vietnamese?" The teacher was being friendly and wanted to chat with her. But the girl looked outside the window and said, "I do not know." Since her classroom recited "good morning" and "good-bye" every day in Japanese, Korean, and Vietnamese, reflecting the backgrounds of the foreign children in the class,[66] everyone in Kim's classroom knew the answer. Any child in Kim's homeroom could have answered that question. Moreover, Kim was familiar with Vietnamese words and phrases from her Vietnamese ethnic club activities. Her reply to the teacher could not have been out of ignorance. Rather, she no doubt did not want to be singled out because of her different ethnic background. The teacher may only have wanted to show her appreciation of Kim's culture, assuming that Kim was communicating with her siblings and parents in Vietnamese, but in Kim's eyes, saying "good morning" or "*sin-cha-o*" in unison with the other children with a Japanese accent was only a matter of Japanese school routine. In daily conversation, by contrast, the Vietnamese greeting was an ethnic marker that separated Kim from the other students.

Reflecting back on the after-school activities that are required only for foreign children, Kim-Ly (pseudonym), a woman in her early twenties at the time of my February 2000 interview, who was born in Nha Trang, Vietnam, and had migrated to Japan at the age of one, expressed negative feelings about Vietnamese children having to register in an extracurricular activity just because they were not Japanese. "I did not do well at school, but it is only because I did not study. How come the Vietnamese children are kept after school when they want to play with their friends? It is none of their business to keep the children after school for the Japanese language classes and ethnic club activities." Kim-Ly's reflections on being an immigrant child mesh with Kim's case (above), demonstrating that those who lived in Japan for most of their lives identify more with Japan and the Japanese and are not comfortable being treated differently as a foreigner. I analyze Kim's and Kim-Ly's responses as expressing frustration as a result of their being identified as a member of an "ethnic minority" in a Japanese school.

Differences between the views of communities and teachers were also evident in educational practices such as using ethnic names and teaching heritage language in order to enhance ethnic identity. This educational approach, which goes back to ethnic education for resident Koreans in Osaka in the 1970s, uses ethnic identity and ethnically distinct names (for foreign children) as identification markers for members of minority groups. As a result of this practice and approach, teachers who strongly believe in this tradition were critical of foreigners' "assimilation" to Japanese culture and their preference for using Japanese names.

Since the beginning of Korean ethnic education in Osaka in the 1970s the practice of "calling Korean children by their real names and asking them to use their real names" (*honmyō o yobi nanoru*) has been regarded important in their version of ethnic education.[67] Teachers who believe in ethnic education use ethnically distinct names to signify that the community has overcome discrimination against resident Koreans. At the same time, however, students who choose to use ethnic names are marked as non-Japanese. Their school-time experiences — coupled with the difficulties that foreigners continue to encounter in Japan — make it understandable that some elect to switch back to their Japanese names later in life.[68] Teachers who value ethnic education for resident Koreans and "newcomers" as well have been known to operate on the principle that "Japanese names = hiding ethnicity = an effort to escape discrimination."

During a visit that a female Japanese teacher and I made to a Vietnamese family in February 2000, the father told us delightedly that their family's surname is Murakami and that their daughter, who went to work after graduating from junior high school, was considering using her Japanese name. The Japanese teacher objected, "It is not right to use a Japanese name when you have your own Vietnamese name. It is so wrong." Both the husband and wife were wide-eyed, as if they were shocked to hear her words. I heard other parents express concerns that their children would be bullied if they were to use their Vietnamese names. Some students, both Chinese and Vietnamese, preferred to use their Japanese names. During my field research in Miyako in 1998–2000, nine out of the school's twelve Chinese children used their Japanese names and five out of the school's nineteen Vietnamese children used their Japanese names. Ten years later in 2008, the preference for Japanese names among the Vietnamese students has increased. The Vietnamese instructor at Tomoni stated, "Switching to Japanese names is like a fad among the Vietnamese in Miyako now."[69]

Another case deals with mothers' expectations about school and the school's interest in teaching heritage language at school. In response to my question regarding mother-tongue/heritage language teaching in ethnic club activities at school, a Vietnamese immigrant mother of three children in her mid-thirties, a naturalized Japanese, said,

> I want my children to learn the Japanese language more than the Vietnamese language. When they become older and if they want to learn [Vietnamese], they can study the language as a foreign language, like English. It is inevitable that children will forget the Vietnamese language as they learn the Japanese language. I want the school to teach the existence of Vietnam as a country by showing videos on Vietnamese culture and society so that the children will not be ashamed of Vietnam. But the most important thing for the children is to learn the Japanese language and to do well at school. Since the children do not understand the Vietnamese language that much, it may be too much for the children to learn the Vietnamese language at school.

She insisted that the teachers should help her children do well academically at school.[70] This vision fits well with a criticism made by two Chinese mothers and a student, who commented that teachers in Miyako are not strict enough and that schools in China are more academically rigorous. Having immigrated to Japan, these "newcomer" mothers wish their children to become academically successful in Japan, their new homeland.

The Politics of Heritage: Owned or Assigned?

The above-mentioned opinions of immigrant parents and their children suggest that ethnic educational practices are not always favored or welcomed and that immigrants have ambivalent feelings about heritage language and multicultural educational activities, despite their enthusiastic promotion by schools and instructors. Here, I analyze this contradiction by examining heritage language teaching and learning within the contexts of my field site and the social forces of the larger Japanese society.

First, ethnic cultures are not necessarily regarded as a source of empowerment in Japanese society: Japanese society has yet to acknowledge other cultures as resources for the enrichment of Japanese society, despite the guidelines set by national and local governments. Emphasizing ethnic cultures in Japan today has noticeable negative effects such as the reinforcement of the boundary between the Japanese and other ethnic groups via the re-creation of ethnic minority categories that associate immigrant children with their countries of origin. Suzuki's findings regarding the preference of Okinawa-Bolivians to learn standardized Japanese over their heritage Okinawan dialect has similarities with the situation of Miyako's immigrants.[71] The strategic management of differences by schools and other institutions within the framework of assimilation and integration does not always yield positive results — a point illustrated by the ambivalence that communities feel about their assigned heritage in institutional settings.[72]

Second, not many immigrants/ethnic minorities are "actively" involved in learning their heritage language or maintaining ties with their ethnic communities due to the above-mentioned factor, despite the fact that heritage language can be a positive symbol of their heritage. This is especially explained by very few third- and fourth-generation ethnic Korean immigrants enroll in heritage language classes in Miyako community (only four students) and in the after-school Korean ethnic club (two students). The low enrollment prevails in spite of the fact that resident Koreans were the largest ethnic minority in my field site (numbering about sixty at the time of my research). As for resident Korean children, many express no identifying link with their ethnic-based collective identities.[73]

Third, heritage language teaching was offered to Chinese and Vietnamese elementary school students in Miyako as an extracurricular activity Japanese language class under the name of "mother tongue" teaching. The Ministry of Education "recommends" this class for those who are unable to speak Japanese, but "requiring" children whose parents are from China and Vietnam to register for this class has created a boundary between Japanese and non-Japanese children. Thus, immigrant children view heritage language teaching and Japanese language classes as signs of their being "non-Japanese." This finding contrasts with cases where schooling in heritage practices can be rendered as authentic cultural heritage (Yamasaki) or as a space where learners attach diverse meanings to heritage language and culture (Doerr and Lee).[74]

Fourth, the minority educational practices in evidence during my field study encouraged ethnic minority students to identify themselves with their ethnic backgrounds, as represented by their countries of origin. This educational approach had two results: (1) it suppressed the shaping of subjectivities that would be out of sync with students' ethnic backgrounds or countries of origin, and (2) it has not allowed the emergence of "hybrid" identities that crosscut national boundaries. An example of the latter is Cantonese-speaking ethnic Chinese immigrants from Vietnam being told to identify themselves as Vietnamese, i.e., by their country of origin and not by their Chinese heritage. In this way, minority education teachers overlook the complex social and cultural backgrounds of their students, reducing them to children from China or Vietnam.[75] Yet studies have shown that identities are not primordial or ascribed, but rather are "a positional choice of the group with which they wish to be associated," more political, and associational.[76]

Moreover, identities change over time and are constantly being formed in our everyday life. In Miyako, however, the concept of identity as a "process" or as a "hybrid" is not in evidence in the stated beliefs and minority educational practices in the local elementary school. Given Japan's society's lukewarm embrace of diversity, immigrant and ethnic minority children prefer to assimilate into the dominant culture, as seen from the cases in which resident Koreans or Buraku prefer to "pass" as Japanese, as well as from the cases in which Chinese and Vietnamese people opt to use their Japanese names. John Lie argues that the resident Koreans and Buraku could become Japanese as individuals as a result of passing, but could not be integrated into society as collectives and may reinforce discrimination. The invisibility and silence of minority groups are, according to Lie, due to monoethnic ideology of Japan.[77] This practice of passing promotes the "homogenization" of society, in spite of the politics of recognition by minority groups.

Discussing globalization as one of the factors that has created the conditions of multiculturalism, Stuart Hall lists "homogenization" and "differentiating effects" as its dominant cultural tendency. According to Hall, globalization is a system that "con-form[s] difference, rather than a convenient synonym for the obliteration of difference."[78] Japanese society shares this cultural trait of "homogenization" while the process of "differentiation" proceeds. "Homogenization" furthers assimilation in the cultural sphere without actualizing any structural differentiation and without protecting cultural differences as rich social resources. As such, in Miyako, the politics of heritage are played out in the limited domain that both hegemonic and anti-hegemonic forces have constructed for supporting ethnic and cultural minorities in Japan. As discussed above, one of these spaces is Tomoni, which provides activities for ethnic minorities in Miyako and Aoyama City.

If the languages taught in Miyako are those of the heritage created and re-created in a specific context, what do these practices and processes legitimize and exclude? As my ethnographic research has shown, heritage language teaching in the school setting brands the Chinese and Vietnamese languages as the heritage "resources" of students enrolled in the Japanese language classes. Through heritage language educational programs and ethnic club activities, Vietnamese and Chinese students acquire the heritage "knowledge" of their countries of origin, however much this might differ from their actual ethnic backgrounds, as seen in the case of ethnic Chinese children from Vietnam being classified as Vietnamese. Those who determine what heritage is for these children are teachers, and these individuals represent the dominant Japanese. Accordingly, heritage language teaching and related educational activities, which aim to foster and ensure the appreciation of the students' heritage, have the opposite effect. Under the state-recommended Japanese language class system, they ironically legitimize the non-Japanese character of the Chinese and Vietnamese students — and thus contribute to their exclusion from the community of ordinary Japanese.

Heritage language teaching outside of the school system in Miyako, which was first organized by a woman of Vietnamese origin and then later introduced systematically at Tomoni, does not involve such contradictions because the learners themselves decided and selected their own heritage or "root" language by choosing to participate in these activities. In this educational setting, both the creators and the providers of their heritage are members of ethnic minorities: the organizing staff members are resident Koreans and the participants are Chinese and Vietnamese children and their parents. The Korean educational center, Tomoni, incorporates non-Korean immigrant children from the neighborhood into a restricted domain in which heritage politics are played out free from the larger sociocultural forces of society. The fact that Tomoni's main players are foreigners can have empowering and encouraging effects on those with roots outside Japan. Those who participate in Tomoni programs are empowered by "owning" their heritage through the center's activities. One Chinese high school girl, who was born in Jilin, China, and had migrated to Japan when she was four, as the great-grandchild of a war-displaced Japanese, explained that she feels empowered by Tomoni because the center provides a space to gather for those whose roots are in foreign countries. She said, "Due to Tomoni's activities, we gather. Without Tomoni, my friends with foreign backgrounds and I are scattered. If I am by myself, I am afraid, but thanks to Tomoni, I feel that I am not alone."[79] Her remarks show that by identifying herself as a member of an ethnic minority in Japan and not necessarily as Chinese — and specifically through her participation in Tomoni — she has been empowered as a foreigner in Japan.[80]

The boundary between resident Koreans and Chinese/Vietnamese immigrants in Tomoni is not as rigid as the one between ethnic minorities/foreigners and Japanese in the institutionalized school setting. The center is inclusive of all who identify themselves as "people with roots in foreign countries." Thus, the boundary here is similar to what Uchibori (1989), in discussing the concept of ethnic groups, calls "announcing one's names" (*nanori*) as opposed to "naming" (*nazuke*) by outsiders.[81] This resonates with Takamori's case of Japanese-Americans in Japan for whom the Japanese language simultaneously excludes and provides them a space of belonging and gives voice to their alterity.[82]

Outside Tomoni, however, the boundary separating minority participants/supporters and the Japanese functions in the same way as does "naming" them as foreigners, reinforcing the difference between Japanese and non-Japanese. Accordingly, the effects of the politics of heritage do not go beyond the space created by Tomoni, and thus, fail to have an effect on the broader Japanese society. Since the boundary dividing ethnic minorities/foreigners from the larger body of Japanese reinforces the differences between the two, heritage language and educational services for immigrants/ethnic minorities in Japan (whether in an institutionalized setting or in the local community) unexpectedly reinforce that boundary and reproduce asymmetrical power relationships between the dominant culture and the minorities. This is even truer when heritage language teaching is institutionalized as the cases of Kim and Kim-Ly demonstrated. The institutional force of schooling makes the boundary between Japanese and ethnic minorities more visible and rigid. Institutions, after all, do not exist in a vacuum: they reflect the symbolic values of the dominant culture, and in this case the dominant culture wishes to distinguish ethnic minorities from the larger Japanese society. Labeling ethnic minorities as "foreigners" arouses a sense of "nationality" (meaning feelings collectively shared)[83] in Japanese, and this in turn results in reinforcing the boundary between the two. The political meanings attached to activities that facilitate the rediscovery of heritage are yet perceived as purely positive within the context of Japan's limited form of "multiculturalism."

Conclusion

With cultural politics constituting the time-space in Miyako where ethnic minorities are engaged in heritage language, I argue that heritage language teaching — along with other educational practices such as ethnic club activities that come under the heading of multicultural education in schools — is not always a means of empowerment. In reality, it may result in further marginalizing these children. This is because the educational practices set students apart as minorities vis-à-vis the dominant Japanese, encouraging them to claim their ethnic identities through the use of ethnically distinctive names and by requiring them to learn their heritage language and cultural traditions. This process goes together with the cultural homogenization of long-term or historical minorities (Buraku and resident Koreans), while not addressing or actualizing structural differentiation. The marginalization of immigrant children deepens even more when the state-recommended Japanese language class system requires children in Miyako "whose parents are from China or Vietnam" to learn a heritage language. Heritage language learning in non-school community settings is voluntary and can empower participants, but even here the dominant Japanese society still "names" the participants foreigners/ethnic minorities. Hence the division between the two remains. The two distinct heritage language teaching practices — heritage language teaching in school and at Tomoni — took place in the same geographic space and are the same in that both involve heritage languages; however, each needs to be examined within its specific context as cultural politics in order for us to understand the full implications for those involved.

ACKNOWLEDGMENTS: I would like to thank participants of my research who generously assisted me during my field research. My research in Japan was supported by the Sasakawa Scientific Research Grant from the Japan Science Society, the Center for Japanese Studies at the University of California, Berkeley, as well as by the postdoctoral fellowship of the Faculty of Arts and Social Sciences, National University of Singapore. I would like to thank Neriko Doerr, Robin DeLugan, Kiri Lee, Yuri Yamasaki, Michiyo Takato, Laura Miller, John Davis, and three anonymous reviewers for their feedback in revising this article. I also appreciate Nelson Graburn's advice and help in suggesting references on heritage over the course of this process. Finally, I would like to thank Tom Fenton, managing editor of *Critical Asian Studies*, for his professional editing and helpful suggestions.

❑

4. Inheriting "Japanese-ness" Diversely

Heritage Practices at a Weekend Japanese Language School in the United States

Neriko Musha Doerr and Kiri Lee

THE MAIN TENET OF STUDIES ON HERITAGE LANGUAGE[1] is that promoting heritage language proficiency "will not only give us more individuals proficient in these languages, it will also dignify our country's heritage language communities and the cultural and religious values that their languages represent."[2] For example, reports indicate that early heritage language education can have a positive impact on the personal and collective self-esteem of minority language students.[3] Language reflects, reinforces, and acts upon relationships of political and economic dominance and inequity: "Because it is used to attain and retain power and control, prescribed language practices and language policies impact various groups differently."[4]

While existing scholarly work illustrates the complexity and nuanced character of heritage language education — due to diverse personal backgrounds and changing political economy and cultural politics[5] — the studies all assume that an individual's link to "heritage" is given and stable, unaffected by schooling processes. This article complements these studies by examining schools as a site of heritage practices, especially regarding the role schools play in an individual's "inheriting" Japanese-ness.[6]

The notion of heritage practice has recently been put forward to stress the fact that heritage is a dynamic process. The moment a particular daily action is thought of as heritage by the person doing the action, meta-cultural awareness emerges, transforming the person's relationship to the action.[7] For example, when playing a card game like *hanahuda* is considered to be a part of passing on Japanese heritage, the card game is approached differently. Heritage is thus better conceptualized as a practice (of considering and treating hanahuda as heritage) than an artifact (the hanahuda cards themselves). "Heritage" thus consists of an assemblage of such "heritage practices" of various social actors and institutions.[8] Drawing on this framework, we view the process of attending heritage language school as a process through which individuals develop a meta-cultural awareness of the language they learn at the school.

Studies by Pierre Bourdieu and Jean-Claude Passeron have shown that schools legitimize certain knowledge, certain ways of being, and certain actions.[9] In so doing, schools differentiate students according to how closely they approximate a valued ideal, e.g., "academic success"[10] or desired habitus,[11] or in terms of the categories schools employ to differentiate students: ethnicity,[12] gender, or a combination of these.[13] Also, standardization processes of language, fostered by mass schooling[14] — in line with the one-nation, one-language ideology of modern nation-states[15] — have differentiated students and made speakers of some linguistic varieties more valued than others in multilingual societies.[16] Schools, however, do not foster a single axis of differentiation or system of hierarchy. In addition, schools are the sites of ideological struggles, as nationalism and cosmopolitanism, monoculturalism and multiculturalism, or public and corporate interests compete to provide students with interpretations of reality and guidelines for future actions.[17] Exposed to such diverse and often contradictory ideologies, schools become productive sites that nurture various, sometimes unexpected, subject positions.[18]

Informed by the understanding of heritage as practice and these dynamics of schooling processes, we argue in this article that heritage language schooling proliferates ways that heritage language learners imagine and "inherit" their "heritage." Our ethnographic research in 2007–2008 at a weekend Japanese language school in the northeastern part of the United States indicates that heritage language schooling processes accentuate the diversity of students' personal backgrounds, the dialects they speak, and their linguistic proficiencies. This schooling transforms what had otherwise been understood merely as "speaking Japanese" into diverse ways to "inherit" Japanese language.[19]

In analyzing diverse ways to imagine "Japanese-ness" (hereafter without quotation marks), we employ the term "regimes of difference" and examine how such regimes of difference are *cited*. Regimes of difference are systems of categories, in which an item is defined in relation to another item that it is contrasted with. For example, "Western" culture is defined as the opposite of "Eastern" culture by selectively pointing out items that are different from the "Eastern" cultures. We draw on Louis Althusser's understanding that we experience the world through systems of categories. We are positioned or interpellated into such categories, and our practices are structured by them. In turn, individuals' behavior and language articulate the perceived differences of people, thereby making ideology manifest in concrete categories of people.[20] We also draw on Judith Butler's notion of performativity[21] in order to elucidate the process of materializing regimes of difference: by being cited as the norm, certain regimes of difference become naturalized and materialized as meaningful sets of categories in which to classify people.[22] For example, the practice of categorizing individuals according to nationality leads to positioning those whose ancestry includes two nationalities and/or who have lived in several countries in an in-between category (e.g., "half," "double," "hybrid") rather than a full-fledged category of being in itself. Individuals are *always already* subjects, Althusser contends, as they are born as subjects in a particular cate-

"Studies by Pierre Bourdieu and Jean-Claude Passeron have shown that schools legitimize certain knowledge, certain ways of being, and certain actions. In so doing, schools differentiate students according to how closely they approximate a valued ideal…or in terms of the categories schools employ to differentiate students…." (Neriko Doerr, February 2007)

gory and stay that way for the rest of their lives. Others believe that subjects are constituted by contradictory interpellations throughout their life (thus creating a multiplicity of subject positions within a subject) and individuals with diverse histories are interpellated differently by the same ideology.[23] Drawing on this framework, we view students' experiences at a heritage language school as processes of being interpellated into various subject positions.

Japanese heritage language education offers fertile ground for analyzing the many ways of inheriting language and determining what the act of inheritance represents. Heritage language education raises questions about what it means to be "Japanese," how "knowing Japanese language" relates to "being Japanese," and who has the right to certify that someone knows the Japanese language. Issues such as these have risen due to the involvement of the Japanese government[24] and as a consequence of the decision taken by some alternative heritage language programs to sever their ties with the Japanese government.[25] Our research site, the Jackson Japanese Language School (JJLS, all the names in this article are aliases), offers both a conventional Japanese government–supported heritage language program and its own program independent of such government support. We show that the existence of these two kinds of programs vying for legitimacy produces competing imagining of what Japanese-ness is, further complicating relationships among regimes of difference through which students position themselves and others.

In what follows, we introduce our field site and our fieldwork, describe and analyze interviews with five students and two specific episodes in heritage language classrooms, and suggest a new focus of research in heritage language education as well as heritage politics.

Weekend Japanese Language Schools

Japanese heritage language instruction began in Hawaii in the 1890s shortly after Japanese immigration to the United States started, but the type of schools discussed in this article were not established until the early 1960s, when Japan's economic development led to increasing numbers of companies sending employees and their families to the United States for short-term assignments, thus creating a need for the schools.[26]

In May 2009, there were seventy-eight *hoshūkō,* weekend supplemental Japanese language schools, in the United States. These schools provide children from the first to the ninth grades (ages six to fifteen)[27] with the same education the students would have received in Japan's compulsory educational system except that five days of general instruction are compressed into one school day with a focus on language arts. The schools aim to enable these children to continue in the Japanese school system upon their return to Japan.[28] When the number of "Japanese" students in such schools reaches one hundred, the Japanese government provides a subsidy that covers the salaries of the principal and other senior teachers.[29]

Beginning in the 1990s, these hoshūkō are having to accommodate a growing diversity of students. In order to cater to students whose aims in studying Japanese do not fit the hoshūkō scheme, a *keishōgo* (Japanese-as-a-heritage-language) program has been developed in some United States cities.[30] The hoshūkō schools follow the *kokugo* (national language/language arts) curriculum in compulsory education based on Japanese government guidelines and they use government-certified textbooks. The kokugo, in Toshiaki Yasuda's words, is "an institution that is used to create and unify a nation in modern nation-states."[31] In contrast, keishōgo programs provide locally produced curricula created by teachers and approved by administrators with no necessary relation to government-sanctioned curriculum guidelines.[32]

Many parents told author Kiri Lee and other administrators that they do not consider the kokugo instruction in the hoshūkō to be *heritage* language education: they argued that it was more about learning Japanese as a school subject (language arts) — as "Japanese children do in Japan" — than about inheriting the Japanese language as Japanese Americans.[33] Guadalupe Valdés defines a heritage language learner in the United States as one "who is raised in a home where a non-English language is spoken, who speaks or at least understands the language, and who is to some degree bilingual in that language and in English."[34] If we use Valdés's definition, the kokugo and keishōgo programs can be seen as two kinds of heritage language education: one is Japanese-government-prescribed (kokugo) and the other is independent (keishōgo). Most JJLS parents, however, do not share this view. The different understandings of these two programs create a fertile ground in which to analyze how students, parents, administrators, and researchers construct, give meanings to, and contest other's perceptions of what "knowing Japanese language," thus "being Japanese," entails.[35]

Jackson Japanese Language School

Our research site, the Jackson Japanese Language School, is distinctive in that it has a well-established keishōgo program (grades two to nine) alongside a hoshūkō that provides kokugo education. Established in 1980 in a suburb of a major metropolitan area in the northeast United States, the JJLS education program caters to students, from preschoolers to adults, who wish to learn Japanese. JJLS is a private nonprofit organization and is overseen by a board of trustees; it supports itself by funding from tuition fees, Japanese government grants, and donations from local businesses. The school meets from 1:00 P.M. to 4:20 P.M. on forty-two Sundays a year in a rented building at a local university.

In April 2008, JJLS had two education divisions (see fig. 1): the first is the hoshūkō (grades one to nine) and the second includes a keishōgo program called the Jackson Course along with other Japanese language programs in the school. The Jackson Course was established in 2004 for students who have no plans to go back to Japan and therefore do not wish to follow the hoshūkō curriculum. Thus students and parents have a choice between two programs: hoshūkō and the Jackson Course.[36] The Jackson Course's curriculum was designed by school administrators and teachers independent of the kokugo curriculum, and Japanese government certified textbooks are not used exclusively. The medium of instruction is Japanese.[37] To accommodate students with a range of Japanese language capabilities the Jackson Course offered three classes grouping children together according to their age (see fig. 1).

JJLS's student body can be roughly categorized into three groups[38] according to the length of their intended stay in the United States: (1) The *chūzai* or "short-term residence" group: students who live in the United States for three to five years due to a parent's intra-company transfer. Japanese tends to be the "first language"[39] of students in this group. (2) The *chōki-taizai* or "long-term residence" group: students who plan to stay in the United States for more than five years. Their return to Japan depends on a parent's being transferred within the company. Chōki-taizai students typically use English in their conversations with one another; they use Japanese only in limited situations, such as at home to their parents or at JJLS. (3) The *eijū* or "permanent residence" group: students who have no plans to live in Japan.[40] In the eijū case Japanese is not often the "first language" of one or both of the student's parents. For eijū students who were born and raised in the United States, English tends to be their "first language."

This article is based on ethnographic fieldwork at JJLS between February 2007 and March 2008, the first year of a four-year project to investigate how different types of classes influence the students' sense of national belonging.[41] Doerr performed the participant observation, conducted most of the interviews, and analyzed the data; and Lee handled permissions, conducted interviews, provided information regarding JJLS, and offered critical feedback to the analysis. Doerr and Lee have been part of the JJLS community as parents,

Fig. 1. Structure of JJLS in April 2008

Grade			
PreK		Pre-School Program	
K		3-5 years old	
1	*Hoshūkō*		JFL Program
2	Elementary School	Jackson Course	Grade 1-8
3	Grade 1-6	Level 2	
4		(Grade 2-4)	
5		Level 3	
6		(Grade 4-6)	
7	Middle School	Level 4	
8	Grade 7-9	(Grade 7-9)	
9			JFL Program
10		High School program	Grade 9-12
11		Grade 10-12	and adult
12			
Adult			

Note: The arrows show the possible advancement to the upper grades and the possible transfer to a different program within the school. Changing a program is determined based on discussions among a pertinent student, his/her parents, and a pertinent

and Lee is principal of the second division of JJLS. These relations allowed Doerr and Lee to gain trust from participants while situating them in particular power dynamics within the school.

For fieldwork, we followed a group of students who were in the sixth grade in the hoshūkō and Level 3 in the Jackson Course in the academic year of 2006–2007. During the research period covered by this article, we carried out participant observation in nine sessions of the hoshūkō and nine sessions of Jackson Course classes. Of seventeen sixth grade hoshūkō students, we interviewed ten students and nine of their parents. We also interviewed all five Jackson Course Level 3 students and their parents, and one new Level 4 student and his parent. We interviewed four teachers: teachers of sixth and seventh grade hoshūkō and Jackson Course Levels 3 and 4 classes.[42] Interviewees were asked a set of standard questions regarding their family background, how they came to live in the United States, their experiences at JJLS and of dialects of Japanese, their views on the hoshūkō and Jackson Course, and their and their family members' ethnic "identities." Most interviews were carried out before or after classes either in the school library, the lobby of the building, or an empty classroom; some interviews of parents and teachers were done at a coffee shop. We gave the interviewees a choice of language (English or Japanese) as a medium of interview. Interviews done in Japanese were translated to English for this article by the authors. The authors are fluent in both English and Japanese, but research was conducted mainly in Japanese.

"Inheriting Japanese-ness" in Hoshūkō Classes

In the sixth grade hoshūkō class in 2006–2007, roughly half of the seventeen students were chūzai and chōki-taizai, and the other half were eijū students. The hoshūkō class differed from the Jackson Course in several ways. For example, in keeping with the original aim of the hoshūkō program, the teachers we observed seemed to presume that all of their students intended to go back to Japan, addressing them as Japan's future labor force, for example.[43] Also, unlike in the Jackson Course, where all students were eijū and socialized in English during recess, hoshūkō class social groups were split by the language used, which overlapped the chūzai/eijū distinction: the former speaking in Japanese and the latter in English. Chōki-taizai students wavered between these groups. It was in this peer dynamics that the students we introduce below interpreted their actions and Japanese-ness.

We introduce our interviews with three hoshūkō students and their parents in order to illustrate students' diverse experiences in the hoshūkō and how that influenced their subjectivities. Then we examine a class discussion to show that what constitutes Japanese-ness can change.

Yaichi: Standardized into Heritage

Yaichi was talkative in class, fluent in Japanese, and eager to change the direction of classroom discussions by making casual comments to the teacher. On 11 March 2007, Doerr tape-recorded an interview with Yaichi in the school library.

Doerr began by asking Yaichi, who was born and raised in Japan, how he came to the United States and how he felt about the transition. Yaichi answered that he came in 2004 when he was in the fourth grade due to his father's intra-company transfer. He thought then that he would go back to Japan in 2008. Thus, he was a chūzai student. (In fact, Yaichi returned to Japan in December 2009 with the rest of the family for educational reasons; his father remains in the United States.) In response to Doerr's questions Yaichi explained that his parents sent him to JJLS so he could study in Japanese. He told Doerr that he liked JJLS because he felt comfortable there and could talk comfortably in Japanese with friends; there was nothing he disliked about JJLS. He valued the diversity of JJLS's student body because this enabled students to communicate different ideas. His teacher seemed to be relaxed about covering the materials, unlike his experience in the American school he attended, and took time to cater to diverse students' needs, Yaichi said.

When asked about his Osaka dialect, Yaichi explained that he shifted to the Tokyo-based "standard" Japanese at JJLS because "there are more Tokyo-*jin* [a person from Tokyo]" in his school.[44] When asked how others responded when he spoke in the Osaka dialect, Yaichi replied: teachers "didn't really comment on it." They just said "that's a dialect." His classmates said, "You speak the Osaka dialect.... You are an Osaka-jin." When asked whether he would like teachers from Osaka to use the Osaka dialect at JJLS, Yaichi responded, "that would be nice." Later on, when discussing his two-month summer visit to the Osaka area in the previous year, he recalled that now that he had become more comfortable speaking standard Japanese, "the Tokyo-jin's dialect, like '*ne*' comes up at the end of my sentences. My friends [in his old school in Osaka] said, 'What? What kind of language are you using?'... They would say, 'Are you a girl?'"

What his mother, Ms. Yoshida, told Doerr a week earlier in her interview illuminates Yaichi's experience with dialects in JJLS. When asked whether or not they speak the Osaka dialect at home, she responded that she and her husband use the Osaka dialect, but Yaichi speaks with a mixture of the Osaka and Tokyo dialects. She explained that Yaichi felt he would get on better with his JJLS friends from Tokyo if he spoke the Tokyo dialect, so he began using that dialect, though not without difficulty, Ms. Yoshida added. In response to the inquiry whether Ms. Yoshida wants the teachers from Osaka to speak Osaka dialect at JJLS, she said Yaichi would feel at home if they did. Yaichi once reported to her nostalgically that he heard someone speaking the Osaka dialect at JJLS, she added. When discussing the place of dialects in JJLS in general, Ms. Yoshida commented that in the past some of Yaichi's friends had laughed at him for speaking the Osaka dialect and this had led to some fighting.

The above interviews suggest that Yaichi felt somewhat marginalized as an Osaka-dialect speaker, but he felt secure in his Japanese-ness when responding to more abstract questions about his difference from Americans. To questions such as "what is your identity?" "what affects your identity?" and "what makes a person Japanese?" Yaichi responded that he is Japanese because he can speak Japanese very fast. What makes a person Japanese is whether or not one would stay for dinner at a friend's home after a play date. Japanese, he explained, would not accept such an invitation, thinking the acceptance rude, whereas Americans would.

These interviews indicated that attending JJLS helped Yaichi adjust to life in the United States, providing him with space to feel comfortable in an English-speaking environment. Yet, Yaichi also felt alienated at JJLS from what is valued as Japanese — the Tokyo dialect — and he was unhappy about not being able to speak the Osaka dialect freely. In Japan, children who transfer to a school in a different region where another dialect is spoken must make an adjustment. The hoshūkō, however, is not located in a particular region in Japan. Rather, it is "Japan" transplanted and built on the Tokyo model, distinctly reflecting the ideology of the standardization of the Japanese nation-state. Using standard Japanese at JJLS amounts to becoming standardized into an imagined ideal Japanese, not only in interactions with friends who speak standard Japanese but also with teachers who notice and thus mark one dialect from another. This "marking" cites a normative regime of difference that hierarchizes one region (i.e., Tokyo) over another. It also changes the perception of the act of speaking: his experiences at JJLS showed Yaichi that when he thought he was merely "speaking Japanese" he was actually "speaking the Osaka dialect of Japanese."[45]

Dotonbori Street, Osaka. When asked about his Osaka dialect, one Jackson Japanese Language School student explained that he shifted to the Tokyo-based "standard" Japanese because more students come from Tokyo. (J.M. Suarez)

Kumiko: Dual Heritage

Kumiko often participated in classroom discussions, but rarely sought to drive the discussion. Her little brother and Doerr's son are classmates. Thus, Doerr knew their mother before interviewing her. This made the interview seem like a casual chat.

Doerr interviewed Kumiko on 17 February 2008, almost a year after the interviews with the other students, because Kumiko's mother was too busy to sign the participation consent form due to the birth of a baby. Responding to Doerr's questions, Kumiko said that she was born in Japan but had lived in California (1999–2000), Italy (2001), and Canada (2002–2005) before moving to the Jackson area in 2006. At the time of the interview she had no plans to go back to Japan to live. In 2000, after the divorce of her parents (both of whom, she said, are Japanese), Kumiko began living with her mother and her stepfather, who is Greek.[46] Kumiko attended kindergarten in Japan and then enrolled in a weekend Japanese language school after she moved to California. She explained that she goes to JJLS "because my mother is Japanese…and my cousins and friends in Japan only speak Japanese.… Besides, I cannot read *manga* [Japanese cartoons] otherwise."

When asked to compare her friends in JJLS and in the American school she attended, Kumiko said her JJLS friends speak Japanese — a point that was actually not that obvious because, as she clarified right after, there were two groups in her hoshūkō class: "One is a group of *hāhu* [half, meaning half Japanese and half non-Japanese] students who mainly speak English and one is a group of students who just came from Japan and speak Japanese better than English."

Kumiko had mentioned earlier that English comes more easily to her than Japanese, but she added, "I get along well in Japanese, with the Japanese group." She explained that the "Japanese group" talks about "magazines in Japan and other weird stuff, new slang words." The hāhu group talks about "games and about the American school." Kumiko said she likes the fact that all chūzai, chōkitaizai, and eijū students attend the hoshūkō class because this means that she can choose which conversations to join.

Regarding her identity and what forms her identity, Kumiko said she is Japanese because "when I am in Japan[47] or being here [in the hoshūkō], I don't get...excluded [by the Japanese group]. I feel comfortable myself and don't feel weird." When asked if she feels excluded in the United States, Kumiko said no because "I can speak English." To a later question about what makes a person Japanese, Kumiko replied, it is "the ability to speak and hold a conversation in Japanese...and appearance, a little bit."

Kumiko's mother, Ms. Kato, also mentioned Kumiko's ability to recognize and move between two groups of students. Describing how JJLS influenced Kumiko, Ms. Kato said that Kumiko learns Japanese culture at JJLS and sees its difference from American culture, especially regarding behavioral codes. Ms. Kato reported that Kumiko says that with her American friends she can be frank, but with her Japanese friends she cannot, especially if what she says sounds like bragging or disagreeing with others. Ms. Kato said, "When I say what I think in front of Japanese people, Kumiko scolds me saying, I should not be frank when I am around Japanese." "Kumiko often chuckles that she has multiple personalities depending on who she is with," Ms. Kato reported.

In short, Kumiko feels she is accepted by the chūzai students in JJLS and by her schoolmates when she visits Japan. Her sense of fitting in — due to her linguistic competency, her sense of ease with familiar topics of conversation, and her knowledge of behavior codes — is connected to her sense of being Japanese. She also feels she is accepted by American friends. For Kumiko, to "inherit Japanese-ness" in JJLS is to develop a meta-cultural awareness of the differences between Japanese and American cultures and to be able to *cite* performatively the regime of difference of Japanese vs. American, moving between the two "groups." Feeling comfortable with both, Kumiko has a dual heritage. She developed this dual heritage by attending JJLS where her interactions with chūzai and eijū students helped her see the contrast between what she considered to be Japanese behavior and American behavior.

Jake: Heritage as Alienation

Jake was one of the most friendly students to Doerr during her participant observation, although he was not very talkative in the classroom, in which Japanese predominated. When he talked casually to other students, he used English.

In an interview on 4 March 2007, Jake said that he was born and raised in the United States (making him an eijū student). Jake comes to JJLS because "it makes my mom happy," he explained. He felt that the homework for JJLS was too much; he would rather play with friends on Sundays. Once he gets to school, however, he said "it is not too bad." To a question about the heterogeneity of students in the hoshūkō class, Jake replied: "Most of the kids who, like, come from Japan and have both Japanese parents know and learn things more quickly than people who just have, like, one parent English and one parent Japanese." Also, he said, "I think that's good because that helps the kids who don't have both parents that are Japanese learn more words."

While Jake was positive about the diversity of students in the hoshūkō class, his mother, Ms. Jones, reported otherwise in her interview. When asked about the difference between Jake's friends in JJLS and in the American school he attends, Ms. Jones singled out the "sense of humor." She said that Jake would complain at home that "Japanese kids" interrupted their teacher with silly jokes in order to make others laugh. "Japanese kids" laugh at such jokes, but Jake does not get it; instead, he complains that it is annoying and rude to the teacher, and disrupts learning, his mother said. Such feelings were also expressed by several other eijū students in our interviews. In fact, during a classroom observation in October 2007, the following episode occurred: Many chūzai students were teasing a male chūzai student about being in love with one of his female classmates. They tried to make the female student sit next to him, giggling and teasing the two of them the whole time. When the teacher asked the class what topic they wanted to choose for a group discussion, one chūzai student suggested, "My friend wants to confess his love to a girl. We could discuss how we could help him accomplish this." Most of the chūzai students burst out laughing. Jake looked puzzled and said, in English, "I don't get it." A chōki-taizai student explained to him in English. Jake responded out loud in English, "I get it now. But, it's not funny." Other eijū students were staying out of the teasing, some totally ignoring it, and others acting as amused observers. When asked if she encourages Jake to make more friends in JJLS than in the American school, Ms. Jones replied obliquely that Jake seems to be able to make friends only with children who are hāhu, who are mainly eijū students, at JJLS. In the past, there were several verbal fights between "Japanese" and hāhu children in class, she said. While they had few fights recently, there still is an invisible wall between them, which Jake resents, reported Ms. Jones.

However, Jake did not seem to want to move to the Jackson Course, where there were mostly eijū students. To the question whether or not he thought about joining the Jackson Course, he said that his mother suggested he attend. However, he decided against it because he felt it is "for people who, not that they don't know it but, like, they don't know, they can't, they don't learn as fast as kids in this [the hoshūkō] class."

When asked about ethnic identity, Jake did not want to identify himself or his parents in ethnic terms.[48] Later in the interview, however, when asked what makes a person Japanese, Jake responded: "how they feel, I guess. If they think they were…like I am Japanese but that's because my mom is and she passes it down. So, it's, like, I guess if your parents' heritage is Japanese then you are included."

In sum, Jake found the mix of chūzai/chōki-taizai and eijū students good, using the regime of difference of chūzai/chōki-taizai vs. eijū implicitly. According to his mother, as well as from classroom observation, however, Jake seemed to feel a sense of alienation from chūzai/chōki-taizai students whom he reportedly considered "Japanese kids": they had a different sense of humor and classroom behavior. Jake befriended other eijū (hāhu) students, but not chūzai students, according to his mother. JJLS allowed Jake to interact with chūzai, chōki-taizai, and eijū students and it provided him with an opportunity to personally experience "Japanese kids" whom he equated with chūzai and chōki-taizai students.

In this analysis, a question emerges: If Jake is differentiating himself from "Japanese kids," what is Jake then? Given the regimes of difference of chūzai/chōki-taizai vs. eijū students that Jake tends to evoke, viewing chūzai/chōki-taizai students as "Japanese" put eijū students, including Jake, in an ambiguous position: are they "American"? But, Jake described himself as inheriting Japanese-ness from his mother. Jake's refusal to explicitly identify himself in terms of ethnicity suggests his resistance to such a normative regime of difference of ethnicity in which there was no place for eijū and/or hāhu students.

For Jake, then, while he inherits Japanese-ness from his mother, he sees that inheriting Japanese-ness in a heritage language school means being *alienated* from his heritage, represented by those he viewed as "Japanese kids." Here, Jake *cited* two kinds of Japanese-ness: individual-focused Japanese-ness (heritage, identification) and community-focused Japanese-ness (getting along with other "Japanese"). The latter is what Kumiko cited when she defined herself as Japanese. It was the schooling at JJLS that provided a space for such community-focused Japanese-ness to come into play.

Negotiating Heritage: How Much Rice Do You Eat?

Students' perceptions of themselves affected the ways they interacted with each other and with the teacher in class, but they were also influenced by such interactions. Below, we introduce one episode in which Japanese-ness came to the fore as students and teacher[49] discussed how much rice their families eat. In this class in March 2008, a student asked how much four *gou* is. "Gou" is a unit used to measure uncooked grains, especially rice. One *gou* is 175ml. That question elicited an active discussion about how much rice the students' families eat per day. The discussion, translated from Japanese, went as follows:

Yaichi: In my family, my dad eats five gou, five gou…six gou. Six gou.
Teacher: In a day?
Yaichi: He eats six gou of rice. My little brother eats four bowls of rice. My little brother. [His rice bowl is] this big (gestures with his hand to show a bowl about the size of basketball). Much bigger than mine. Mine is about this big (gestures a smaller bowl). My dad's is about this big (gesturing a smaller bowl).

…

Kumiko: There are five members in my family, but we make two gou and have leftovers. A lot of leftovers.
Yaichi: Usually, people eat nine gou. Well, eight gou.
Kumiko: No, two gou is enough for a family of five.
Taro: No way. Never heard of that. My family eats about four to five gou.

Yaichi: You [Kumiko] are unusual! You are unusual! Unusual.
Teacher: Two gou is too little, isn't it?

...

Kumiko: No, the reason why two gou is enough for my family is because we eat salad and other food. Rice is usually not the main course of the meal. Rice is a side dish. I don't eat much rice.
Yaichi: Usually, a family would eat nine gou of rice.
Kumiko: Also, bread comes with dinner.
Yaichi: My father is not normal, though.
Kumiko: We eat fish, meat, salad, and rice.

...

Teacher: Boys in Japan, they eat a lot of rice.
Kumiko: I don't eat much rice.... I eat rice only as rice balls.
Teacher: On TV [in Japan], young guys eat rice in big bowls.
Atsuko: When I attended a school in Japan for a couple of weeks, ...all the boys made leftover rice from lunch into rice balls and finished it all.
Yaichi: Really?
Atsuko: Not this big [gestures the size of tennis ball, which is the regular size of a rice ball], but this big [gestures the size of small soccer ball]!
Teacher: I like that.... Kids in Japan. Boys eat a lot of rice.
Yaichi: I, I....
Atsuko: My little brother used to eat a lot, but not anymore lately.

In the above interactions, Yaichi boasts about how much rice his family eats. Kumiko dared to differ from Yaichi, saying that her family eats very little rice. Yaichi insists that his family eats a lot. Taro, another chūzai student, also feels that Kumiko's family eats too little rice. Yaichi and Taro found Kumiko's family to be "unusual." This utterance reveals a subtle position that Kumiko occupies. The concept of "unusual" positioned her as Japanese because it would be unusual *for a Japanese* family to eat only two gou of rice a day. For an American family, this would hardly be "unusual." If an eijū student with one parent being non-Japanese said his/her family ate only a little rice, the discussion might have shifted toward Japanese vs. American in terms of the amount of rice they eat. In Kumiko's case, however, the discussion continued on the assumption that it is a matter of "usual" or "unusual" (the regime of difference of usual vs. unusual Japanese). Thus, by calling Kumiko "unusual," they were positioning her as Japanese, albeit an unusual one; here, there is some confidence in Kumiko's being Japanese in contrast to the silence of all the other eijū students.

Kumiko explained herself by saying that her family eats other things besides rice. In a typical Japanese meal, rice usually comes with vegetables and meat, fish, and more. That is, when Yaichi says his brother eats four bowls of rice; he meant he eats four bowls of rice along with other food. So, technically, Kumiko's explanation does not explain why her family eats less rice. Yet, there were no particular reactions by the other students to Kumiko's explanation.

The fact that the comparison was done on a family basis also points to Kumiko's subtle position. Among those who participated in the discussion,

Kumiko was the only one who was living with a non-Japanese parent, her Greek stepfather. That fact could explain the difference in her family's eating habits. Kumiko did not raise this as an explanation, however; nor did the others.

The interaction changed gears when the teacher said that "boys in Japan" eat a lot of rice. This comment not only introduced the gender aspect into the discussion but also shifted the frame of comparison from that between students' families to that between "boys in Japan" and students at JJLS (the regime of difference of Japanese in Japan vs. Japanese in the United States). Atsuko, a chōki-taizai student, agreed with the teacher by drawing on her school experience in Japan.

The discussion then shifted to another level: the teacher showed explicit approval of boys in Japan who eat a lot of rice by saying, nostalgically, "I like that...." Yaichi tried to respond to the teacher in vain. Atsuko responded by saying that her little brother, "a Japanese boy," used to eat a lot of rice. Here, Yaichi and Atsuko (in the proxy of her little brother) seem to have tried to live up to the teacher's expectation in being "Japanese who eat a lot of rice." The teacher's approval defined what Japanese-ness is, thus rendering male chūzai students less Japanese.

Following Emiko Ohnuki-Tirney's argument that Japanese view rice as a metaphor for themselves,[50] the classroom engagement itself may indicate the Japanese-ness the students are "inheriting." The silence of the eijū students, then, tells us a great deal.

When asked why she enrolled in a weekend Japanese language school after moving to California, one student replied that she goes to JJLS "because my mother is Japanese...and my cousins and friends in Japan only speak Japanese.... Besides, I cannot read *manga* [Japanese cartoons] otherwise." (Neriko Musha Doerr, February 2010)

The interaction above shows that what constitutes Japanese-ness can shift in relation to how people view one another's Japanese-ness. In a heritage language classroom, students related themselves to their heritage — Japanese-ness — differently not only from their diverse family backgrounds and personal experiences but also in relation to other students and the classroom teacher and according to the level at which they contrast Japanese-ness and non-Japanese-ness.[51]

"Inheriting Japanese-ness" in the Jackson Course

We now draw on our interviews to describe the perceptions of two Level 4 Jackson Course students selected for this study for their contrasting expressions of Japanese-ness. Then, we examine a classroom discussion in which students and a teacher negotiated their relationships to their heritages. In 2006–2007, there were five students in the Level 3 Jackson Course. All of them were eijū students.

Sasha: Heritage as Alterity

During a classroom observation, Sasha impressed Doerr as being easygoing, independent, and able to make friends with everyone. When Doerr interviewed Sasha on 27 May 2007 she said she was born and raised in the United States (thus an eijū student) and had been attending JJLS since preschool. She did not remember when she moved from the hoshūkō to the Jackson Course, but her father, who supported the Jackson Course from the beginning, later told Lee in his interview that she moved upon entering the third grade when Jackson Course opened.

When asked what she wants from JJLS, Sasha said she wants to learn "how to write and speak in Japanese so that I can go around in Japan by myself." When asked what influence JJLS has on her identity, she responded that it allows her to learn Japanese. She added, "Nobody in English school knows Japanese. They think it's cool that I do."

To the question whether her parents speak any dialects of Japanese, Sasha responded, "my mom is Chinese or Chinese-Malaysian. My dad is Japanese." When asked later about her parents' identities, however, Sasha replied: "I am not sure…. My mom says she is alien, immigrant. She knows English but is not [an American] citizen. My father…not sure." About her own identity, Sasha said, "I do think I am American because I was actually born here, even though I do also think I am Asian because my parents are and I know how to speak two different languages [Japanese and Chinese][52] besides English." When asked about what had influenced her identity, Sasha responded:

> Personality, looks different. It doesn't really bother me if somebody, like, excludes me or something because that's what they think but that's not what I think about myself inside. Like my mom, some people have, like, not exactly excluded her but not treated her the same as the white people because she is Asian. So, some people are still like that…. Actually, my mom sort of laughs about it. There are funny stories that she tells us. And also she sort of accepts that people don't exactly, like, understand her, I guess you could say, but once you get to know her, to me she is, like, very

nice and stuff and she wouldn't be different from anybody else; just looks different and maybe has an accent or something, but she's not different, not that different.

When asked later about what makes a person Japanese, Sasha answered: "I don't want to be racist or anything, but black hair, darker skin, and an accent in English."

She recalled that the hoshūkō was "a bit harder and it sort of challenges you more and I couldn't exactly keep up and that's why my dad put me in the Jackson Course so that I can enjoy it better." The Jackson Course is at her level, she said. In the Jackson Course, when students do not understand something, students ask in English, and the teacher uses English words to explain, which she found useful. In the hoshūkō, the teacher never speaks English in class, she said.

Sasha's interview suggests a mainstream (white) American frame of reference. Sasha mentioned physical appearance, the ability (but not the degree of proficiency) to speak Japanese, and accents in English as markers of Japanese-ness or Asian-ness, assuming a mainstream American audience. While she commented on her appearance as having somewhat negative effects in the American context, her Japanese language ability has had a positive effect on how her American friends view her. Here, we can see the regime of difference of (white) American vs. Asian American based on the norm of the former. The notion of "accent" also implies hierarchies among English varieties. This normative regime of difference Sasha evoked differs from that of Kumiko, who put both American and Japanese on equal terms.

For Sasha, difference within JJLS was interpreted mostly as linguistic with little effect on her sense of heritage. Being in the classroom with chūzai and chōki-taizai students in the hoshūkō led her to realize her limited proficiency in Japanese, but Sasha did not mention any sense of alienation from these students or from Japanese-ness. Sasha did not conflate the regime of difference of chūzai/ chōki-taizai vs. eijū or hoshūkō vs. Jackson Course with that of Japanese vs. American.

In sum, Sasha defined her heritage — Japanese-ness — not in relation to Japanese but against the normative mainstream American point of view: her heritage was alterity to mainstream American. JJLS helped her gain such alterity.

Mayumi: Heritage beyond Government Prescription

Mayumi is one of the students who moved from the hoshūkō to the Jackson Course during our research period, upon entering the seventh grade. Doerr observed a drastic change in Mayumi's personality after her move to the Jackson Course: from a quiet student she became an active participant in classroom discussions and even teased the teacher.

In an interview on 25 February 2007, a month before her move to the Jackson Course, Mayumi told Doerr that she was born and raised in the United States (thus, an eijū student). She went on to explain that she began JJLS in preschool because her mother wanted her to be able to speak Japanese to her grandparents. As to the influence of JJLS on her, she mentioned that it "gives me a sense of being Japanese."

When asked why she wanted to switch to the Jackson Course, Mayumi replied that the hoshūkō

> is fast-paced because we have to do a week's worth of work in one day. So, they don't take time to explain, and it is hard for me to understand because I'm not advanced in Japanese.... Some find it just the right speed because they came from Japan and are here for a short time. Japanese is their native language and it comes naturally to them. For me, Japanese is my second language and it takes a while to think in Japanese.... I cannot understand things sometimes. It is frustrating. When I give up, it becomes boring. In regular school, I know all the language and I can form questions better.

As for her identity, Mayumi said she is "half Japanese, half Russian." Regarding what influenced her identity, Mayumi said, "Parents...Japanese language school, definitely. And going to Japan. Having a kimono." When discussing what makes a person Japanese, she answered: "one of the parents is any portion Japanese," but added, "I feel I am more Japanese [than Russian] because I speak it."

When Doerr asked several questions regarding how she used to view the Jackson Course, if she thought about joining it before, and why she was moving to the Jackson Course, Mayumi explained as follows. When her mother first introduced the idea that she move there several years earlier, she felt "why change now." However, Mayumi's mother, Ms. Michaels, recalled in her interview with Lee on 10 June 2007 that Mayumi's first response was negative. Mayumi felt that the Jackson Course "was for dropouts." Mayumi explained in her interview that, upon graduating from elementary school, she thought about changing her course and went to a trial class. She liked it and moved to the Jackson Course.

In these interviews, Mayumi related to her heritage — Japanese-ness — from various angles: her mother's ethnicity, her experiences (attending JJLS and visiting Japan), and her possessions (a kimono). Her view of the Jackson Course changed from a class for dropouts (according to her mother) to a class in which the teacher can take time to explain things. This latter perception of the Jackson Course comes from the fact that the Jackson Course does not follow the government-prescribed curriculum and does not have to rush to cover the material.

The difference between the hoshūkō and the Jackson Course then is about linguistic ability as well as connection to the government-prescribed constraints. Mayumi views the institutional regime of difference between the two as that of government-prescribed vs. independent. She does not see the difference in ethnic terms. Mayumi's sense of heritage, then, exists *beyond the government prescription*. In contrast to Jake who remained in the hoshūkō class despite feeling alienated, Mayumi's decision to move to the Jackson Course reflects her sense of heritage, free from government prescriptions about what knowledge of the Japanese language should be. It was her schooling in heritage language and the decision she made to switch to the Jackson Course that provided her a new way to frame what and how she "inherits."

On Disgusting Food: Cultural Differences and Connections

Classroom interactions, as in the hoshūkō class, show how students' Japanese-ness is negotiated — a process illustrated in the following episode. In the second session of the new Level 4 class in April 2007, the teacher was lecturing about hunter-gatherers.[53] Responding to Sasha's question whether or not hunters ate dogs, the teacher mentioned that some dogs are for eating. Mayumi said out loud, "Eeee-yuuuu!!!" showing her disgust for the idea of eating dogs. This scream began a series of exchanges about eating food that some found disgusting. The following exchanges are translated from Japanese. Words spoken in English are underlined.

Teacher: You say "Eeee-yuuuu," but that's from the sensitivity of people in America. Right? From the sensitivity of a Japanese, or even, as a country bumpkin.... Well, I've eaten an insect [*konchu*]. Do you know what a konchu is? <u>An insect</u>.

Mayumi: I have eaten insects.

Teacher: Really? What did you eat?

Mayumi: Mmmm... I don't know what to call it in Japanese, but... <u>mealworm</u>?

...

Teacher: Wow! Some people in America eat bugs! I did not know that!

...

Teacher: There's a place called Yonezawa in Yamagata. It's a countryside in northeastern Japan. There, on a farm, not a farm [but] rice fields, tons of grasshoppers come out. Grasshoppers. You catch them all and cook them with soy sauce, sugar, and *mirin* [rice-based sweetener]. Then, eat them.

Kim: I have eaten them, too.

Teacher: You have? Their long legs are very crunchy and they are pretty good. I ate them for the first time when I was around six years old. I didn't like the guts coming out from the tummy, but I came to like them. Eating them while drinking cold beer is the best!

Sasha: [giggles].

Teacher: So, there are people like that. By the way, which country was it? Thailand? In the place around there, when chicks grow in the egg and be ready to hatch, they eat them.

[Some students make faces.]

Teacher: Making faces like that! Americans kill cows and eat them, right? Cows. Moooo! [Students laugh.] Americans kill them and eat them.

...

Teacher: Well, there is no ending when we start talking about which is more cruel when it comes to eating meat for food. Plants are alive, too, right?

Mayumi: No. When you eat meat, what's on the plate does not match the animal. No, there is no small cow sitting on the plate when you eat beef.

...

Teacher: From my point of view, it's all the same. But, emotionally, we learn to not accept certain things, I guess.
Kim: Well, it's a difference between cultures.
Teacher: Exactly!
Kim: I can respect difference in cultures. But, I just cannot eat an almost-born chick myself.
Teacher: Me, neither. But, we don't look down on people who do eat them, do we? I think that's their culture. Okay, it became less about history and more about food and culture, but, going back to hunter-gatherers....

In the interactions above, at first, the teacher and Mayumi positioned themselves as opposites. When Mayumi was disgusted by the idea of eating dogs, the teacher labeled this an "American" reaction: an accusation of ethnocentrism against those who are disgusted with dog eaters. The teacher then aligned himself with the dog eaters by confessing that he, a Japanese person, eats bugs: thus the teacher himself eats what may be disgusting to Americans. Here, the regime of difference between an American (Mayumi) vs. a non-American (teacher as bug eater aligned with dog eaters), was evoked. Given that this took place in a *heritage* Japanese language class, this contrast is notable.

Mayumi collapsed that dichotomy, however, by saying that she also ate bugs: mealworms. Here, Mayumi aligned herself with the teacher as a bug eater. Kim joined in by saying she had eaten bugs as well. Here, the teacher and these students all became bug eaters over and beyond an initial contrasting of their sensitivities regarding dog eating. After the first "shocking confession" that he eats bugs, the teacher softened his tone and explained that he actually felt bad eating grasshoppers at first. This showed him reaching out to those who would be disgusted by the thought of eating grasshoppers. Note that Mayumi was not aligning herself as Japanese, even though she could have done so. Instead, the experience in the United States, i.e., mealworm eating, was used to connect to the teacher's "Japanese" experience.

Then, the teacher moved to another level — the chick-eaters in Thailand. Students did not say "eeee-yuuuu" this time; they only made faces. The teacher responded by noting that Americans eat beef also. This put "animal" eating in perspective. Americans and non-Americans are all meat eaters; no eating preference is more or less cruel.

Mayumi resisted by saying that beef does not come in its real shape of the animal. Kim agreed with the teacher that eating meat is eating meat. However, she hedged and said that although she could accept chick eating, she could not do it herself. This was a justification of her entitlement to being disgusted, as long as it does not lead to an accusation of inhumanity against chick-eaters. The teacher agreed with her. Here, the teacher and students were united as non-Thai in the sensitivity toward chick eating. Then the discussion was connected to the issue of general cultural tolerance.

In the course of this conversation, the regime of difference of Americans vs. non-Americans was brought up (dog eating), erased (bug eating), brought up again (beef eating), and erased again in a shared disgust but tolerance toward chick eating. Here, although the class is a Japanese heritage language class, the students' relationships to Japanese-ness, their heritage, was not automatically acknowledged. The teacher and students negotiated their subject positions through several phases as they worked through their sensitivities and more abstract understanding of how to relate to other heritages. In our interviews, students self-identified themselves in various ways: Sasha, as American or Asian; Mayumi, as half Japanese and half Russian; and Kim, as Korean. Despite these self-identifications students we interviewed connected and aligned themselves with or distanced themselves from various heritages depending on the context. Students could be Japanese, American, both, or neither

In an interview with the teacher in the following week, Doerr asked his feelings about having students with diverse backgrounds. He at first said it was fun. Then, he said he tries to be sensitive and not to hurt the feelings of students. He tries to make sure the discussion does not become an attack on a particular country, especially when there are students in class who have personal connections to that country. In short, in the Jackson Course, the ways students related to Japanese-ness were ambiguous and other heritages could become highlighted.

Inheriting Japanese-ness Diversely

This article has delved into how heritage language schooling multiplied the ways that individuals imagine and "inherit" Japanese-ness in the United States. The diversity of personal histories, family backgrounds, linguistic proficiency, and future intentions came to be accentuated and given shape at JJLS with two tracks of heritage language class.

In the hoshūkō class, Yaichi felt forced to standardize himself into a Japanese-ness that differed from his own experience in Japan. What he had thought of as merely "speaking Japanese" came to be considered as "speaking the Osaka dialect of Japanese" in the hoshūkō class, transplanted "standard Japan." In the hoshūkō class, which was filled with chūzai, chōki-taizai, and eijū students, Kumiko learned to code switch between the behavior pattern of "American" students (in which category eijū students are ambiguously included) and that of "Japanese"/chūzai students. In the same class, Jake felt alienated from the chūzai students whom he viewed as "Japanese kids." His connection to his heritage became ambiguous — he was "Japanese" via his Japanese mother but not quite Japanese in relation to the chūzai students. Here, through attending JJLS, one's regional background (Yaichi), one's personal tastes in topics of conversation (Kumiko), or sense of humor (Jake) were accentuated and came to represent one's relationship to heritage. What would be all vaguely considered as merely "speaking Japanese" and "being Japanese" outside JJLS came to be differentiated into specific ways of being Japanese by their experiences of schooling at JJLS, where students were faced with community-focused Japanese-ness. Classroom interactions further complicated students' relationships to Japanese-ness, *citing* various regimes of difference and revealing different layers of imagined Japanese-ness depending on the topic of conversation. In discussing the amount of rice consumed, Yaichi's and Kumiko's Japanese-ness was reconfirmed at one moment, but reduced at another.

In the Jackson Course, where what constitutes Japanese-ness was not implied by the Japanese government-prescribed curriculum, and students were not expected to be monolingual and homogeneously "Japanese," Sasha did not discuss her Japanese-ness in relation to her fellow students. Rather, Sasha viewed Japanese-ness in contrast to the "American-ness" represented by people outside JJLS: JJLS provided Sasha with alterity to "American-ness." Attending the hoshūkō made Mayumi realize that her linguistic competence was lower than that of her chūzai classmates, although this did not affect her connection to Japanese-ness. By moving to the Jackson Course, Mayumi found a concrete way to connect her linguistic proficiency to Japanese-ness: outside the Japanese-government-prescribed curriculum. She no longer perceived that she spoke Japanese with "less proficiency" for her age (being a dropout); she spoke a different kind of Japanese. However, both Sasha and Mayumi also contrasted themselves to Japanese when it came to what they would eat. In the Jackson Course, the teacher associated students' links to Japanese-ness in more fluid ways. Thus students' other-than Japanese heritage was also emphasized.

In this article, we sought to highlight the importance of the schooling process as a heritage practice: it provides a space to change one's relationship to the language one speaks, creating a meta-cultural awareness of one's relationship to the language and what it represents. That is, language education entails more than inculcating language proficiency; it helps learners develop subject positions.

We suggest four new areas of investigation regarding heritage language education: (1) investigation of the ways a learner develops his/her relationships to heritage; (2) critical examination of what it means to call a language one's heritage; (3) analyses of how a learner relates to his/her *other* "heritage" and reconciles differences or "contradictions" in doing so; and (4) investigation of how a leaner develops his/her sense of belonging in relation to various groups of people. These offer researchers a potentially fruitful field of investigation. Heritage language teachers should also be aware, we suggest, of these processes and allow students to examine and gain a deep understanding of these issues as part of heritage language education. We thus conclude that heritage language education should not just be a site for language education but one for understanding heritage politics as well.

ACKNOWLEDGMENTS: We would like to express our gratitude to all the research participants in the Jackson Japanese Language School for sharing their views and allowing us to observe the classes. We thank John Davis, Laura Miller, Yuko Okubo, Taku Suzuki, Ayako Takamori, and Michiyo Takato for commenting on earlier drafts, anonymous reviewers for their constructive comments, Christopher Doerr and Paul Schalow for copy-editing earlier drafts, and Tom Fenton for the final thorough copy-editing. All responsibility for the material discussed here remains our own.

❏

5. Rethinking Japanese American "Heritage" in the Homeland

Ayako Takamori

HERITAGE LANGUAGE[1] as a concept and object of study emerged in the United States in the context of second language education. It was promoted by the rise of multiculturalist ideologies and cultural activism in the United States to deal with specific challenges around heritage language acquisition and education for minoritized ethnic populations and children of immigrants and to mitigate language shift and cultural alienation (two phenomena that are viewed as linked[2]). Such efforts are motivated by the desire to transform ways in which certain cultural differences have historically been devalued and racialized. The perspectival positioning of much scholarship on heritage language is based on the premise that a heritage language is usually a minority language in what is often a diasporic location (or a place where sovereignty and borders are in dispute). Discourses about "minorities" and the languages they speak remain problematic. In recognition of the contestations around the usage of the term "minority," which reifies identities and renders social inequality in reductive terms, I seek to highlight ways in which people are minoritized in specific contexts. Further, by shifting the perspective and contexts dealing with heritage language, I hope to call attention to the problematics of "majority" and "minority" designations in sociolinguistic objects of study such as heritage language.[3]

What happens, though, when a heritage language is the dominant language and its speakers are using a language in the place of so-called heritage? Since heritage language education is often used as a resource to help maintain a person's connection to a usually distant ethnic "homeland" and is therefore often described as an avenue for cultural return, what happens when heritage language learners actually "return" to the place, or nation, of heritage? The case of "return migration" is a particularly fruitful site in illustrating how the meaning and significance of "heritage language" for heritage speakers is situationally specific.

Between 2005 and 2006, I conducted twelve months of participant-observation fieldwork research about Japanese Americans who reside in Japan and their social networks to investigate how ethnic and national identities are reshaped and reproduced in return-migration contexts. My informants — most of whom lived in the greater Tokyo metropolitan area — included Japanese Americans, *nikkeis* of other national origin, and Japanese individuals who associated with nikkeis.[4] Early in my research, I became aware of the centrality of language — pragmatically and ideologically — in structuring Japanese American experiences in Japan. Drawing on ethnographic data from this research, I examine the connection between heritage language and "heritage." I focus on how heritage language speakers use and communicate in their heritage language in their homelands and in their countries of heritage. In this research context, the heritage language, Japanese, is also the dominant or majority language. Further, Japanese Americans are not minoritized and racialized in Japan in the same way that they are in the United States. Yet they are also often clearly marked through language and other performative markers as being not "Japanese." Their experiences communicating, interacting, and living as heritage language speakers (whether or not they are recognized as such) in Japan illuminate and radically reframe how processes of cultural identification are implicated in language ideologies. That is, the national context fundamentally constructs transnational subjectivities at the same time that those subjectivities disrupt the very ideologies that attempt to define them.

My argument is threefold: I suggest that heritage language (and by extension minoritized identities) should not be regarded as having a stable referent. Rather its meaning and value is only produced (as all language is) through interactions and discourses in locationally and historically specific contexts. I further suggest that heritage language education is not necessarily empowering for heritage language speakers. Rather than providing a means of connection to a heritage, heritage language education can paradoxically serve to heighten a heritage language speaker's sense of alienation and non-belonging from his or her "heritage." Finally, I argue that Japanese Americans, insofar as they disrupt ontological coherence in Japan by being simultaneously Japanese and not Japanese, represent an uncanny presence in Japan. In being both familiar and strange, their disturbing presence in Japan unveils processes of how modern national identity is constructed and maintained.

Language and Assimilation in the United States

How Japanese Americans refashion themselves in Japan through language is dependent on the history of language politics in the United States as much as it is on language ideologies in Japan. Social scientists have often used "language shift" toward English among immigrant and minority ethno-linguistic communities in the United States as an indicator and measure of their assimilation, along with other demographic data such as rates of intermarriage, class status, and spatial dispersal.[5] Sociolinguists have observed a pattern among many immigrant and ethno-linguistic communities in the United States of language shift toward English over the course of three generations.

> [T]he typical pattern has been for the first generation to learn enough English to survive economically; the second generation continued to speak the parental tongue at home, but English in school, at work and in public life; by the third generation, the home language shifted to English, which effectively became the mother tongue for subsequent generations.[6]

From an anthropological perspective, this pattern, while generally descriptive, is also deterministic. It neglects to consider the contingencies of particular cultural, historical, and political contexts, such as the effects of education and immigration policies. Nor does this model account for discourses and language ideologies generated about specific minority groups in relation to the nation. Such meta-linguistic discourses not only articulate minority and national identities, they also shape the emotional valence that heritage language speakers develop for their heritage language.

This dimension of language shift is particularly salient for Japanese Americans who have been less successful than other minoritized ethnic populations at heritage language maintenance. Japanese Americans, in addition to being cast as "perpetual foreigners," have been deeply affected by the collective memory of internment during World War II. And prior to World War II, widespread anti-Asian sentiment and legislation severely limited opportunities for Japanese Americans in the United States.[7] Even those born and raised in the United States and who were university educated during the first half of the twentieth century found few career options outside of Japanese American communities and support networks. Explanations of language shift among Japanese Americans also must acknowledge the profundity of the rupture of World War II and its aftermath for Japanese Americans, as Toyotomi Morimoto as done in his historical study of language maintenance among Japanese Americans.[8] Morimoto describes the vibrant and committed efforts of Japanese American heritage language education in the communities prior to World War II. If one is to accept that language shift among Japanese Americans has made it so that they can no longer be considered an ethno-linguistic community, then the specific historical context of war, displacement, and anti-Japanese sentiment along with economic struggles to rebuild livelihoods must be considered as factors in the failure of Japanese language maintenance in the United States. For example, after their release from internment camps, former Japanese American communities along the west coast never completely regained their former strength, presence, or vitality.

The overwhelmingly dominant wartime and postwar discourse pressuring Japanese Americans to disavow cultural affiliation with Japan played no small part in Japanese language shift among Japanese Americans. The pressure to prove their citizenship (as well as government recommendations to disperse and assimilate after the dissolution of the camps) no doubt led many of the wartime generation to renounce and forsake interest in their Japanese "heritage" and their heritage language along with it. For Japanese Americans, then, the significance of their heritage language in constructing their identification as Japanese American was in large part determined by language and race politics in the United States as well as by the trajectory of their historical experience.

The historical specificities of Japanese American experiences in the United States are significant for a more nuanced understanding and theorization of language shift and assimilation among Japanese Americans. While Mary Waters and Tomás Jiménez argue that the body of contemporary research reveals enough evidence to claim that the three-generation model still holds today,[9] such models tend to ignore the specific experiences and meanings attached to language for those such as Japanese Americans who are demarcated as ethno-linguistic minorities.

The three-generation model of language shift notwithstanding, in a four-volume overview of language maintenance and language shift within Native American, Latino, and Asian American ethno-linguistic communities in the United States, David Lopez[10] contends that compared with other ethno-linguistic communities in the United States, Japanese Americans are exceptional for not maintaining their bilingualism and should therefore not be considered a language minority. What determines and constitutes an ethno-linguistic community according to Lopez is unclear. He attributes language shift among Japanese Americans to the relative upward mobility, affluence, and assimilation of Japanese Americans in U.S. society. Lopez's claims reinforce the postwar characterization (and implicit accusation) of Asian Americans, and especially Japanese Americans, as being model minorities. Given the fragmentation and dissolution of Japanese American communities, a more nuanced explanation for language shift should include an analysis of war and postwar contexts and how Japanese Americans struggled to remake their lives after leaving the internment camps.[11]

The difficulty in maintaining the use of Japanese across generations cannot be reduced to increased socioeconomic status alone. Analyses of the significance of Japanese as a heritage language must account for historical experience, collective memory, and cultural reproduction among Japanese Americans in addition to shifts in class status and upward mobility. Ethnographic methods enable a more complicated and phenomenological understanding of the relationship between Japanese language and constructions of Japanese American identities. By privileging ethnographic narratives, I hope to resist reifying Japanese American identity and leave space for the diversity of experiences.

While Japanese Americans living in Japan generally have enjoyed greater employability and upward mobility in the last couple of decades than their Latin American nikkei counterparts,[12] the diversity in the class backgrounds of the Japanese Americans I interviewed was noticeable. For those younger Japanese Americans[13] who described themselves as coming from economically struggling families, Japanese language education often did not play a significant role in the narratives of their upbringing. For example, one of my informants, Michael, was a *nisei* (second generation)[14] university student from California who, in his interview, talked about how he did not conform to the model-minority stereotype. He was spending a year abroad studying in Tokyo and was having a difficult time adjusting to life in Japan. Prior to enrolling in university in Japan, he had no formal education in Japanese. He had not even heard of the term, "J-school," the common shorthand for Japanese language schools and *hoshū-*

kōs in the United States, until he met other Japanese Americans at his university. I assumed that Michael's parents made a deliberate decision not to teach Michael Japanese. When I inquired whether he regretted not studying Japanese, he quickly dismissed my tacit evaluative assumption that his parents did him a disservice by not teaching him Japanese: "My parents were struggling just to survive. They didn't have time to teach us Japanese. Worrying about passing on Japanese culture was the least of their worries."

Most Japanese Americans I interviewed in Japan who were not confident about their Japanese language skills said they wished that they had made more of an effort to learn Japanese earlier. They had internalized the idea that learning Japanese was something they should have done as Japanese Americans. Michael, however, refused to assume a natural link between his cultural heritage and his heritage language. He consciously rejected hegemonic expectations of both American multiculturalism and Japanese national ideologies that each in their own way mandate that heritage and identity is inextricably tied by blood/ethnicity to language. However, Michael's refusal is not equivalent to or indicative of cultural assimilation or dis-identification as Japanese American.

Michael's experiences placed within the context of a broader history of Japanese American heritage language maintenance hint at a more complex dynamic between class and language maintenance. The relation between class mobility, heritage language, and constructions of ethnic identity among other Asian diasporic communities in the United States should provide rich sites for further research and theorization. Recent scholarship has begun to address class, heritage language, and identity to varying degrees; these case studies reveal, however, that the relationship between heritage language and class status resists generalization across Asian Pacific American communities.[15]

As John Edwards argues, language shift should not be made synonymous with diminished ethnic affiliation or identity.[16] Language can also maintain its symbolic significance, Edwards contends. Indeed, "Japanese language" — however it is imagined and defined — still has lexical use and symbolic significance in the Japanese American cultural imaginary, even for those who are third, fourth, or even fifth generation. My informants who claimed to have no knowledge of Japanese and were raised in English-dominant home environments said they still used words such as *gohan* (rice), *shōyu* (soy sauce), and *itadakimasu* (a set phrase spoken before eating) in their households.

Another illustration of the continued lexical use and significance of Japanese for Japanese Americans is found in the novels of *sansei* (third generation) mystery writer Naomi Hirahara. Japanese language remains a central component of ethnic identity as it is lived and experienced in the everyday lives of the Japanese American protagonists and characters in her novels.[17] Hirahara writes in English (though the novels are also translated and published in Japan). The dialogue and speech patterns of the Japanese American characters, and especially that of protagonist Mas Arai (an aging gardener who solves murder mysteries), are laden with slang, both English and Japanese. His use of language in this way marks his identity as Japanese American and as a laborer. The linguistic variances from "standard" English of Hirahara's characters are not exceptional peculiarities but part of the fabric of mundane, unremarkable speech. Hirahara does not write her novels for a specifically Japanese American audience, but her characterization and transliterations of Japanese American speech patterns and pronunciations remain largely unexplained and untranslated in her texts. The protagonists in her novels are often working-class Japanese Americans for whom concepts contained in words such as *bachi* (roughly, "what goes around comes around") and *gasa gasa* (onomatopoetic description of children who are particularly restless and active) remain meaningful and integral parts of their moral framework as well as understandings of themselves. A couple of her Japanese American readers told me that her books caught their attention because her titles contained words or phrases with which they could relate. One nisei woman explained that she purchased Harahara's book, *Gasa Gasa Girl*, precisely because as she put it, "I was a gasa gasa girl." Harahara believes that concepts and terms such as these no longer circulate as frequently among contemporary young Japanese, but she insists that they are still used and understood by Japanese Americans.

While Japanese Americans often describe a sense of cultural loss or alienation in diasporic contexts, the lexical significance of Japanese and other performative and ritual enunciations in Japanese lead many Japanese Americans to claim that they adhere to what they view as an older or more "traditional" Japanese moral order and system of values such as *gaman* [perseverance or endurance], self-sacrifice, and hard work without complaining.

Even if the characters in Harahara's novels do not often carry on entire conversations in Japanese, lexical use of Japanese is prevalent and crucial to enacting ethnic identities against the backdrop of American society. Japanese language, then, continues to play a central role in constructing Japanese American cultural identities and communities.

Lopez's work in the 1980s was situated against the backdrop of a history of scholarship arguing that bilingualism and maintenance of heritage languages in ethnic communities had deleterious effects on those communities and children's education.[18] Scholars such as Lopez were attempting to intervene in and shift the thinking of American society as well as academia toward a multiculturalist and educational framework that would provide (in theory at least) a space of participation for those who had been largely excluded through institutionalized racism. As such, these interventions played an important part on the academic front of social justice movements informed by an era of activism, both in academia and American society at large (i.e., civil rights, antiwar, and feminist movements, the formation of ethnic and women's studies). Terence Turner warns, however, that a simplistic conceptualization of multiculturalism

> risks reifying cultures as separate entities by overemphasizing their boundedness and mutual distinctness; it risks overemphasizing the internal homogeneity of cultures in terms that potentially legitimize repressive demands for communal conformity; and by treating cultures as badges of group identity, it tends to fetishize them in ways that put them beyond the reach of critical analysis....[19]

Critics have also pointed to forms of tokenization in what they call "food court multiculturalism," a facile celebration of diversity that covers over relationships of power in the production of difference.[20] In practice, institutionalizing multiculturalism may also essentialize cultural and ethnic identities and create prescriptive expectations of those who fall under these identity categories.

A reconsideration of the relevance of heritage language and language shift among Japanese Americans should also take note of global economic changes in the latter half of the twentieth century, particularly Japan's rapid economic growth and power in the postwar period. Debates about multiculturalism and bilingual education in the United States coincided with heightened pressures to be economically competitive and cosmopolitan persons in a globalizing marketplace as new forms of transnational movements were shaped by neoliberalization. Data from my research suggest that the shifts in Japan's place in the global economy over the last sixty years are reflected in the generational differences among Japanese Americans in their attitudes toward Japanese language. Sanseis who came of age in the 1960s, for example, often spoke jokingly of themselves as "bananas" alienated from anything Japanese, and they used to be proud of their lack of knowledge of Japanese culture and language. Later generations of Japanese Americans, including *shin-niseis*,[21] were more likely to embrace their biculturalism. Informed by the popularization and global circulation of manga, anime, Japanese toys, and other forms of Japanese pop-cultural production (which Douglas McGray has labeled "Cool Japan"), younger generations of Japanese Americans are less hesitant about identifying themselves with Japan, consuming Japanese products, or expressing curiosity about or interest in Japan.[22] Many of the younger Japanese Americans I interviewed — those like Michael who had moved to Japan within the last ten years — have chosen to study, work, and live in Japan not just because of their cultural heritage and curiosity about their ancestors' homeland, but also because of their interest in global pop culture.

"Returning" to Culture: Heritage Language in the Land of Heritage

Lopez believes that "however much they might like to 'return' to their culture, [Japanese Americans] will not do it through their ethnic language."[23] This claim is accurate in many ways, but not always in the ways Lopez intended. For Japanese Americans who choose to live in Japan, for instance, fluency and competence in Japanese is a fraught site of cultural negotiation. This is so not simply because of language shift among Japanese Americans but because Japanese language ideologies, or the "complex systems of ideas and interests through which people interpret linguistic behaviors,"[24] place Japanese Americans under much greater scrutiny in Japanese society since they are not immediately recognized or categorized as foreigners.

Japanese Americans are, in a sense, returning to "their culture" by choosing to move to Japan.[25] They do not necessarily view their move to Japan as a "return," hence my reluctance to describe this movement as "return migration." Their homeland is and always will be the United States, and if they return anywhere, it will be to the United States. When I asked my informants why they had decided to move to Japan, many explained that their desire to learn or improve their knowledge of Japanese was a significant motivating factor. Whatever their personal reasons and motivations for moving to Japan may have been, the relationship Japanese Americans develop with their heritage language and the sentiments they feel toward Japanese become complicated and acquire new significance in the context of "return migration." Learning and speaking Japanese as a Japanese American in the United States is a very different experience from speaking Japanese in Japan. Japanese language acquisition, and heritage language education more generally, is viewed by U.S. educators and heritage language learners alike as an empowering way for Japanese Americans to connect with their cultural roots. However, competency in their heritage language, I suggest, sometimes serves counterintuitively to further distinguish and separate Japanese Americans from Japanese beyond other forms of cultural and social alienation, rather than creating a cultural bridge to their Japanese heritage. A few of my informants spoke of what they felt was a double standard for them in Japanese language classes. They described their Japanese language teachers as expecting Japanese American students to have a "naturally" greater facility with the language. Conscious or not, such expectations may be rooted in an assumption that the propensity for Japanese is somehow innate and blood-linked. That many Japanese Americans feel beholden to learn and speak fluent Japanese indicates the continuing salience of an ideology of Japanese identity through which blood, race, nation, and culture are elided.[26] Those who struggled to learn Japanese resent being judged as poor or lazy students when they fail to measure up. Japanese American narratives about studying their heritage language as youths foreshadowed their experiences in Japan, where they again felt judged in their use of Japanese.

In a place such as Los Angeles, heritage language education can be seen as a multicultural victory and an empowering expression of cultural identity; in Tokyo, by contrast, heritage language education may be seen as shaking the very underpinnings of Japanese national identity. Alternately, discourses of internationalization often position bilingual Japanese Americans as cultural mediators, helping to establish Japan's place in the world. The regimes of value by which Japanese language education for heritage learners comes to be seen as compulsory are just as constricting, exclusive, and reifying of identities as ideologies of monolingual nationalism. I argue that acquisition of Japanese is not always coded as positive. How language is used, its relationship to the (re)production of identity, and what language itself comes to signify are all specific to particular contexts. Further, expectations that Japanese Americans must have an educational background in Japanese reinforce language ideologies in which identity, language, and belonging are configured and elided.

Linguistic Birthrights

Discourses about blood underlie Japanese language ideologies. Jennifer Robertson and Michael Weiner have both shown that attitudes about blood and about how blood has come to signify race and nation are not unique to Japan.[27] Nonetheless, in tracing the history of eugenics and discourses of blood in Japan,

Robertson explains how blood "remains an organizing metaphor for profoundly significant, fundamental, and enduring assumptions about Japanese-ness and otherness."[28] Below I introduce several case studies of Japanese Americans living in Japan.[29] These examples illustrate how Japanese Americans in Japan (and their experiences as heritage language speakers) contradict dominant discourses of Japanese culture and language being rooted intrinsically in blood. The ideology of blood in Japan is a significant factor in the nation's strict immigration policies. The assumption that people with Japanese blood would be able to assimilate readily into Japanese society and fears that racially different foreigners will give rise to social problems and unrest were responsible for the 1990 revised Immigration Control Act and the so-called nikkeijin visa, which allows nikkeijins to fill labor shortages in Japan's manufacturing sectors. As with Latin American nikkei migrants in Japan who "illuminated deep ruptures in the dominant ideal of the coeternity of blood and culture,"[30] Japanese Americans living in Japan similarly reveal how Japanese blood has little to do with cultural identification and behaviors, Japanese language ability among them.[31]

On a lazy winter Sunday afternoon in the outskirts of Tokyo, I sat with Ted, a nisei in his mid thirties from New Jersey, and a few of his friends. We were watching television in his apartment. His spoken Japanese, although slang-ridden (or perhaps because it was), was fluent. Ted spoke Japanese and English with seemingly equal ease. He rapidly code-switched with his other Japanese American friends, a few of whom were childhood or "J-school" friends who also happened to reside in the Tokyo area. He also had a tight social circle of young Japanese male friends. In other words, Ted seemed to have no social insecurities about his Japanese language skills. That afternoon, the normally talkative and boisterous group had fallen into a sleepy and comfortable silence. I was only half paying attention to the talk-show program on the television when a *gaijin-tarento* (foreign celebrity/television personality) appeared on the set for an interview. This particular gaijin-tarento was a young, articulate white American woman; the television hosts were asking her about the *gaikokujin* (foreigner) perspective on some aspect of Japanese society. Gaijin-tarento are not uncommon on Japanese television and, even if they play comic characters who make grammatical mistakes stereotypical of foreigners, they generally speak Japanese fluently. Just as I was marveling to myself how this particular gaijin-tarento was not only very fluent but also had no perceptible accent, Ted, as if reading my thoughts and sensing I would be able to relate as a fellow Japanese American, looked over at me and blurted out in English, "It's not fair that a gaijin can speak better Japanese than I can."

Ted's sentiment reveals his internalization of two hegemonic assumptions relating Japanese language and identity, even if he experientially understands their constructed-ness. The first is that the Japanese language is inherent in Japanese "blood." The claim of fairness or unfairness indexes the way in which Ted links entitlement and heritage with Japanese language ideologies. Regardless of Ted's actual fluency in Japanese, he feels he has not fully inherited that which should have been rightfully his by blood: language. The practice of inheritance entails receiving an object that was not previously in one's possession via kin/blood relations. Inheriting such an object makes it one's own. The flaw in the concept of heritage language is that a heritage language speaker will always remain a heritage language speaker. That is to say, heritage language cannot be a completely assimilated object and a heritage language speaker will never be able to be a native speaker. Fairness can also relate to the way in which Japanese Americans may feel they are being unfairly judged or to their feelings that the expectations placed on them to speak "perfect" Japanese — whatever that may mean — are unreasonable. The second assumption is that if people who are Japanese should naturally speak perfect Japanese then people who are not ethnically Japanese should not be able to speak such seemingly flawless Japanese. These assumptions reinforce the isomorphism of language, race, and nation. It is precisely Ted's realization that he is unable to fit neatly within these language ideologies about Japanese national identity that fosters his sense of unfairness and reinforces his feelings of marginality and non-belonging in Japanese society.

Japanese Americans not only have widely varying degrees of ability and competency in Japanese, they also have divergent views, attitudes, and feelings about language and how it relates to their identities. Many of the Japanese Americans I interviewed, however, described how they have become more concerned, or at least more aware, than they were previously of other people's evaluations of their language competence (and implicitly about their level of "Japanese-ness" or proximity to cultural "heritage") after moving to Japan. Among the most commonly asked questions I heard exchanged between newly acquainted Japanese Americans is "How good is your Japanese?" While this question might just as frequently be asked of non-nikkei foreigners or residents in Japan, for Japanese Americans, it appeared to carry greater significance in the social interactions I observed. This question is often asked among Japanese Americans not so much to evaluate each other's language ability as it is to situate each other within a shared sense of diasporic experience. Hence, the question "How good is your Japanese?" might be followed by other questions such as "What generation are you?" and "Did you attend J-school?" — questions specific to experiences in diasporic contexts. These questions not uncommonly serve as entry points into more meta-linguistic discourse. On a pragmatic level, however, they also serve to help Japanese Americans locate one another in terms of possible shared ethnic communities and historical experiences. Japanese American discourses, then, serve as points of connection or divergence at the same time that they contribute to constructing and producing broader knowledge about Japanese American diasporas. These informal social interactions allow Japanese Americans to survey and aggregate Japanese American experiences and identifications as a whole and relationally to situate themselves. Language and talk about language not only play a significant role in shaping Japanese American experiences in Japan; they also re-frame their identifications as Japanese American and constructions of ethnic identity in the context of Japan.

Meta-linguistic talk among Japanese Americans is often shaped around experiences of interactions with non-nikkeis in Japan. Japanese Americans are typically highly sensitive to the way in which Japanese and foreigners alike monitor and evaluate their linguistic practice and self-presentation in various situations. These evaluations in turn not only reinforce their sense of non-belonging in Japan but also affect how Japanese Americans strategically and creatively present themselves through language in various contexts in Japan. This was the case with Yumi.

Linguistic Strategies for Self-presentation

Yumi is from California, is a mother of three children, and teaches English part-time. Prior to having children, she worked as a translator for a Japanese publishing company. Although she was clearly proficient in Japanese, she spoke extensively about her struggles with learning Japanese in the United States and being transferred to various schools because of her struggles. I was looking forward to meeting Yumi since the mutual friend who had introduced us described her as funny, a bit clumsy, and foul-mouthed. I made my way to the department store café just outside Tokyo where Yumi and I had agreed to meet for an interview. Five minutes before I arrived Yumi sent me a frantic text message saying she was running late dropping off her kids. (I was somewhat relieved to find that I was not the only one in Japan who runs late to appointments.) Shortly after I ordered coffee, Yumi rushed in waving at me but looking flustered, juggling multiple bags, and talking rapidly and curtly on the phone in fluent Japanese. Impressed with her fluency during her phone conversation, I detected only a hint of an accent that would give her away as not Japanese. As she put away her phone, she apologetically explained that she and her husband, who is Japanese, were discussing who would to pick up the children from school later that day.

Almost as soon as Yumi took off her jacket, however, her phone rang again. She looked at the caller-ID, grimaced, and apologized, saying, "Oh, I'm really sorry. It's one of the other mothers. I'm meeting up with them later. I have to take this call. It'll be quick." I noticed this time that as she talked on the phone she had a perceptible American accent and she spoke in a measured, slower manner with more hesitations and filler words. She threw in a few English words here and there such as "Ok," "right," "park," and "you know." When she hung up this time, she let out a big sigh and said conspiratorially (before I could say anything), "I can't let the other mothers at the school think I am fluent in Japanese. They'll expect me to act like a Japanese mother. Shall we get some lunch and then talk?"

We approached the service counter to browse their menu. She ordered first, but I was surprised when she didn't speak any Japanese at all to the café employees. She said in a slow and loud voice that I normally associate with tourists in Japan, gesturing widely and pointing at the food, "Coffee, please. And this sandwich please. Yes, that one. Thank you." I was impressed by her boldness. When we sat down, she said, "You get so much better service if they think you're American and can't speak Japanese. I only speak English when I order tickets at the train station and places like that." This claim came as no surprise since I had often heard Japanese Americans utter similar statements throughout my fieldwork.

The friend who introduced us was right: Yumi was funny. She spoke seriously of her experiences and challenges living in Japan, but she also had a seemingly endless supply of humorous stories. She launched immediately into the first story about how she was the target of a bet made by two American men in a bar. They assumed she was Japanese. She gleefully played along for a while pretending she didn't know English since, as she said, "they can't distinguish the nikkeijin accent." That was the first time I had heard anyone talk of a distinct nikkeijin accent. In that single interview, Yumi illustrated a creative range of communicative strategies for living in Japan and negotiating various kinds of relationships. Among close relations and family, she felt comfortable speaking freely in Japanese. She said she chooses not to have close "real" Japanese friends. But among her Japanese acquaintances and in her dealings with her children's school, that is to say among people with whom she has ongoing relationships requiring frequent communication and who may be familiar with her personal background as a Japanese American, she strategically and deliberately speaks "poor" Japanese with an American accent. Among strangers, particularly in customer service–related jobs, bureaucrats, and government employees, she only speaks in English so that they will not judge her or behave otherwise condescendingly to her. Similarly, a few of the more mischievous Japanese Americans I knew told stories of feigning complete ignorance of Japanese when faced with situations where they had to interact with those in positions of governmental or institutional power such as the police.

Linguistic Identity and Belonging

While Yumi developed linguistic strategies for managing day-to-day interactions and relationships in Japan, Frank's personal history and experiences of growing up as a sansei in New Jersey dramatically shaped the choices he makes regarding his children's language education in Japan. He believes these choices in language education have profound repercussions for their psyches. Frank lives in Tokyo with his Japanese wife and three young children. He works for a major U.S. company in Tokyo. He is a long-term resident with no immediate plans to return to the United States. He also claims to speak somewhat limited Japanese. He nonetheless hopes to be able to spend more time in the future studying Japanese. Frank's children, being raised in Japan, communicate almost exclusively in Japanese. They understand the English spoken to them by their father, but are self-conscious about speaking English. His children occasionally take part in Japanese American functions that involve some form of presentation or ceremony in which they say a few words or set phrases in English. For Frank's children, being raised in Japan and having a Japanese American father, English could be considered their heritage language. Explaining why he had decided not to teach his children Japanese and English simultaneously, Frank said: "I know for many Japanese Americans, there's this self-consciousness, stigma of being a minority. For [my children] to grow up in the environment here, their core self is much stronger...." Thus, his rationale for not going out of the way to teach his children English is because he does not want his children to have the same cultural conflicts he had had. He wants to spare them the difficulties he encountered in the United States. Frank is convinced that in the future his children "will be able to withstand the discrimination because they didn't experience it as children. I do not want them to be self aware that they are different." Frank's view strikingly contrasts with Kimi's perspective. Kimi, a nisei whose parents prioritized her Japanese language acquisition, was determined to raise her children multilingually in hopes that competence in multiple languages would open possibilities for upward mobility in a competitive global economy in which cosmopolitan subjectivities are increasingly valued. Frank, on the other hand, associated multilingualism with exclusion, struggles to belong, and being marked as other. His fears are shared by other Japanese Americans who feel embarrassed and marked by language.

Helen, a sansei, has been living in Japan for over twenty years. When we first met, sitting next to each other at a large Thanksgiving gathering for Japanese Americans, I was trying to engage her in conversation. Although polite, she seemed unresponsive. So I left the gathering that evening with the impression that she did not like me. I learned the next time we met that she had wanted to talk to me, but she thought I was Japanese and was afraid to speak. She is still shy about speaking Japanese for fear of sounding rude. Her sense of embarrassment indicated an awareness that others, especially Japanese, might have negative perceptions of her based on her utterances. This awareness and sense of embarrassment extended to her father. She also described feeling utterly mortified and embarrassed when her nisei father came to visit her in Tokyo. Although it was the first time he had been to Japan, he grew up in Hawai'i assuming he was fully bilingual, being the son of Japanese immigrants. Thinking he could speak Japanese fluently and unproblematically, he unabashedly went up to a middle-aged woman on the street and asked: "*Obasan! Obenjo doko?*" (Aunty, where's the toilet? [He left out a verb and used an archaic and vulgar form of "toilet."]) Her father, who did not live in Japan and came from a place where heritage language speakers are not minoritized or stigmatized had no experience on which to base any sense of self-consciousness or shyness. Furthermore, regardless of his class and educational status in Hawai'i, the Japanese he learned came from a population of Japanese immigrants who had worked as plantation laborers. The Japanese he spoke was not only perceived as odd by Japanese, but it also marked him as rough, uneducated, and working class.

While accents, mistakes, and other minor inflections mark Japanese Americans in Japan as not Japanese, there are Japanese Americans who speak flawless, native-level Japanese. One of these is Brian, a sansei who works as an accountant in Tokyo. He is fully bilingual and lives his life, for the most part, as a regular Japanese salaryman in Japan. He is one of the few Japanese Americans I met in Japan who actually "passes" as Japanese. However, his demeanor when we spoke was marked with pathos. He told me he considers his language ability a double-edged sword because his Japanese colleagues refuse to acknowledge his American identity. He feels that a whole aspect of his identity is effaced, disavowed, and without voice; it goes unrecognized by other Japanese. This frustration, in part, led him to seek out other Japanese Americans in the Tokyo area. Perhaps he experienced what Dorinne Kondo experienced when she caught a glimpse of herself while running errands, but did not recognize the person in the reflection. While Kondo's sense of self-erasure was over a period of months, Brian's sense of alienation from himself in the attempt to fit in in Japanese society spanned decades, creating a profound sense of loss.

Uncanny Returns

As Paul Garrett and Patricia Baquedano-López discuss, recent studies of language socialization in multilingual contexts show that those who are multilingual are uniquely positioned as agents (rather than minoritized objects of assimilation and language loss) who are able "to renegotiate, challenge, or transcend the existing social categories that are constituted and indexed by the codes and communicative practices at their disposal."[32] The Japanese Americans described above are constrained and frustrated by the existing social categories in Japan, but it is precisely in their in-between-ness and within unclear boundaries of identity that they also find creative ways to navigate, subvert, and play with these delineations. As I have illustrated above, language often serves as a means for exclusion, definition, and social surveillance. It is also a means for asserting agency through creative and subversive play.

Within their limitations as heritage language speakers, Japanese Americans nonetheless make choices, strategically drawing on language to position and present themselves in Japanese society. Inasmuch as they are constantly marked and reminded of the ways in which they fail to perform Japanese-ness (linguistically or otherwise) they also find ways to claim their belonging and articulate their alterity and identification as Japanese Americans, even as the construction of their ethnic identity as Japanese Americans is reframed. A number of Japanese Americans were interested in participating in my fieldwork research precisely because they wanted to promote knowledge, awareness, and visibility of Japanese Americans among Japanese. I would argue that the ontological incongruity and ambiguity of Japanese Americans in Japanese society provides one of the most potent possibilities for intervening in the genre of Japanese discourse theorizing Japanese-ness and national character, known as *nihonjinron*.[33]

I frequently asked my informants how they felt Japanese viewed or regarded Japanese Americans. Yumi and a number of my other informants suggested that most Japanese have no concept of Japanese Americans — the category simply does not seem to exist in hegemonic discourse.[34] Japanese Americans experienced what Dorinne Kondo described as being a "living oxymoron" or "conceptual anomaly"[35] in which they seem to occupy an impossible ontological status as both Japanese and not Japanese. This idea speaks to the power and possible negative effects of the way in which blood, culture, and language are aligned in constructions of modern nationhood. At the same time, this lack of definition allows Japanese Americans to refashion themselves creatively in Japan. Further, in escaping easy categorization, Japanese Americans in Japan can potentially present an uncanny epistemic rupture that is ontologically (and ideologically) threatening.

I became aware of this potential one muggy summer evening in Tokyo when my friend Lina, a Brazilian *sansei*, invited me to join a small group of friends and acquaintances at a casual Brazilian restaurant. After introductions, I settled in at the table where the conversations taking place were mostly in Japanese since it was a mixed group of both nikkeis and Japanese. A young Japanese man in the group commented on how my friend Lina and I had the same smell [*nioi*]. A little surprised and unsure of what he meant, I asked him to explain. He paused for a few seconds, not sure how to respond. "Well, for example, you're both dressed alike," he replied, pleased that he came up with something. Lina and I both protested. The only thing in common about our dress was that we both happened to be wearing tank-tops on that sweltering evening. Our attire, I surmised, though not altogether unusual, could seem out of place in a city where many adult women wear crisp, long-sleeved twin sets even in the hottest part of the summer. Later in the evening, as we were making our way to a local salsa club popular among Brazilian nikkeis, I found myself walking next to the same Japanese man. As we were chatting, he turned to me abruptly and said that he feels strange around me. Taken aback, I asked him why he felt this way. He replied: "You, and Lina as well, you both look completely Japanese, and yet you talk like a foreigner and act like a foreigner. You even move and walk like a foreigner. It gives me a strange feeling and I'm not sure how to act around the two of you." He seemed to me to be genuinely unsettled and troubled. His interactions with Lina and me produced for him a cognitive dissonance. His earlier remark about our smell started to make more sense to me. Both Lina and I were uncanny embodiments of a seemingly irreconcilable contradiction of social categories he believed to be mutually exclusive. That is, being ethnically (and phenotypically) Japanese and yet also foreign. At first he could not pinpoint what there was about our presence and material form that was uncanny to him. The term he used earlier, "smell," indexes an intangible but real sensation: what he perceived as our shared and strange aura (*fūniki*).

This kind of experience is not unique among Japanese Americans, especially among older generations of Japanese Americans who have been living in Japan for decades. One of my informants, Mrs. Kawamoto, was an elderly Japanese American nisei woman in her eighties who was born and raised in Hawai'i. She had been living in Japan for more than sixty years, having moved to Japan with her parents just prior to the bombing of Pearl Harbor. While still a teenager, she was forced into a marriage with a Japanese man and warned not to let anyone know she was American. Like most Japanese Americans who lived in Japan during the Allied occupation and postwar period, English language skills were in high demand despite her attempts to blend in as quietly as possible as a Japanese housewife and mother. Throughout our conversations, Mrs. Kawamoto spoke of her fear of being judged (and outed as American) by others, because, as she put it, "Other people think I speak *hen na nihongo, dakara ne*" (I speak strange Japanese). As the examples above suggest, to be a Japanese American heritage language speaker in Japan is to be uncanny. While Mrs. Kawamoto uses Japanese in most of her daily interactions in Japan, she says she still dreams in

English. Her statement reveals the way in which English, as it is relegated to but nonetheless expressed in her dreaming life, represents the excess of identity that refuses to be repressed.

As in the cases of Mrs. Kawamoto and Helen, it was not unusual to hear Japanese Americans living in Japan speak of their self-consciousness communicating in Japanese because they fear being perceived and evaluated as *hen*, or strange, by Japanese. In some cases, Japanese Americans who are embarrassed and hesitant to communicate in Japanese have what Stephen Krashen calls "language shyness," a trait not uncommon among heritage language learners.[36] If Japanese American communicative competence is evaluated as strange and discomforting, it is because Japanese American performativity is read as both familiar and strange, violating the assumed boundaries between self and other and the naturalized coherence of Japanese identity. In this sense, Japanese Americans can be said to constitute an uncanny presence in Japan in unsettling the very ideological underpinnings of national identity. As Mladen Dolar suggests, "ideology perhaps basically consists of a social attempt to integrate the uncanny, to make it bearable, to assign it a place."[37] The uncanny then is an inherent part of constructing Japanese modernity at the same time that it threatens to reveal and undo it at its very sutures. The failure of integration or assignation of place produces disruptive re-surfacings of the uncanny.[38]

At the same time that Japanese Americans fail linguistically to pass as Japanese, they are also often described as being more Japanese than the Japanese. Matthew Hamabata, the Japanese American anthropologist who struggled with how to position and identify himself while conducting fieldwork in Japan, was regarded suspiciously by a cabdriver for not knowing the Chinese forms for "right turn" or "left turn" in the early part of his fieldwork. Later, when he become more adept at presenting himself as Japanese American in social interactions, Hamabata was praised by another cabdriver for preserving what he considered to be older, Meiji-era Japanese values of discipline and hard work (implying that Hamabata enacts a supposedly more authentic Japanese culture, which Japanese youths today have lost).[39]

The historical conditions that fostered the formation of Japanese diasporas were directly tied to the significant social transformations taking place in the making of modern Japan following the Meiji Restoration. It should come as no surprise then that the descendents of those largely disavowed populations who went abroad should reappear in Japan uncannily embodying corrupted traces of the habitus of their ancestors that have all but vanished in Japan. These forms of linguistic and embodied practices lead to some descriptions of Japanese Americans as being "more Japanese" than Japanese. These perceptions are attributed to the maintenance of selected aspects of what are read as more "traditional" Meiji-era practices and values. In this way, Japanese Americans are specters of an imagined unadulterated, premodern past. They are otherworldly in their strangeness and in their familiarity. This aspect of Japanese-American–ness can be jarring when they, perhaps unlike their South American counterparts, also simultaneously and contradictorily identify with the most iconic and significant "Other" in Japanese national discourse: the United States.

In contradicting these self/Other dichotomies reinforced in both orientalist and nihonjinron discourses, Japanese Americans destabilize articulations of modern Japanese nationhood. Naoki Sakai describes the way in which, through what he calls the "regime of translation" and the "schema of cofiguration," nations as homogeneous, coherent, and essentialized entities are defined and imagined against what is construed as linguistically discrete and incommensurable others.[40] Sakai contends that the ideology by which Japan is mythologized as a monoethnic society is premised on "the assumption that, since the Japanese people are one ethnos, communication of ideas and sentiment among them is guaranteed from the start."[41] While Japanese Americans are part of the Japanese ethnos, seamless communication is not a given. Japanese American heritage language speakers undermine the elision of race and culture in these processes of national construction and cofiguration as they navigate their day-to-day lives in Japan. Their linguistic and bodily strategies of self-presentation are uncanny anomalies that shake the very underpinnings of Japanese national identity.

Conclusion

As William Safran notes, "[l]anguages are not only tools of nation-building but also means of political control."[42] Language for ethnic minorities and immigrant communities in the United States has accordingly been a central aspect of the struggle cultural activists have waged in order to shape debates around national identity. Efforts to gain legitimacy for bilingual education and heritage language programs have often served as a means of asserting cultural alterity and of carving a space of belonging in the face of pressures to assimilate. While ideologies and assumptions about the relationship between language and identity are rooted in the culture of the United States, they also dramatically inform how Japanese Americans perceive themselves and negotiate social relationships when they are in Japan.

The relationship between Japanese Americans and the Japanese language is about as varied and fluid as Japanese American identity itself, but it is also inextricably and structurally tied to specific geopolitical contexts and local hegemonic discourses about belonging and nationhood For my informants, language has come to be an arena for reinforcing their difference, strangeness, and exclusion from Japanese society. Language, as a marker of ethnicity, class, and citizenship, not only differentiates individuals within a "language community," but it also helps to enforce boundaries of national identity. Japanese Americans may regard learning Japanese as a way to reclaim their cultural "heritage" (however phantasmatic that may be), but the experiences of Japanese Americans living in Japan reveal how language ideologies serve to police Japanese and Japanese American identity. Access to heritage language education has opened up career opportunities to Japanese Americans not often available to other foreigners or immigrants. Nonetheless, I hope to have shown how, for Japanese Americans living in Japan, despite their typically privileged status as transnational elites, being a heritage language speaker is not always empowering. Language ideologies in Japan reinforce their difference and non-belonging in Japan by erasing their identifications as Japanese American and disavowing their alterity and historical experience.

Yet language is obviously also a site for asserting alterity. As Martin Manalansan illustrates in his work on Filipino gay men living in New York, language — in this case, the innovation and dynamism in Swardspeak (queer vernacular) — is a resource for creative and agentive use in shaping identifications and forging diasporic spaces of belonging despite the marginalizing realities of transnational migration.[43] Japanese Americans generally occupy a different class status as transnational migrants; however, Japanese American linguistic practices similarly constitute a medium by which spaces of belonging are created in Japan at the same time that they delineate Japanese American alterity and historical experience. This tension articulated through language is characteristic of the uncanniness of Japanese Americans in Japan, an uncanniness that often reveals the gaps and impossibilities within ideologies unifying and naturalizing specific configurations of nationhood, ethnos, and language.

Japanese and Japanese Americans alike tend to view not learning Japanese as a willful rejection of Japanese (American) identity. This sentiment is marked in conversations by comments such as "you should" and "why don't you?" Those who feel their language abilities are insufficient are often guilt-ridden, as is evident in statements such as "It's embarrassing that I've lived here for so long and haven't improved," "I know I have no excuse," and "I haven't had the time yet, but I plan to study." Heritage language and being a heritage language learner/speaker, as these comments imply, is in many ways a burden — a source of guilt, shame, and inadequacy. Attempts to celebrate "heritage" and efforts to promote heritage language education reinforce these forms of guilt and inadequacy. These expectations sometimes become a prescriptive and reifying aspect of reclaiming and constructing ethnic identities. Assumptions about the assimilation and internalized racism of Japanese Americans reinforce the trope of cultural loss, causing further anxieties over authenticity and claims of belonging among ethnic minorities. These anxieties are played out through language and discourses about language.

I have argued that the idea that Japanese Americans should learn Japanese as a way to maintain ethnic affiliation (in U.S. multicultural discourse) paradoxically plays into Japanese nationalist language ideologies even as those ideologies serve to exclude heritage language learners. Language, however, is also the medium by which Japanese Americans create spaces of belonging in Japan and give voice to their alterity and historical experience/identities. Language itself — and the anxieties and aspirations surrounding it — became a prominent theme in my discussions with Japanese Americans living in Japan. This preoccupation with language reveals the way in which language is inextricably tied to the production of Japanese Americans identity.

ACKNOWLEDGMENTS: I am grateful for the help I received on this article from Neriko Musha Doerr, Michiyo Takato, Taku Suzuki, Yuko Okubo, Laura Miller, Faye Ginsburg, Bambi Schieffelin, Sarah Mountz, and two anonymous reviewers.

❑

6. Afterword: Japan-Related Linguistic Intervention

Laura Miller

IN A MOVING ESSAY ABOUT HER PERSONAL EXPERIENCE with the Japanese language, Ayukawa Michiko, a Japanese Canadian, relates how love and pride in the native language used by her immigrant parents transformed into a curse after the trauma of 1940s wartime removal and incarceration.[1] Competence in her once beloved childhood language deteriorated and eventually she rejected the language altogether as symbolic of a stigmatized identity. As an adult, her disfluency causes her great shame and mortification. On one occasion she reports on a conversation she had with Mrs. T of the Japanese Embassy, who had inquired about the health of Ayukawa's baby daughter:

> I hesitantly replied in my "lost" Japanese that she was fine but did cause quite a commotion when she was hungry. The exact words I used now escape me, but whatever I said caused Mrs. T to laugh derisively at my "quaint" Japanese. Then and there I vowed that I would never try to speak Japanese to any native Japanese anymore! And this vow was kept for years.[2]

Nevertheless, in her later years she diligently studies and reclaims a degree of Japanese language proficiency, reestablishing a positive identity as a Japanese Canadian. Ayukawa's story is instructive for us as we consider this thematic collection of articles on heritage language in Japan-related settings. The radical shifts in language attitudes, skills, and symbolic meanings held by a single person, as in Ayukawa's case, are mirrored in countless other narratives and community stories from around the globe.

The authors of the articles in this collection ask us to look closely, and ethnographically, at the notion of heritage language and the ways in which the teaching and learning of a heritage language is molded by the context in which it occurs. As the authors show through a richness of ethnographic detail, the host nation's socioeconomic and political milieu, the global status of Japan, and the learner's individual history and psychology — all modify any simplistic assumption that heritage language learning is a straightforward form of identity manufacture and maintenance. Similar to Ayukawa, learners of Japanese as a heritage language and learners of other heritage languages in Japan vary widely in their experiences with and reception to this type of linguistic intervention. If the Japanese heritage language situation is so diverse, and occasionally displays contradictory trends, why should we care? The studies in this collection force us to acknowledge this diversity and what it says about the complex relationship between language and identity. The sparkling new research found here offers needed lessons to scholars of Asian diasporas, migration, ethnic identity, and ethnolinguistics.

In these heritage language studies we see a pattern in which the ideologies held by instructors and educational institutions do not often match individual lived reality. This is most poignant in cases in which institutions map a one-to-one correspondence between national language and ethnicity, obliterating hybrid and transnational identities and subjectivities. Both the institutional and in some cases the individual desire for an isomorphic match between self-identity and language masks the social science understanding that one's ethnic slot is never immutable and fixed, but rather is negotiated and made relevant through interactive talk. The case of Kumiko described by Doerr and Lee aptly illustrates this, as her identity depends on who she is speaking to, which language she is using, and the nature of the interaction.[3] In a classic theorization of this issue, Moerman asks us to rethink how we ascribe ethnic identity.[4] Based on his fieldwork among an ethnic group in Thailand who refer to themselves as Lue, he was forced to radically reconsider the way scholars used to go about delineating ethnic groups on the basis of observable traits or cultural features such as language or food habits. Unable to find any unique or specific criteria that could be used to mark the boundary between the Lue and other neighboring ethnic groups, Moerman concluded that "[s]omeone is Lue by virtue of believing and calling himself Lue and of acting in ways that validate his Lueness."[5] The use of a group member's own self-identification as the basis for how we might describe them is now recognized by most anthropologists, but it may not be acknowledged by all the people and institutions individuals in diaspora come into contact with. Therefore, the role and function of language as an observable criteria to mark identity takes on heightened meaning, and a second or third language that is linked to ethnicity becomes more than simple language learning.

Additionally, these struggles with linguistic identity in transnational settings also highlight a basic sociolinguistic finding: an "authentic" language can never be completely learned, by children in Japan, Peru, Bolivia, or the United States, because the concept of an "authentic" language is a fiction. We see this poignantly in the words of Yaichi, the boy from the Kansai region introduced in Doerr and Lee's study, whose regional dialect is not the one taught in his heritage language program and is ridiculed by fellow students and teachers.[6] It surfaces in the experiences of Japanese Peruvians described by Yamasaki who return from Japan with contemporary colloquialisms never to be found in the textbooks of their schools.[7] The students, armed with updated snazzy teen-speak, were not viewed as having command of good or authentic Japanese. It should be noted that ideas about the authenticity and correctness of language are promoted not only by teachers and schools and enshrined in the textbooks they use, but are often held by many speakers and language learners themselves, who see authorized forms of language as more "authentic" than the forms of language they might actually hear being spoken by native speakers.[8] For example, in research on Americans doing study abroad home stay in Kyoto, it was discovered that host families refused to teach the Japanese language learner their own dialect.[9] Instead, they spoke to each other in Kyoto-ben but always switched to the standard form when speaking to the foreigner.

In North American research there is often the assumption that heritage language instruction serves as a method for opposing or mediating an official mainstream imposition of a standard national language. Yet as these articles make clear, the heritage language itself is an imagined standard that is presented as the true, authentic version of a language. Particularly in settings where schools and teachers are sponsored by or are affiliated with the Japanese government, the form and content of heritage language instruction may be imposing a privileged class and regional model of Japanese-ness. This deserves careful scrutiny.

This last point brings us to another uneasy realization. The research in these articles cannot help but expose the hand of the Japanese government and other formal elite institutions in determining the nature and forms of heritage language instruction. World English is a widely recognized research domain and way of conceptualizing the legitimate varieties of English that exist in Europe, North America, Australia, Jamaica, India, and elsewhere. In the case of the Japanese language, however, the Japanese government does not envision the possibility of World Japanese. Indeed, it appears that government and business elites are re-colonizing former subjects through language monitoring, funding, and the provision of "real" native speakers for heritage language instruction.[10]

In Suzuki's description of the heritage language situation in Bolivia, we learn of the economic, cultural, and symbolic significance of selecting Japanese over Okinawan Ryūkyūan as the language of instruction.[11] The settlers' original Okinawan identity, the basis for the foundation of the expatriate Okinawan community in Bolivia in the first place, is subjugated to larger sociopolitical concerns in which the dominant prestige language is Japanese. Of course, funding from the Japanese government plays a role in this relocation of heritage. Once a formerly banned language of instruction in Peru during World War II, Japanese language ability is now a desired type of cultural capital.

The shift in Japan's global status has also created a burden for anyone with any type of Japanese ancestry to consciously make a choice about this language. For others around the globe such a choice might not ever be theirs to make. Among descendants of people from Mexico who emigrated to California decades before that state ever became part of the United States, a decision to not pass on the Spanish language was often made by grandparents and parents who saw that it was a stigmatized language in a land now under Anglo rule. Another example: I have an acquaintance who was born in the former Yugoslavia and emigrated first to Israel and later to the United States. He and his wife taught their children English and Hebrew. When I asked him if he would ever teach them his Croatian mother tongue, he replied, "Never. I myself refuse to ever speak it again." In other words, it is best not to assume that a person wants to retain or implant their native language in their children. Language shame held by speakers of minority languages who have been the target of years of discrimination, such as the Ainu in Japan or Native Americans in North America, has often led to the near extinction or disappearance of these languages.

Scholars need to keep in mind that the continuing existence of heritage language schools around the world has much to do with the prestige value of learning Japanese in the current historical moment. Let us also remember that Japanese language teaching itself has become a booming global cultural industry. The new visibility and attractiveness of the Japanese language (many heritage language learners are motivated by a desire to read manga) has meant increased involvement of Japanese embassies and consulates in the structure and content of Japanese language instruction outside university settings. Through funding, sponsorship of speech contests, cultural events, and other activities, provision of books and materials, and funneling of selected language instructors, the Japanese government promotes an ideology of a pure, correct form of the language. (This is similar to the Foreign Ministry's attempts to monitor and "certify" as authentic the thousands of new Japanese restaurants that are being established outside Japan.) The Japanese Chamber of Commerce in Chicago set up a day school and Saturday school for expatriate Japanese families who expect to go back to Japan. According to their promotional literature and website:

> The JCCC founded the Futabakai Saturday School, the first Japanese school in the Midwest, in 1966 and the Day School in 1978. The Day and Saturday Schools provide a place where children of Japanese expatriates can retain close contact with the customs, traditions, and education of their native land. The schools allow Japanese families to fully participate in their U.S. assignment without compromising their Japanese culture or the education of their children.[12]

In other words, the official organs of the Japanese business community want to convince those who are sent on overseas assignments that they will be living in a transplanted Japan that simply happens to be located in the American Midwest. Yet, as research on returnee children has shown, no matter how many precautions parents take, their offspring will still be marked by the foreign experience in some manner that children and adults back in Japan unerringly sniff out.[13] The forms of ethnic socialization and linguistic immersion that are desired will always be mediated in some unexpected manner. As Doerr and Lee illustrate in their research, regardless of the type of ideologically marked language tracks students are placed into, and no matter how much parents and educators imagine it, both tracks are, at the end of the day, forms of heritage language instruction.[14]

Heritage language as approached in this collection of essays is always grounded in local language politics, be they at the national or community level. Together these studies allow us to reexamine the very notion of heritage language, recasting the concept as one less grounded in North American identity politics. We see that the imagined heritage language takes many forms, from forced family obligation to a special endowment or object of intense desire. Notably, however, these authors uncover the counterintuitive finding that linguistic intervention, no matter how well meaning and well intentioned, often entails a certain degree of psychological pain for the targeted individual. For many people in diasporic circumstances, belonging to an a priori category of "Japanese" (or "Vietnamese" or "Chinese") is often imposed, or else is under threat of reassignment or withdrawal depending on various displays of linguistic or cultural competence. In a rush to celebrate multilingualism, bilingualism, and multiculturalism, and the putative tolerance and broad-mindedness these are supposed to engender (but which in fact may thwart their own noble intentions, as seen in Okubo's essay[15]), governments, school boards, teachers, administrators, and parents may ignore the personal costs of having feet in more than one world.

In some cases the psychological pain derives from what happens when a formerly private language, one associated with the safety, tolerance, and acceptance of home life, is turned into a public language. The private Chinese or Vietnamese spoken with family in Osaka, the evolved and new form of Japanese spoken in Bolivia or Peru — all are transformed into a public or outside language in the heritage language situation.[16] Language choices and performances in these situations thereafter become fraught with intense self-surveillance and outside evaluation. The heritage language learner might be fully at ease with her language competence in one space, but uncomfortable in another. The "bad" or "incorrect" Japanese that is acceptable with family and friends is suddenly scrutinized for its adherence to some abstract notion of what is "proper."

Although the same situation confronts many native speakers of nonstandard forms (attested to in Japan by the huge market in language etiquette books), it is often experienced more intensely by heritage language learners. Yumi's deliberate disfluency performances, described by Takamori, remind us of the importance of research that uncovers the local concerns that impact individual linguistic choices.[17] Japanese is Yumi's private language, the one she uses with her husband, but she assumes a different public persona in Japan. Yumi's private language from her American past is a counterpoint to a language of public life in Japan. Depending on the person and where they use this now-public language, the consequences may vary dramatically, from language shyness to oblivious use of casual speech in formal contexts.

Like Yumi, many other speakers grapple with the politics and consequences of language socialization and choice. In sharing the narratives of Korean women who strive to understand their linguistic and ethnic identities, Sonia Ryang describes the distressing experiences of Yuhi, the main character in an autobiographical novel written by *zainichi* (born-in-Japan) Korean writer Lee Yangji:

> The ethos of the lost tongue, the pathos of the lost or hidden self, and the sadness that is completely private and hard to verbalize overlap with those of Yuhi in inversion, whose true, secure language remains Japanese, yet who wants to recover her mother tongue, the language of everyday life in South Korea, which comes to her as only an incomplete means of self-expression.[18]

I found Ryang's words echoing in some of the sentiments that bubble up in a range of settings described in this set of articles. Similar to Yuhi, people with Japanese ancestry who are primarily speakers of other languages are always expected to want to reconnect with an imagined lost tongue, the ancestral root language that may never quite live up to their linguistic dreams or needs. We should therefore question the implicit notion that heritage language is something "mislaid" that must be reclaimed or reinstalled, in some cases generations after an original migration.

These articles also inspire a final unnerving thought: Is there any language that can be said to be the best, most perfect one for any of us? Will not all languages inevitably fall short of the idealized notion that a real, true, authentic form of speech exists for each person that fully fits their unique history, identity, and sense of self? After all, the languages we speak are often the product of historical, sociopolitical, and socioeconomic trends, accidents, and forces. They are insufficient to completely define or enclose our identities.

❑

7. Afterword: Cross-Cultural Implications of Japanese Heritage Language Policies and Practices

Krista E. Van Vleet

IN THIS COLLECTION OF ARTICLES, the authors bring attention to the interrelation of language, identity, and power in the teaching of "heritage languages" in Japan and the Japanese diaspora. Although the relevance of this collection to scholars who focus on Japanese language and culture is clear, by taking seriously the heterogeneity of speakers and of social and historical contexts in which individuals learn and use Japanese, the authors also contribute significant theoretical perspectives and ethnographic cases to cross-cultural scholarship on language. For specialists of other geographical regions these articles offer insights into the interrelationships of linguistic hierarchies and political economy, the navigation of ethnic and racial subjectivities, and the active roles of children and adolescents who may (or may not) claim belonging to various communities through their linguistic practices.

Linguistic Hierarchy, Political Economy, and Remembrance

That languages are always parts of larger systems of sociality, politics, and economy is almost a truism in sociocultural and linguistic anthropology. As Susan Gal pointed out over two decades ago, the capacity of language to denote or represent the world is "fundamentally implicated in relations of domination."[1] At least in part, this is because language structure and use "provide access to material resources" and "become resources in their own right."[2] Several articles in this thematic collection further highlight the ways a particular language, or linguistic variety, may be differentially valued (symbolically and materially) by different institutions and speakers and within complex arrays of political economic conditions and historical contexts.

For scholars interested in linguistic hierarchy in multilingual nations, and the relationship between state power and language ideology, the articles in this volume are replete with telling examples. Suzuki's discussion of heritage language education in Colonia Okinawa, Bolivia,[3] and Yamasaki's discussion of nikkei students in Lima, Peru,[4] for example, explore the complex ways that linguistic hierarchies and transnational political economies may be layered upon each other. In the Andean nations of Peru, Bolivia, and Ecuador, the hierarchy of languages is embedded in a colonial and postcolonial political economy. Bruce Mannheim has argued that in contemporary Peru every act of speaking clearly positions people and reproduces a ranking among languages in which Spanish is more highly valued than Quechua and Quechua is valued over other indigenous languages.[5] Languages are, of course, legitimated by formal institutions (such as schools, governments, and the military), enable access to labor markets, and take on hegemonic dimensions so that even those without access to the "legitimated variety accept its authority, its correctness, its power to persuade, and its right to be obeyed."[6] For hundreds of years Quechua has been the subordinate language of the "indians."[7] And indigeneity throughout the region is often stigmatized as "embodying economic impoverishment and cultural backwardness," while whiteness is valorized as embodying "power, modernity, and the capitalist market."[8]

It is within this particular array of linguistic, social, and political-economic hierarchies of the Andean region, that Okinawan-Bolivians learn Japanese. In some ways ambivalently positioned as "foreigners" who are able to access symbolic and material capital[9] and as "affluent large-scale farm owners"[10] people in Colonia Okinawa have chosen standard Japanese rather than Uchināguchi as the heritage language taught in schools. Suzuki notes that heritage language education for second- and third-generation Okinawan-Bolivians became crucial not only as a way to preserve their ancestral culture, but also "to maintain and bolster their upper-class status within the rural Bolivian society, which was marked by their 'Japanese' (not Okinawan) heritage."[11] Through this choice, the colonia also acquiesced to a linguistic hierarchy centered in Japan and maintained access to financial support from the Japanese state, including disaster relief, public works, and economic assistance, in addition to direct support for schools and the enhanced access of individuals to work and scholarships in Japan.

The significance of the political economic context is reinforced by Yamasaki's article on heritage language education among nikkei in Colegio El Agustino (CEA), a private school in Lima, Peru.[12] Although Peru and Bolivia are similar in terms of the structuring of linguistic hierarchy, the initial insularity of the Okinawan community in Bolivia contrasts to the socioeconomic and cultural differentiation among the approximately 80,000 nikkei in Peru, most of whom live in the large city of Lima.[13] At same time, by the 1980s most non-nikkei in Colonia Okinawa were integrated with the Bolivian-Okinawan community whereas most non-nikkei students in CEA were not integrated into the nikkei community in Lima.[14] Most courses at CEA, which was founded after World War II, are taught in Spanish. At CEA learning Japanese has been emphasized to "prevent the complete loss of ancestral language and cultural traits."[15] Yet in the 1990s enrollment dropped because many nikkei returned to Japan for work, and many adults who stayed in Peru sent their children to American or bilingual schools, which were viewed as more prestigious. At this time, the emphasis on language education at CEA also shifted to English, although Japanese language and other aspects of Japanese culture continued to be taught. The history of heritage language education in CEA aligns with shifts in political and economic policies in Japan allowing for return migration and work in working-class jobs, with shifts in the Peruvian economy, which by the 1990s was experiencing an increase in foreign tourism, and with the elaboration of a linguistic hierarchy that has incorporated English as well as Japanese into the mix.

These articles on Japanese heritage language education in the eastern lowlands of Bolivia and coastal city of Lima, Peru, remind scholars of both Asia and Latin America that linguistic hierarchies and political economies are not static and that "heritage" may be defined according to local as well as transnational parameters. Even in the last decade a person of Asian descent may be disparagingly referred to as "chino" in Bolivia or Peru, but their often higher socioeconomic class status (at least as compared to Quechua-speaking farmers) and perceived social and economic connections to technologically advanced or "modernized" nations outside South America, make learning Japanese a potentially valuable resource. From a different perspective, these cases suggest how debates around "heritage language" education or linguistic revitalization can potentially take on hegemonic dimensions, ignoring the diversity of claims and identities that language policy may invoke. Bilingual intercultural education (in Quechua or Aymara and Spanish) was a hotly contested issue throughout the twentieth century and continues to be so today in Bolivia, Peru, and Ecuador. In many communities, Quechua-speaking parents resist bilingual education and reject the view that bilingual or heritage language education is a tool of social mobilization or cultural maintenance. In contrast to the ideology of Japanese language in Japan, which emphasizes that education in a heritage language enhances the learning of Japanese,[16] in the Andes language ideologies promote the view that education in native or heritage languages inhibits the learning of Spanish.[17] Many Quechua speakers view the ability to speak, write, and read in Spanish, or English, as far more important to the lives and livelihoods of their children than Quechua. Although Japanese has been at best tangential to debates about or curricular development of bilingual intercultural education in these nations over the past fifty years, much can be learned by scholars and activists from attending to these cross-cultural similarities and differences.

The other articles in this book also extend understanding of linguistic hierarchy, political economy, and state influence. Linguistic hierarchy is evinced by the sometimes poignant cases of teachers correcting a fluent speaker of Japanese because he uses a different (local) variety or more informal register, of return migrants whose archaic turns of phrase cause consternation or humor in Japan, or of a child who is labeled as "Vietnamese" or "Chinese" though born in Japan and able to interact in the same way her Japanese companion does. Clearly some language varieties (such as standard Japanese) are understood to be more correct, or are more valued in the marketplace, or are spoken by individuals who are, at least in some contexts, understood to be more authentically Japanese than others. Here the political economy of language intersects with questions of identification and belonging.

Language, Indexicality, and Identity

A second set of themes that emerge in the articles in this book is the situatedness of racial and ethnic discourses and the production of identities through the use of language by individuals in various social contexts. As Mary Bucholtz and Kira Hall note, one of the mechanisms through which people (consciously and unconsciously) "construct identity positions" linguistically or lay claim to belonging to particular collectivities is through indexicality.[18] An index might be a word, phrase, or some linguistic form that depends on the context for its meanings. For example, many pronouns (I, he, she, we, here, there, that) change meaning depending on who speaks and in what context the words are spoken. The "overt mention of identity categories and labels" or the "use of linguistic structures and systems that are ideologically associated with specific personas and groups" may also be "indexical processes through which identities emerge."[19] In their language classes or at the kitchen table, people may explicitly name an identity category or index their associations with various collectivities (such as family, Colonia Okinawa, or Japanese-American community) by code-switching between languages or varieties, by using particular phrases, mobilizing symbolic resources such as talk about food, or by embedding other people's words through direct and indirect quotation and reference to other texts. This collection of articles highlights the ways that individuals consciously and unconsciously use language to position themselves within social relationships and contexts.

The heterogeneity of Japanese society, the ways in which discourses of multiculturalism, language, and ethnicity interrelate, and the importance of individual interactions in producing or transforming ethnic subjectivity is beautifully described in Okubo's article on after-school heritage language classes.[20] These classes and club activities are required — but only for certain children — in the multiethnic city of Miyako, Japan. Although Okubo concentrates primarily on the children of Vietnamese immigrants, she also weaves in strands of the history of Korean residents, Chinese residents, and Buraku. Those who "lived in Japan for most of their lives identify more with Japan and the Japanese and are not comfortable being treated differently as a foreigner."[21] Nevertheless, the children of Chinese and Vietnamese immigrants are required to take after-school classes in Japanese and participate in ethnic heritage classes, and they are encouraged to use their Vietnamese or Chinese rather than Japanese names.

When individuals are referred to as "Chinese" or "Vietnamese," even though they were born in Japan, a particular constellation of racial and ethnic associations is triggered. Some of these discourses are explicit among teachers and include assessments such as "not taken care of at home," "not disciplined as Japanese children," "having a difficult family background," or "without the ability to absorb complex and abstract ideas."[22] In spite of the state mandate for multiethnic education, Vietnamese parents may want their children to learn Japanese, or even English, before learning Vietnamese, and children's experiences inside and outside school may sensitize them to the social hierarchies that make retaining their heritage language less than appealing.[23]

Although sobering, it is not surprising that when a teacher asks second grader, Kim, "What is 'hello' in Vietnamese?" Kim refuses to answer. Kim says "I do not know," even though her class recites greetings in three languages each morning. Although the teacher may not have intended any harm, she also indexes ethnicity through her question. Kim correctly recognizes a contextual difference between her entire class reciting greetings in Japanese, Vietnamese, and Korean each morning and her teacher addressing her directly as a child who may speak Vietnamese at home. Individuals sometimes respond to these kinds of linguistic cues, linked to social contexts and much broader social discourses around race and ethnicity, below an explicit level of awareness.[24]

The conscious navigation of identities through language is also clearly demonstrated in Takamori's description of Yumi.[25] Refusing to claim an essentialized identity, Yumi skillfully identifies herself in different ways — indexing ethnic, gendered, and class positions through the *way* she speaks — in various social situations. Takamori recounts that Yumi spoke fluently on the phone in Japanese with her husband, but shifted her speaking when interacting with another mother on the phone. For example, "she had a perceptible American accent and she spoke in a measured, slower manner with more hesitations and filler words. She threw in a few English words here and there such as 'OK,' 'right,' 'park,' and 'you know.'"[26] Yumi obscured her fluency in Japanese from the other mothers at the school because they might expect her "to act like a Japanese mother," and she completely hid her ability to speak Japanese from service workers in restaurants so that she might be perceived as an American and get better service.[27]

Just as facilely code-switching between Japanese and English, or standard and local varieties of Japanese, might enable an individual to access particular communities, a lack of fluency in particular linguistic varieties or a lack of social knowledge about when and how to use a variety might mark an individual as other. Among the nikkei in Lima, particular Japanese terms and everyday expressions, some of which are archaic and some of which are mixed with Spanish, may reinforce belonging within their families or communities but may not be acceptable in language classes, school, or other contexts.[28] Japanese Americans in Japan, in contrast, are "constantly marked and reminded of the ways in which they fail to perform Japanese-ness (linguistically or otherwise)" yet may "look Japanese."[29] The degree of attentiveness to particular varieties of a language that may ensue within a community intersects with an individual's abilities or desire to "claim their belonging and articulate their alterity and identification" through how they speak as well as what they do.[30]

Takamori also explores the tension between different systems of racial identification in the experiences of Japanese Americans who live in Japan for education, work, or family reasons. The assumptions that people who are not ethnically Japanese should not be able to speak Japanese perfectly — and conversely that those who are ethnically Japanese should be able to "inherit" language skills — are tied to notions of blood, nationality, and race.[31] For example, Michael who studies, works, and lives in Japan refuses a "natural link" between his identity as a Japanese American and his ability (or lack thereof) to speak Japanese.[32] However, many of the other young people in the Japanese-American community in Japan buy into U.S. ideologies of multiculturalism and Japanese ideologies of nationalism that link ability to speak a language with ethnicity. Some of the Japanese Americans who Takamori interviewed expressed consternation that their Japanese language teachers expected "Japanese American students to have a 'naturally' greater facility with the language."[33] Another Japanese American complained that he could not speak the flawless Japanese of a white American television celebrity.[34] Youth position each other not only in terms of language proficiency but also in terms of cultural and social experiences and commonalities — but the ability to speak non-accented fluent Japanese (however full of slang) — is a significant way of fitting in.

Youth and Agentive Use of Language

As much as these articles speak to the importance of state roles in solidifying and extending language (and other) hierarchies and of individual interactions that index ideologies of ethnicity and nationality, the authors also contribute ethnographic and analytical perspectives on youth. Most of the individuals engaged in heritage language learning are children and adolescents who have variable fluencies and substantially different relationships with Japanese than do their parents. Within this collection we find a tension — and a productive one — between the efforts of parents, educators, and policy-makers to remember, revive, and transform the language as a way of maintaining an identification with a living, breathing culture and the subjectivities of children, who are themselves learners and speakers of "heritage" languages. Of course, not all individuals of Japanese descent accept the notion that the Japanese language is an important part of their self-identification. How might individuals endeavor to remember, make themselves at home in a place that feels strange, maintain a sense of their own subjectivity as Japanese (or another ethnicity), extend their love of nation or desire for a better life to their children? How might children and adolescents who are born in a place other than that of their parents' birth take up and/or transform these projects? By incorporating attention to children within the frame of "heritage language," the authors contribute to wider discussions about socialization, education, migration, and language in meaningful ways.

Children of migrants may feel homesickness for a place they never "knew" or pride to be associated with a particular nation other than the one of their birth. Alternatively children and adolescents may be less connected to the idea of maintaining a heritage language and keenly aware of the ways speaking certain languages or language varieties position them according to racial, class, and other status hierarchies. In Doerr and Lee's article on two different types of heritage language teaching — *kokugo* (national language arts curriculum of Japan) and *keishōgo* (language as heritage) — children's positionality is taken seriously methodologically.[35] The authors' attention to interviewing children as well as adult parents and teachers illuminates the ways "heritage language schooling processes accentuated the diversity of students' personal backgrounds, dialects they speak, and linguistic proficiencies and transformed what had otherwise been understood merely as 'speaking Japanese' into diverse ways to 'inherit' Japanese language."[36] For example, Yaichi, realizes that rather than speaking Japanese he was speaking the Osaka dialect of Japanese.[37] The explicit focus on talking with children to find out how they see their own language learning and their identity — and the extent to which different groups of students or types of courses affect this — is overlaid upon children's views of heritage language that emerge in the classroom. As students and teachers discuss how much rice each family eats, how well and which dialect one speaks, who one's friends are, whether one reads manga or owns a kimono, and what ethnicity one's parents are, they also highlight the cultural aspects of Japanese subjectivity that are imbricated with language.

The children in these articles at times challenge or question adults who elide their own experience of Japanese even as they acquiesce to the hierarchies imposed in their heritage language classes or society more generally. For instance whereas teachers in the Lima school assumed that returnees would speak "better" Japanese — and placed them in the advanced class — many either did not speak well or spoke in dialects or registers other than the standard Japanese taught at the school. Some students passed exams at high levels, but refused to speak in class; others relied on fellow students to translate the teacher's questions into Spanish and to provide the answers in Japanese. Those students who could speak well at times questioned standard forms or requested additional information based on their experiences at home and in Japan. When Claudia asks about when to use "need to" as opposed to "have to" she is drawing on language use outside of class, but the teacher refuses to answer her. Claudia sees Japanese class as boring.[38] Others such as Yuriko see little value in Japanese education. For Yuriko, Peru is "horrible but cool" because in Peru she has friends. Making no effort to "hide her negative attitude toward the Japanese class from her teacher" or the interviewer, she says she has no intention of returning to Japan.[39] As Yamaguchi notes, one of the consequences of heritage language education in Lima is that students are sometimes encouraged "to 'dis-inherit' what they have learned outside school: this may relate to their family's social status in their ancestral country."[40]

As Begoña Escheverria demonstrates based on research in a very different ethnographic context (that of Basque medium schools in Spain), when children and adolescents "buy into" the importance of language revitalization and the link between language and identity, heritage language education has much greater success.[41] But children also need to have opportunities to use language informally. Even students in Basque medium schools, who are taught all subjects in Basque and may come from Basque-speaking homes, spoke to each other in the hallways, while flirting or arguing or joking, in Spanish. Teenagers report being embarrassed using the standard Basque forms they learned in school when vernacular Basque forms are expected. For "not only does this mark the speaker as not 'authentically' Basque, he or she is also marked as 'uncool.'"[42] Youth sometimes lack everyday access to vernacular forms of Basque, but Spanish informal forms pervade the lives of children whether they go to Basque medium of Spanish medium schools. Being able to sound "cool" rather than "proper" or to engage in "fun or 'hip' communicative purposes," Escheverria concludes, might encourage greater use of Euserka (the Basque language) among youth.[43]

Similarly children and youth in Japanese heritage language classes recognize that personal forms of expression, from various dialects learned in Japan, to slang, to informal or vernacular speech, conflicted with the standard dialect taught by teachers.[44] Adolescent girls in Lima, especially, were interested in Japanese popular culture (music, comic books, television shows) and attempted to redirect classroom activities. But for most of these students, their diverse experiences and language practices did not work to their advantage in school. Many students recognized that Japanese as spoken (in Japan) was different from the Japanese spoken and taught in their classes. But like the Vietnamese children and parents in Japan, they had little control over what was taught to them as heritage.

As Nancy Hornberger has argued, "we need to ask not just *what* language means in a particular social context but also *how* that meaning is accomplished interactionally and *why* those meanings (out of all possible available meanings) are expressed in that particular case."[45] The articles in this collection explore the ways that Japanese, and other languages, are taught and learned as "heritage." The historical and ethnographic details of the various cases illuminate the importance of interrogating how, for whom, and by whom, heritage is defined. The linguistic hierarchies that shape particular interactions, the relationships between state policies and individual desires, the heterogeneity of communities linguistically, socially, and otherwise all are significant aspects of understanding Japanese as a heritage language — and of the Japanese state as an entity that promotes both multiculturalism and linguistic hegemony. These articles also show that as much as state policies shape heritage language education, the everyday use of language is also crucial to its maintenance and transformation. As individuals navigate social relationships, they draw upon and transform linguistic resources and identify themselves in various communities. Scholars of regions where multiple languages are spoken, thus, have much to gain by considering remembrance, heritage, identity, and power through these ethnographic and historical cases.

❑

8. Afterword: Dreaming in...English?

The Complexity and Unexpectedness of Japanese Being and Becoming through Language

Barbra A. Meek

"[T]o be a Japanese American heritage language speaker in Japan is to be uncanny. While Mrs. Kawamoto uses Japanese in most of her daily interactions in Japan, she says she still dreams in English."[1]

IN HIS BOOK *INDIANS IN UNEXPECTED PLACES* Philip J. Deloria reflects on the appearance of Indians in unexpected social arenas through an analysis of historical photographs and accompanying narratives: the Native American woman at the beauty parlor, later photographed enjoying a treat at an ice cream parlor, markedly adorned yet seeming to be out of context.[2] To ameliorate the dissonance of seeing a woman in Native American regalia seated in a drugstore, the observer might ask: What language do you speak? What language do you dream in? Were the subject to respond in Lakota, the observer might consider the unexpectedness resolved; still odd to see her sitting there, but certain of her Indian-ness. Were the subject to respond in "broken" English, the observer's conundrum would also be resolved — a sign of partial assimilation. Were the woman to respond in the same dialect as the (English-speaking, non-ethnicized) observer, the unexpectedness would be magnified. On the other hand, were the observer to be Indian, the unexpectedness might be realized in relation to the fact that the woman is sitting at a counter in regalia when the situation does not call for such attire. In any case, such images not only disrupt certain taken-for-granted conceptualizations of Indian-ness (while at the same time resurrecting them), but also highlight the social provenance of the imagined and the everydayness of disjuncture — between the imagined and the real, the assumed and the unexpected. The ethnographically rich and theoretically provocative articles in this book provide plenty of fodder for reflecting on and re-imagining processes of regimentation, conventionalization, and fiction —

processes that result in the confused gaze of an observer who imagined things differently.

Through the lens of language shift, language socialization, and (sociolinguistic) disjuncture, the goal of this brief commentary is to draw out some of the complexity and contradictions in conceptualizing some languages as heritage languages and not others. I begin with a brief review of the conceptualization of the term "heritage language" in North America framed by language shift, focusing on the ambiguities entailed in its use and the challenge that the standardization of this phrase raises in relation to processes of identification relating languages and peoples. I then turn to language socialization in order to highlight the processes of regimentation (through discourse/language) that standardize interpretive frames and thus conventionalize certain language ideologies, influencing individual interpretations of and reflections on their own and others' subjectivities as well as the recognition and status of a language. Finally, in these acts of recognition and processes for identification, opportunities for misinterpretation (or alternative interpretation) abound. Though constrained by linguistic performance, physical appearance, and other meaningful embodied comportments, the interpretive frame — an ideological conglomerate as Doerr and Lee might say, or a semiotic bundling à la Webb Keane[3] — for recognizing such socially laden signs will vary across interactions and interlocutors, highlighting the importance of language socialization and individual biographies in rendering interactions interpretable *and* opening up a space for indeterminacy and redefinition.

What is a heritage language and how has this concept been regimented or standardized in relation to other similar terms such as first language, mother tongue, ancestral language, and minority language? As these articles illustrate, significant overlap and confusion abounds. In a 1991 publication on heritage language programs in Canada,[4] for example, the Canadian Education Association (CEA) noted that

> The language of origin, the first language, the language of one's parents or one's ancestors, the ethnic or minority language has commonly been called a "Heritage Language." Yet we find ourselves in some difficulty trying to define heritage language: we have seen much use made of the definition established by the Ontario Ministry of Education, that is, "any language other than French or English."[5]

To clarify the concept the authors drew on an earlier report by Jim Cummins and Marcel Danesi,

> The term "heritage language" usually refers to all languages other than the aboriginal languages of Native and Inuit peoples and the "official" Canadian languages (English and French). A variety of other terms have been used in Canada to refer to heritage languages: for example, "ethnic," "minority," "ancestral," "third," and "non-official" have all been used at different times and in different provinces. The term used in Quebec is "langues d'origine." In other countries the term "community languages" is used (e.g., Australia, Britain, New Zealand) and the term "mother-tongue teaching" is also common. A number of Canadian

proponents of heritage language teaching have expressed misgivings about the term because it connotes learning about past traditions rather than acquiring language skills that have significance for children's overall educational and personal development. In the Toronto Board of Education the term "modern languages" is used partly in an attempt to defuse the strong emotional reactions that the term "heritage languages" evokes.[6]

This passage highlights two issues related to "heritage language": (1) the term may exclude aboriginal or indigenous languages and (2) it emphasizes cultural tradition over linguistic practice. Other, and more recent, scholarship, including the growing literature on indigenous language revitalization and reclamation, conceptualizes this term in relation to sociohistorical context and as process, as noted by Doerr and Lee, rather than by types — of languages, populations, or traditions.

According to Jim Cummins, coauthor of the above-cited report and a scholar who has written extensively on heritage language initiatives and programming, "the term 'heritage language' generally refers to the community ethnocultural language which is not necessarily the child's first-learned language (or even used in the home)."[7] Similar to the notion of an ancestral language, a heritage language has become defined as a linguistic variety indexical of an individual's ethnic affiliation.[8] Or, as Miller notes in her remarks in this book, a heritage language can and does function as a visible sign of ethnolinguistic belonging.[9] The difference then between the term "heritage language" and those such as "first language," "minority language," and "mother tongue" hinges on a distinction between processes of acquisition and competence and processes of identification. That is, while the terms first language, minority language, and mother tongue presuppose some degree of naturally acquired linguistic knowledge and communicative competence, the concept of "heritage language" does not. As each of the articles in this collection explains, the key conceptual component of heritage language is the process of identification through a particular linguistic variety in relation to some sociolinguistic landscape, and then secondarily, the process of acquisition and evaluation of competence as facets of that landscape.

As alluded to by Takamori and elaborated on by Doerr, the concept of "heritage language" and the inception of heritage language programs in the United States arose in conjunction with the Civil Rights Movement.[10] They gained prominence in North American bureaucratic discourse in the 1970s and 1980s when governments in tandem with academics began to address the multilingual realities of their citizenry and the social disparities of particular ethnically and racially defined groups of people.[11] Educational agendas focused on bilingualism took center stage, and the Canadian and U.S. governments passed legislation in support of various language initiatives, such as Canada's 1988 Multiculturalism Act and the U.S.'s Bilingual Education Act of 1968 and Indian Self-determination and Education Assistance Act of 1975. While some of these efforts were intended to facilitate the acquisition of English rather than the maintenance of the minority or heritage language, the complex sociolinguistic terrain affecting the lives of people, especially students, teachers, and parents, gained firmer ground as language planning efforts and educational programs were developed and instituted. Most prominently articulated by Joshua Fishman in *Reversing Language Shift*, heritage language programs became a crucial step toward recovering the lost linguistic ground of non-dominant/minority languages resulting from the institutionalized dominance and privileging of English (and to some extent French in Canada).

Since then local and international agencies have productively leveraged the term "heritage language" in their attempts to recognize and promote marginalized languages, languages under-represented, under-supported, and often under-valued within a particular socio-political context or regime (usually a nation-state). Not only has this phrase seemingly grown in circulation, its articulation has undergone further specialization.[12] For example, the website for the Center for Applied Linguistics (CAL), which houses a center devoted to heritage languages,[13] recognizes three subcategories of heritage language borrowed from Fishman's "300-plus Years of Heritage Language in the United States."[14] These subcategories acknowledge the different socio-historical provenance of language communities and the language(s) they speak: immigrant heritage languages, indigenous heritage languages, and colonial heritage languages.[15] What these more nuanced ameliorations do not remedy, however, are the complications and the contradictions that arise in practices of choosing, labeling, and performing a singular heritage (and language).

Complicating the acquisition of a heritage language, and the imagined legitimacy accompanying its acquisition, are the processes of institutionalization which entail notions of fluency and correctness. Such processes facilitate the development of a curriculum as well as the methods and expectations for evaluating successfulness. Underlying such processes are the dominant discourses and ideologies which emerge from the pervasive, taken-for-granted ideas about language. That is, language socialization in the classroom is usually an extension of the dominant socializing trends and narratives circulating elsewhere. As Elinor Ochs and Bambi Schieffelin have pointed out on many occasions, language and culture, practice and theory are mutually constitutive; that is, we are socialized (become subjects) into and through language.[16] Discourses circulating about appropriateness, correctness, and value mediate our judgments of our own and others' practices, in this case speaking Japanese. The valuing of a particular style or register of Japanese over other varieties creates links between linguistic practice and social context such that the performance of speech becomes indexical of the performance of heritage and the evaluation (or self-evaluation) of the speaker's "authenticity."

Additionally, such patterns of socialization and institutionalization involve the marketing and circulation of heritage language programming, motivated by socioeconomic opportunity and/or the ratification of one's identity. As Doerr and Lee show through their interviews with students, students choose different tracks in relation to their imagined trajectories and concepts of "Japaneseness." For those in the Jackson course, the practice and performance of their heritage is more fluid and negotiable, realized, for example, in the discussion of "disgusting" foods. By contrast, the discussion of quantities of rice in the *hoshū-*

kō class allowed limited negotiation, if any, suggesting a stricter regimentation of both language and social identity. The difference here lies in the ways in which sameness and difference are managed and negotiated,[17] though perhaps most explicitly in terms of the pedagogical styles of the different curriculums and the authors, voiceless or not, who authorize and validate the acquisition of and socialization into the Japanese language. The remaining conundrum, however, is still one of language socialization, where socialization into and through a language (even the "same" language) may have varied results — even within a single village, as Don Kulick's work on language shift and socialization has shown.[18] Or, to put this differently, Ayako Takamori points out that "heritage language cannot be a completely assimilated object and a heritage language speaker will never be able to be a native speaker."[19] What, then, can be satisfactorily achieved through such programs? Reframed as a language socializing event, the goal of "native speaker" status would be untenable. Perhaps the more relevant question is, how might the expectations and the assessment of success be recalibrated in order to achieve success? In what ways are such programs, including language revitalization programs, successful, and how might these revisions also disrupt or modify the language politics frequently entailed in the acquisition or non-acquisition of a particular language, dialect, or style?

Inspired by discussions of modernity and the changing use of "gaps" and "tears" in recent scholarship, any analysis of ideology-making and ideological regimentation requires the complementary investigation of the disconnections or disjunctures that arise as such theoretical configurations emerge and are negotiated in interaction — dialogically or monologically, discursively or conversationally, and so forth. Such an investigation may attend to divergence in discourses — and by extension ideologies — circulating around a similar social agenda or goal (such as the importance of heritage language classes), a disconnect between practice and theory (equating certain styles of speaking with ethnic heritage), and disconnections within practices (styles of speaking, teaching, and evaluation).[20] Complicating further the ideological configurations and the concept of disjuncture, additional discontinuities may be recognized or erased in relation to the temporal and spatial contexts or axes of interpretation. For example, expectations of linguistic performance become temporally mediated in relation to individual histories or assumed experiences. The teachers interviewed by Doerr and Lee may have had different expectations of their individual students depending on their knowledge of each student's background. Doerr and Lee show that certainly some of the students had a more playful interaction with their language teacher than other students, reflected in the interview with Jake and his mother and partially accounting for his sense of alienation. Expectations of fluency become spatially mediated by physical location and geography. Takamori provides several examples of the ways in which assessments of fluency, and by extension social positioning, are managed by Japanese Americans living in Japan, from offhand remarks like Ted's ("It's not fair that a gaijin can speak better Japanese than I can") to Yumi's manipulation of her own performance of Japanese in order to portray a certain persona ("I can't let the other mothers at the school think I am fluent in Japanese. They'll expect me to act like a Japanese mother") and to achieve certain ends more effectively ("You get so much better service if they think you're American and can't speak Japanese").[21] Phenotypic characteristics, rendered interpretable by ideologies of race/ethnicity, provide an additional axis for understanding ideological amalgamations or repertoires and moments of disruption. In an interview with Benjamin Bailey, a Dominican American high school student describes his intentional rupturing of interlocutors' assumptions about his ethnicity by speaking Spanish in their presence rather than some alternative variety of English.[22] By contrast, many of the Japanese Americans interviewed by Doerr and Lee and by Takamori discuss their desire to hide their difference, to accommodate the assumptions of certain interlocutors (other Japanese speakers of Japanese descent, if not nationality) in order to feel legitimately Japanese. A question left under-addressed is why these individuals feel this need? Is it only in such institutional or public contexts where evaluation is expected? Do some individuals maintain a counter-narrative or alternative model to the "having their feet in two worlds" interpretive schema?

In Takamori's piece, Yumi appears to have an alternative model, one that recognizes various dominant or pervasive models associated with different styles of speech and the social personae associated with them, and then manages her own public linguistic performances in relation to these conventionalized interpretive schemata. Though not directly interrupting these schemata, the fluidity of her shifting between styles suggests a subtle awareness of disjuncture (if only personally realized), or more exactly, an awareness of opportunities for disjuncture through her recognition of the various ideological connections between language and identity, and the potential for — and potency of — mis-recognition.

Such everyday experiences and practices reveal the mutual constitutiveness of the power of ideology and the problematics of disjuncture. Disjunctures highlight the ideological edges that guide interpretation; disjuncture plays ground to ideology's figure, and vice versa. The difference, however, between this concept of disjuncture and the vernacular use of gap in linguistic anthropology is that a gap indicates the taken-for-granted assumptions which do not require articulation (and perform the tacit act of inclusion-exclusion border maintenance) whereas disjuncture entails the opposite, the divergence of assumptions and the breakdown of communicative "gaps." Unlike "gaps," disjunctures create opportunities for negotiation, or re-negotiation. Remarking upon the ideological dissonance equated with Japanese Americans speaking their heritage language (Japanese) in Japan, Takamori suggests that

> [t]he uncanny then is an inherent part of constructing Japanese modernity at the same time that it threatens to reveal and undo it at its very sutures. The failure of integration or assignation of place produces disruptive re-surfacings of the uncanny.[23]

As miscommunication, speech error, the uncanny, or the unexpected, disjunctures do not belie the hierarchical, authoritative structuring of sociality but render them salient, malleable, and shiftable.

In sum, these articles provide rich analyses for complicating the concept of heritage language and for inspiring more detailed investigations of heritage language projects, from the regimentation of language planning by governments, NGOs, and other institutions to the face-to-face management of linguistic performance in classrooms. They also encourage more globally comparative work on heritage language programs, both cross-nationally and intra-nationally, across different groups and within groups. For example, a comparison of Native American language revitalization programs and Japanese heritage language programs could reveal the subtle ideological differences in the configuring of the relationship between language and blood across these communities. Of similar interest is the relevance of conceptualizing a homeland in relation to heritage language projects; the underlying motivations for different approaches to language learning (maintenance or re-creation), the imagining of a center (and thus a periphery) and the subsequent configuring of authority/legitimacy/authenticity, and finally the embodiment of this spatialization in relation to language learning and evaluations of competence (movement across borders, relocation, educational trajectories). These suggestions only scratch the surface. As the authors of these articles explain, the mapping of the complexity of the relationship between heritage, language, and people moves us beyond isomorphic conceptions of people, language, and nation and challenges the bounded-ness of our own linguistic imaginings. So, what language(s) do you dream in?

❑

Notes

Introduction

1. Eidson 2005; Graham, Ashworth and Tunbridge 2005.
2. Breglia 2006; Kirshenblatt-Gimblett 2006.
3. Hamlish 2000; Kreamer 2006; Stone 2005; Truettner 2008.
4. Basu 2007; Breglia 2006; Moscardo 1996; Nuryanti 1996; Prentice 2005; Richter 2005.
5. Graham, Ashworth and Tunbridge 2005; Handler 1985; Lumley 2005.
6. Handler 1985. He uses the term "culture" instead of heritage.
7. Breglia 2006.
8. Smith 2006.
9. Kirshenblatt-Gimblett 2006.
10. Skutnabb-Kangas and Phillipson 1989. Also, see Takato 2008.
11. Cook 1999; Doerr 2009; Firth and Wagner 2007a; Firth and Wagner 2007b; Leung, Harris, and Rampton 1997.
12. Suzuki 2010.
13. Takamori 2010.
14. Okubo 2010.
15. Guadalupe Valdés (2001, 38) defines a heritage language learner in the United States context as "a language student who is raised in a home where a non-English language is spoken, who speaks or at least understands the language, and who is to some degree bilingual in that language and in English." The term "heritage language," which first emerged in Canada in proposals for the language education of minority groups other than French-speaking, was used to make the point that the languages spoken throughout Canada are the heritage of all Canadians; they are not foreign languages (Tavares 2000). In the United States, the emergence of the term heritage language coincided with the increasing support from the wider public for minority language education due to the new awareness that minority languages enrich not only their speakers but also the American nation as a whole in the globalizing world (Peyton, Ranard, and McGinnis 2001; Wiley and Valdés 2001).
16. Another tenet of "heritage language" education is to serve those whose linguistic proficiency does not fit the pedagogy of either language art class for "native speakers" or foreign language class. Researchers then seek to develop pedagogies that serve them efficiently (Douglas 2005; Lynch 2003; Valdés 2001).
17. Fishman 2001; Li 2006; Valdés 2001.
18. Fishman 2001, 95.
19. See Cho 2000; Moses 2000.
20. Anderson 1991.
21. Baliber 1994; Bauman and Briggs 2000.
22. Balibar 1988.
23. Bourdieu 1991. Also, see Bauman and Briggs 2000; Crowly 1989; Milroy and Milroy 1991.
24. Kroskrity 2000; Woolard 1998.
25. Fishman 2001; Henze and Davis 1999; May 2001.
26. Irvine and Gal 2000.
27. Lee 1996; Mashiko 2003; Yasuda 1999; 2003; also see Takato 2009.
28. Comaroff and Comaroff 2004; Kymlicka 1995; Taylor 1994; Wolf 1994.

29. Appadurai 1990; Appadurai 1996 (Sovereignty); Hannerz 1992.
30. Kymlicka 1995.
31. Fishman 1991.
32. Baker 2006; Henze and Davis 1999.
33. Cummins 2001.
34. Phillipson, Rannut, and Skutnabb-Kangas 1995.
35. Suzuki 2010.
36. Yamasaki 2010.
37. Doerr and Lee forthcoming.
38. Okubo 2010.
39. Also, see Canagaraja 1999; Delpit 1995.
40. Takamori 2010.
41. Meek 2010, 122 {check}.
42. See He 2006.
43. Appadurai 1990; Hannerz 1992.
44. Tsing 2005.

Chapter 1 – Suzuki

1. Cummins 2005, 586.
2. Basham and Fathman 2008, 578.
3. Carreira 2004, 18.
4. Blackwood 2007; Lie 2003; Nicholls 2005. See also Mercurio and Scarino (2005) regarding the ` government's attempts to define and label various languages (e.g., "indigenous," "foreign," "ethnic") spoken within its territory.
5. Horvath and Vaughan 1991. Hornberger (2005) claims that while U.S. policymakers, scholars, and educators have only recently used the term "heritage language" as a neutral and inclusive alternative to terms such as minority, indigenous, immigrant, ethnic, second, or foreign language, their Australian counterparts had long been using the term "community language" to refer to this same range of language resources in their national context.
6. See, for example, Brutt-Griffler and Makoni 2005; de Bot and Gorter 2005.
7. In this sense, Japanese language schools in Colonia Okinawa function similarly to bilingual schools in Argentina. Banfi and Day explain that bilingual schools in Argentina catered initially to the German and Italian immigrant communities as "heritage schools," but more recently established bilingual schools are called "global language schools" for they provide the children of "internationally mobile families" with English, the "global language." Banfi and Day 2004, 404, 405.
8. Scholars have long debated whether Okinawan is a dialect of Japanese or a linguistically distinct language. The Okinawan language remains virtually incomprehensible to the majority of mainlanders of Japan, but most of the words used are in fact the same. It is intonation and the particular pronunciation of words that make the Okinawan language sound different from mainland Japanese "standard" language. The major difference in pronunciation is the number of vowels used. Standard Japanese has five vowels: a, i, u, e, and o; in Okinawa only three are used: a, i, and o. As a result, same words are pronounced differently in two languages (e.g., te [té, hand] in mainland Japanese is ti in Okinawan). In addition, many consonants used in the Okinawan language do not exist in modern Japanese, as well as some verbs that have a unique set of conjugations, which differ from their mainland counterpart, and some adjectives that are not found today in mainland Japanese. The Okinawan language itself has a wide variety of dialects throughout the Ryūkyū Islands. The off-lying islands show the widest diversion from what was considered to be "standard" Okinawan, which is used in the Shuri area of Okinawa Hontō Island. See Molasky 2003, 165; Barrell and Tanaka 1997, 135; and Kerr 1958, xvii, 34.
9. Lan 2006, 11, citing Nippert-Eng 1996, 7.
10. Kimura 1981.
11. Arakaki 2002, 36. Many argue, and I agree, that Okinawans today still do not possess the same political and economic rights in Japan as other Japanese citizens. The

Prefecture of Okinawa remains home to 75 percent of U.S. military facilities and the majority of U.S. military forces in Japan. (The bases occupy 20 percent of the Okinawa Hontō Island.) Per capita income has been around 70 percent of the national average during the 1990s, and Okinawa's unemployment rate has constantly been the highest among all prefectures. See Hein and Selden 2003a, 5–6, for a summary of Okinawa's precarious status within Japan–U.S. relations today. For more comprehensive studies regarding Okinawa's struggles against injustices perpetrated by the Japanese national government and the U.S. military, see Johnson 1999, Hook and Siddle 2001, and Hein and Selden 2003b.

12. The spelling of Ryukyu, using two Chinese characters as is done now, was standardized during the Ming dynasty period in the fourteenth century. The word has been rendered phonetically in more than sixty forms, such as Luchu, Liukiu, Loo Choo, and Roo Choo. Over time, however, the Japanese term, Okinawa, has slowly replaced other alternatives as the generic name for the islands (Kerr 1958, xvii). "Ryūkyū," with elongated vowel signs, is the more phonetically appropriate spelling, but Okinawa's local institutions, such as the University of the Ryukyus and Ryukyu Shimpo, regional newspaper, employ the romanized term without elongation. I use "Ryūkyū" throughout this essay.

13. As a result of Imperial Japan's rigorous assimilation policy from the 1890s to 1940s, Okinawans today, especially young people in the prefecture's urban areas, have little speaking or comprehensive abilities in the language. See Ching 2001, Oguma 1995, and Tomiyama 1997 for the cultural and linguistic assimilation of Okinawans and other imperial subjects.

14. Nakasone 2002a, 17.

15. Sakihara 1981, 15; see also Ishikawa 1973.

16. JICA Okinawa 1985.

17. For Okinawan residents, "Naichi," literally "inner land," refers to the four major islands of Japan. Although the term is also often used to refer to the residents of Naichi, I use the term Naichi-jin, "people of Naichi," to refer to the Naichi residents of Japan, in order to distinguish the geographical areas and demographic groups. See Toyama and Ikeda 1981.

18. Oguma 1995.

19. Christy 1997.

20. Oguma 1995, 388.

21. For instance, although the Meiji constitution, promulgated in 1890, promised wide representation in the law-making body of the nation-state, Okinawans had to wait until 1920 to be allowed to send the prefecture's representatives to the Lower House of the national Diet. See Kerr 1958, 428.

22. Postcolonial theorist Homi Bhabha calls this "colonial mimicry." See Bhabha 1994.

23. Bhabha 1994, 86. See Kaneshiro 2002 for Okinawans in the Philippines whom locals viewed as being different from Japanese Naichi-jin. The Okinawan immigrants' tenuous relations with their Naichi-jin counterparts in Hawai'i are detailed by Ige 1981, Toyama and Ikeda 1981, and Ueunten 2002. Discrimination against Okinawans by Naichi-jin Japanese took place in Naichi as well. The massive exodus of Okinawans to mainland Japanese cities took place in the 1920s, when the decline in the international price for sugar hit Okinawa's monoculture agricultural economy. The serious recession was called "sotetsu palm hell," because people in Okinawa suffered from famine and reportedly had to eat poisonous sotetsu palm leaves to survive. See Mukai 1992 and Tomiyama 1990 for the causes of the recession and subsequent Okinawan emigration to cities in mainland Japan such as Osaka, Kawasaki, and Yokohama.

24. See Peattie 1988 (216–22) for a description of the social hierarchy in colonial Micronesia. Peattie details the occupational ranks among Japanese immigrants: mainland Japanese at the top, Okinawans and Koreans in the middle, and local Micronesians at the bottom. See also Tomiyama 2002, 65, for Okinawan émigrés in Micronesia, who worked in harsher working conditions for lower wages than their Japanese Naichi-jin coworkers at sugarcane plantations, launched "the Lifestyle

Reform Movement" to erase Okinawan features from their bodies (e.g. clothes, language, and food), and amplified discriminatory behaviors against the local Micronesians. See Tomiyama 1990 and Rabson 2003 for similar patterns of cultural self-Japanization and discrimination against non-Japanese Others that were observed in pre–World War II Osaka, where Okinawan domestic migrants worked as construction and manufacturing laborers.

25. The U.S. attacks and the violence caused by the Imperial Army's Naichi-jin soldiers were both responsible for the deaths. The colonial ambiguity of Okinawans as "not quite" Japanese national subjects is believed to have caused the mass killing of Okinawan civilians by Japanese Naichi-jin soldiers during the Battle of Okinawa. Naichi-jin soldiers, who were stationed in Okinawa to protect local Japanese – Okinawan – residents, suspected that Okinawans were potential spies, and killed Okinawan civilians both by execution and in what is often referred to as "compulsory group suicides." See Allen 2003, Field 1993, and Ota 1999.

26. GRI consisted of locally elected officials and was in charge of the administrative and legislative functions of Okinawa, but it was obliged to obey the orders of Uscar, which also maintained the right to nominate the government's chief. Uscar nominated the first four chiefs of GRI, but the fifth chief, Yara Chōbyō, was elected by the Okinawan people. Yara was the last GRI chief before Okinawa's reversion to Japan in 1972.

27. As a gesture of salvaging Okinawa from tyrannical Imperial Japan, Uscar held a democratic election for Okinawans to choose the GRI chief, who served under Uscar. When the first election for the GRI chief in 1950 did not turn out as Uscar had expected, however, it abandoned the system and handpicked a chief it favored.

28. Oguma 1998, 504, 474–76. The minimum wage for American employees at U.S. bases was reportedly fourteen times higher than that of the Okinawan workers. See also Oguma 1995, 504.

29. Under the agreement made between Uscar and GRI in 1952, landowners contracted with the GRI chief, and the chief then rented the land to the U.S. military. Since the rent Okinawan farmers received from Uscar for their land was extremely low, only 2 percent of the landowners agreed to the contract with GRI. Hence, Uscar resorted to compulsory land expropriation in 1953. (See Miyagi 1968, 217.) During 1953 alone, 447 families were forced to move; the U.S. military acquired 175 hectares of farmland as a result. By the end of 1953, U.S. bases occupied 14 percent of the entire Okinawa Hontō Island, or 42 percent of the island's farmland. The land problem triggered island-wide protests by local Okinawans from 1953 to 1954. See Ōshiro 1992, 99.

30. In one survey, approximately 10 percent of Okinawan settlers in Colonia Okinawa stated that their dislike of living under U.S. occupation, particularly working for the U.S. military, was a major reason for their decision to emigrate. According to Amemiya, "nearly all" Issei had been employed at one time or another by the U.S. military bases. Her informants expressed their disdain for "military labor," or gun sagyō, because they were placed below American superiors both in terms of pay scale and administrative rank. See Nakayama et al., 1986, 45, and Amemiya 1999, 58–9.

31. The number of settlers increased from four hundred at the time of departure from Okinawa, due to childbirth on board ship and after the group's arrival in South America. See Higa 2000, 243.

32. Mori 1998; Suzuki 2007; Tsujimoto 1998.

33. The local non-Nikkei Bolivians were, of course, highly diverse in their socioeconomic statuses and ethnic/racial backgrounds. For a more nuanced analysis of complexities of the local class and ethnic/racial relationships, see Suzuki forthcoming and Stearman 1985.

34. Yamasaki 2010.

35. "Becoming Japanese" was a complex process for Okinawan immigrants and their offspring. For details about the historical transformations of the ethnic Okinawan community in Colonia Okinawa, see Suzuki 2006.

36. Mori 1998, 106.
37. Nichibo Kyōkai 1985, 2.
38. Kunimoto 1989.
39. Mitsuhashi 1983.
40. See contrasting cases of the foundation processes of Japanese language schools in Peru and the United States. See Doerr and Lee 2010 and Yamasaki 2010.
41. In 2001, the school charged US$30 a month for students who attended the morning Spanish classes only, and US$50 for those who took both Spanish and Japanese language classes.
42. While the percentage of Okinawan–Bolivian CBJ students decreased steadily from 1987 (100 percent) to 1995 (67 percent) during the "dekasegi fad" (due to the emigration of families with school-age children), Okinawan-Bolivians continued to represent the majority of the student population (84 percent) in 2001. See Mori 1998, 112.
43. Okinawa Daiichi Nichibo-kou 2001, 1. Translation by the author.
44. The actual dynamics of education in the CBJ school are far more complex than what the school's slogans suggest. See Suzuki 2010 (Embodying) for representations and interpretations of Japanese-ness, Okinawan-ness, and Bolivian-ness by teachers, parents, and students at the school.
45. Okinawa Daiichi Nichibo-kou 1998.
46. In the Special Class designed for non-Japanese speakers, non-Nikkei Bolivian students, and the children of intermarried parents, a bilingual Nisei teacher used the JSL (Japanese as a second language) instruction materials. Since the Japanese proficiency of CBJ students was somewhat behind that of Japanese students in Japan, the textbooks used were also behind by one year (i.e., students in Class 5 used a fourth-grade-level Japanese textbook). Some of these textbooks, relatively new editions, were donated by the past JICA teachers or Okinawa Prefecture teachers.
47. In order to protect my informants' confidentiality, individual names used in this article are pseudonyms.
48. Approximately 81 percent of the second-generation Okinawan-Bolivian respondents in Anbo et al.'s survey expressed confidence in their ability to comprehend; 61 percent felt comfortable speaking Uchināguchi. Anbo et al. 1998, 246.
49. See, however, the case of Japanese-Peruvian communities, where terms and expressions in Uchināguchi have become integral parts of the "Japanese" language they speak. See Yamawaki 1996 and Yamasaki 2010.
50. Nichibo Kyōkai 1998.
51. Higa 2000, 251.
52. Gushiken 1995.
53. "Dekasegi" literally means one who "goes out" to earn money, with the intention of returning home in the future. The term originally referred to workers from rural areas of Japan who migrated to cities in Japan in search of work. See Tsuda 2003, xii. See Suzuki 2010 (Embodying) and Tsujimoto 1999 for a more comprehensive study of dekasegi migration of Okinawan-Bolivians from Colonia Okinawa to Japan. Among the many excellent studies on Japanese-Brazilian dekasegi migration to Japan are Roth 2001, Tsuda 2003, and Linger 2001.
54. Tsujimoto 1998. See Yamasaki 2010 for Japanese-Peruvians' dekasegi migration to Japan.
55. For more about JLPE see Yamasaki 2010.
56. In 2008, the annual average unemployment rate in Okinawa Prefecture was 7.4 percent, while the national average was 4.0 percent. See Okinawa Prefecture's labor statistics page: http://www.stat.go.jp/data/roudou/sokuhou/nen/ft/pdf/index.pdf (accessed 20 August 2009) and Japan Statistic Bureau's labor statistics page: http://www.stat.go.jp/data/ roudou/sokuhou/nen /ft/pdf/index.pdf (22 August 2009).
57. See Takamori (2010) for similar practices of "boundary work" among Japanese-American residents in Japan.
58. Lan calls this symbolic value of language "linguistic capital." See Lan 2003, 137.

59. Stephenson 1999, 2–3.
60. Osterweil 1998, 151.
61. Axel 2001, 7–15.

Chapter 2 – Yamasaki

1. Ministry of Foreign Affairs of Japan 2010. http://www.mofa.go.jp/region/latin/peru/index.html (accessed 10 September 2010).
2. Araki 2002; Morimoto 2002.
3. Araki 2002, 76.
4. Takenaka 2003.
5. Ibid.
6. The purpose of the new immigration law was essentially to get Nikkei to engage in unskilled industrial labor, which young Japanese shunned, and to keep undocumented guest workers away from those unskilled jobs. Japanese Ministry of Justice (2005) statistics show that, as of the end of 2004, 55,750 Peruvians were officially registered as residents in Japan. This number includes children and teenagers of Japanese descent who migrated to Japan with their parents. The number also includes non-Nikkei Peruvian spouses as well as non-labor migrants such as students. Masuda and Yanagida (1999) estimated that there were approximately 60,000 Peruvians in Japan, including those who stay illegally, and half of the total number of Peruvians living in Japan are of non-Japanese descent (Masuda and Yanagida 1999).
7. Jo 2001; Luykx 2003.
8. Jo 2001, 36.
9. Bourdieu 1991; Heller 2001; Milroy and Milroy 1999; Silverstein 2003.
10. The concepts and definitions of the term heritage language have been discussed and developed by researchers and educational practitioners over the past decades. In the context of the United States, for example, heritage language refers to a language with which individual speakers have a historical and personal connection regardless of their actual proficiency. See Fishman 2001; Valdés 2001.
11. Kroskrity 2000.
12. Silverstein 1979, 193.
13. Hornberger 1988, 2000; King 2000; Luykx 2003.
14. Since English has become an increasingly important tool for getting a good job, learning English has become a craze in Peru in recent years (Masuda and Yanagida 1999, 290).
15. Undōkai, a full day of athletics, is one of the major events of the Japanese school year and is usually held in the fall. The form and games are remarkably similar from place to place. The children are divided into two teams, red and white and compete against each other. Generally, the students practice and rehearse repeatedly for at least one month preparing for that day.
16. In Peru, many private schools are either religious or related to particular ethnic or foreign communities. The latter type of school, which is locally called escuela associada con communidad extranjera (school associated with a foreign community), includes the Nikkei schools.
17. Suzuki 2010.
18. Ibid. In Peru, private schools are considered better than public schools. Therefore the majority of parents want to send their children to private schools, although many are unable to afford the tuition. Because CEA is a relatively inexpensive alternative among private schools, many non-Nikkei children who live in the neighborhood are enrolled there.
19. In the suburbs of Lima, Japanese immigrants established three educational institutions after the war. At these schools non-Nikkei students now predominate due to the decline in the Nikkei population in those areas.
20. Note that this is unlike the situation in the Bolivian Nikkei school described in Suzuki 2010, which did have teachers from Japan.

21. I participated as a researcher in the school for three months. I regularly visited CEA four days a week from 8:00 A.M. to 3:00 P.M., except during the winter break (27 July–7 August). I spent a total of forty-eight days at CEA, approximately 125 hours of these in classes.
22. All the key informants had a good command of Japanese, however, and conversations were mainly carried on in Japanese.
23. Masuda and Yanagida 1999, 262.
24. During the 1960s, many Nikkei parents looked for high-quality education rather than heritage education, so that their children would achieve socioeconomic success in mainstream society (Masuda and Yanagida 1999, 262). In 1972, the second Nikkei comprehensive educational institution, a large-scale private school, was founded in the middle-class area. This school was designed for college-bound students.
25. Cummins 1995, 137.
26. In fact, some students do not even understand the meaning of the Japanese songs and mottos that are conventionally used at the school. For example, posters hung on the walls in the hallway would have words such as "punctual," "honesty," and "diligence" written on them in Japanese. While I was at CEA, students often asked me what the Japanese characters meant.
27. Fukumoto 1997.
28. Araki 2002, 88.
29. Since people of Okinawan heritage make up 80 percent of the total population of Japanese descendants in Peru, many words that originated in Okinawan dialects are used in the daily conversations of the Nikkei today. Okinawa's distinct culture and traditions, as expressed in music, dance, and rituals, still persist among the descendants of Okinawan immigrants in Peru. (See Suzuki 2010.)
30. The major reason why the returnees were enrolled in CEA was the returnees' limited command of Spanish. For example, the mother of one newly arrived second-grader said that she sent her son to CEA because he had difficulty communicating in Spanish. Parents of the returnees also tend to think their children would find it easier to adapt in the Nikkei schools rather than in Peruvian schools. A reason cited for choosing CEA in particular was largely economic, since the monthly CEA tuition amounts to US$90 while the monthly fee in the other Nikkei school in Lima — also a comprehensive educational institution like CEA — is $200. Although many returnees remain at CEA until they graduate, some leave CEA and transfer to the public schools once they get used to their new environment and become comfortable in Spanish. They do so because the public schools require no tuition. Hisako, an eighth-grader returnee girl, described CEA as "a kind of passing point" for some returnee students, a place that prepares returnees in their transition into the larger Peruvian population.
31. This standardized test is held annually both in Japan and abroad to evaluate and certify the Japanese language proficiency of nonnative speakers. The JLPT has four levels, with level 1 being the most difficult.
32. Original utterances in the extracts in the following sections were spoken in Spanish, Japanese, or a mixture of both. Two different fonts are used to distinguish Spanish from Japanese in the dialogs. The English translation appears in italics. Some extracts, in which code-switching and word-borrowing did not take place, or I did not recapture verbatim utterances, are shown in English translation only.
33. Each returnee student naturally had different experiences in Japan. Some were bullied or treated as outcasts in the Japanese schools, while others said they enjoyed their school life in Japan. Sra. Masako and the other Japanese teachers mentioned that the students' personal experiences in Japan could possibly affect their motivation for studying Japanese in Peru.
34. See Okubo 2010.
35. Jo 2001, 26.
36. Ibid., 27.
37. Fiske 1991 (1989).

38. In this respect, Valdés's definition of "heritage language students" may apply to Nikkei students to some extent. Valdés writes that in the U.S. context the term heritage language student can refer to "a language student who is raised in a home where a non-English language is spoken, who speaks or at least understands the language, and who is to some degree bilingual in that language and English" (Valdés 2001, 38).
39. Bourdieu and Passeron 1977; Bourdieu 1991.
40. Doerr and Lee 2010.
41. Kirshenblatt-Gimblett 2006, 179.

Chapter 3 – Okubo

1. Moore et al. 2003.
2. Chambers 2005, 7.
3. Graburn 2001; Corsane 2005.
4. Graham, Gregory, and Tunbridge 2005.
5. Lowenthal 1994, 41.
6. Graburn 2001, 71.
7. Lowenthal 1994, 43.
8. Tunbridge and Ashworth 1996, 4.
9. Eidson 2005.
10. Graham, Gregory, and Tunbridge 2005, 34.
11. Eidson 2005, 558.
12. Graham, Gregory, and Tunbridge 2005, 34.
13. Fishman 1999 in Deusen-Scholl 2003, 216. Three centuries of heritage language education in the United States. Plenary address given at the First National Heritage Language Conference, Long Beach, Calif., in1999.
14. Nakajima 2003.
15. For example, according to Nakajima (2003), heritage language is functional and creates all semantics for the first generation and bilingualism for the second generation; however, for the third generation, heritage language lacks a function and becomes a symbol of their cultural group.
16. Deusen-Scholl 2003. For a discussion of heritage language teaching in relation to the issues of identity and community, see He (2006) and Carreira (2004).
17. The research is based on ethnographic fieldwork in one multiethnic neighborhood in Osaka between September 1998 and March 2000, August and September 2001, May and June 2004, and July and August 2008. In particular, I examined the educational practices directed toward 1.5-generation Chinese and second-generation Vietnamese children in school and within their local community. I follow Zhou and Bankston (1998) in using the term "1.5 generation" for those who arrived in the new society between the ages of five and twelve.
18. Eidson 2005.
19. Olwig 1999.
20. Ministry of Justice 2009. http:// www.moj.go.jp/PRESS/090710-1/090710-1.html (accessed 16 November 2009).
21. Ministry of Education 2009. http://www.mext.go.jp/b_menu/houdou/21/07/1279 262.htm (accessed 16 November 2009).
22. Ota 2000. According to my search in 2008, the Ministry of Education further defines these children as "those who are not able to speak conversational Japanese adequately, and those who are in need of Japanese language instruction for lacking a language for learning (gakushū gengo) at their grade levels and for having difficulty in participating in learning (gakushū katsudō) despite their fluency in conversational Japanese. Even with these clarifications, the Ministry's focus as reflected in their policies is still on language, as Ota (2000) rightly argues. Ministry of Education 2008. http://www.mext.go.jp/b_menu/houdou/19/08/07062955.htm (accessed 3 June 2008).
23. Castles and Miller 2003.
24. Komai 2006.

25. Ibid., 128. This is the notion of creating the culture of a nation-state merely composed of one ethnic group.
26. In this report, "multiculturalism and coexistence" (tabunka kyōsei) is defined as "the coexistence of people with different nationality and ethnicity as members of a local society, with an appreciation for cultural differences and an effort to create an equal relationship" (Ministry of Internal Affairs and Communications 2006, 6).
27. Yamawaki 2003.
28. Turner 1993; Goldberg 1994; Eller 1997; Kincheloe 2002.
29. Chapman 2006, 100–1.
30. Kajita et al. 2005, cited in Kato 2008. Being aware of this trend, Kato (2008) suggests the limitations of policies of multiculturalism and coexistence (tabunka kyōsei) for assisting foreigners, and questions the notion from the perspective of "the person concerned" as an "individual," and not as an object to be supported.
31. Povinelli 2002.
32. Banks 1995; Korn 2002.
33. Eldering 1996.
34. Ibid., 322.
35. Aoyama City 2003, 16; Aoyama City 2004.
36. Lie 2001; Oguma 1995; Graburn et al. 2008; Willis and Murphy-Shigematsu 2008.
37. Upham 1987, 79.
38. Araragi 2000; Tamanoi 2000; Tamanoi 2003. In 1972, then prime minister Kakuei Tanaka opened diplomatic relations with China. With the release of a joint statement by Japan and China, the search for Japanese in China began. They and their families began returning to Japan with the Japanese government's support. In 2007, the number of returnees from northeast China was 6,393 families, or 20,416 war-displaced Japanese and their children and grandchildren. These Japanese nationals and their descendants, who are Chinese nationals, are collectively referred to as "Chinese" in Japanese society. Following this practice, I refer to them as "Chinese" as well. http://www.kiko kusha-center.or.jp/kikokusha/kiko_jijo/chugoku/mhwdata/index_f.htm (accessed 11 June 2009).
39. The Japanese government approved the settlement of three refugees from Vietnam in 1978, and accepted additional refugees in 1979, even before the Japanese government ratified the International Convention Relating to the Status of Refugees in 1981. In 1979, Japan set the acceptable number of refugees from Indochina at 500; the number was enlared to 3,000 in 1981, 5,000 in 1983, and 10,000 in 1985. The number of Vietnamese refugees who settled in Japan totaled 7,169 in 1994, when the government abolished this system. In 1980, the Japanese government started accepting family members of refugees under the ODP (orderly departure program: family reunification immigration program). This program ended in 2004 (Kitayama 2004, 100–1). Toda (2001) reports that approximately 70 percent of Vietnamese residents in 1999 were either permanent residents or settlers — those who reside in Japan as former refugees or their family members (Toda 2001, 2–3).
40. The number decreased after the war as some returned to Korea, but it has gradually increased again. Miyako 10-nen no Ayumi 1984, 29; interview with a researcher at HuRights Osaka, March 1999.
41. Information acquired at City Hall, Aoyama City, in 2008. Since government's studies and reports classify people according to their nationalities, Koreans, Chinese, and Vietnamese are those who hold nationality of each state. As Japanese nationality is based on descent under Japan's Nationality Law, those who were born in Japan are not necessarily Japanese nationals. Japanese in these reports also include naturalized Japanese of foreign descent. Vietnamese include recent immigrants, students, and Vietnamese trainees (kenshūsei). For a study of Vietnamese residents in Japan, see also Kawakami (2001). As for Koreans in Aoyama, approximately 90 percent were special permanent residents, i.e., resident Koreans (zainichi). According to the latest figures available on Chinese returnees, in 2000, Chinese returnees constituted about 43 percent of Chinese in Aoyama City (Aoyama City 2003; Kaji 2008).

42. The government-assigned Dowa districts are the areas that are officially assigned for the Buraku special measures. Some Buraku communities received benefits of the Dowa special measures given Dowa districts, but not all. Dowa special measures will be explained in the next section.
43. Aoyama City 2001, 2, 3, 5, 24.
44. "The Localization of U.S. Multicultural Education in Japan." Paper presented at the 2003 annual meeting of the American Anthropological Association in Chicago.
45. Yamawaki (2003) argues that guidelines for foreigners developed by local government can be classified into three kinds — those with a focus on "human rights" exemplified by the ones for resident Koreans in Osaka City, those focused on "internationalization" such as the ones in Hamamatsu City in Shizuoka Prefecture, and the "integration" type such as the ones developed in Kawasaki City in Kanagawa Prefecture, which falls between the first two.
46. Between 1998 and 2008 I conducted formal interviews for from 30 to 120 minutes with 123 individuals in person and phone interviews with four others. Only two interviews were tape-recorded.
47. BLL, the Buraku grassroots political organization formed in 1955, demanded that central and local governments improve Buraku conditions (in what was known as the Buraku liberation movement). Their efforts resulted in policies geared toward solving the Buraku problem in the 1960s. These were made possible by the Special Measures Legislation (SML) of 1969 (Upham 1987; Neary 1997).
48. Buraku kaihō dōmei Ōsaka-fu rengōkai 1982, 4–18.
49. Tomoni did receive a budget allotment for social education under Dowa education.
50. Neary 1997.
51. Tomoni 2002.
52. See Tai 2006; Tomoni: http://tomoni.ld.infoseek.co.jp/kihon/soukai.htm (accessed 6 October 2007). Here, "Tomoni" is a pseudonym.
53. The Vietnamese language class for children was conducted mostly in Vietnamese, using excerpted materials from a Vietnamese language textbook printed in Vietnam. The course covered the Vietnamese alphabet, and taught students how to spell simple words that matched illustrations in the textbook and how to pronounce those words.
54. Ogawa 2008; Tomoni 2005. In the academic year 2006–2007, Tomoni received a grant of 200,000 yen (about US$2100) from the Osaka Community Foundation for heritage language classes. This was in addition to other activities offered for immigrant children and adults, such as assistance in studying and instruction in the Japanese language for immigrants.
55. Only two students of Korean background participated in the Korean ethnic club at Miyako Elementary School and three to four students of Korean background joined in Tomoni's activities for Koreans in 1998–2000 when approximately sixty students of Korean background lived in Miyako.
56. Ogawa 2008. Parentheses are added. For more information on Tomoni, see Tai (2006) and Okubo (2005), chapters 2, 3, and 7.
57. Tomoni 2005. Interview with the official of Tomoni in July 2008.
58. The latter was a common belief among teachers mainly in Osaka, who support immigrant children's speaking a language other than Japanese. Their thinking is based on Cummins's "Linguistic Interdependence Principle" (also discussed in Nakajima 2003). Teachers were made familiar with Cummins through workshops on second language teaching and learning held by the teachers' association for the education of foreign children in Osaka.
59. Schools reported the number of children who resided in the government-assigned Dowa districts as those who were in need of special assistance as members of the Buraku community, regardless of their family history and ethnic backgrounds. The official number included non-Buraku Japanese who moved into the government-assigned Dowa districts, as well as resident Koreans, Chinese, and Vietnamese in the districts. See note 42 for an explanation of the government-assigned Dowa districts.

60. By contrast, schools without minority communities generally offer Japanese language instruction only. The combining of ethnic club activities and Japanese language instruction is unique to areas with minority communities. (Personal communication with a former Japanese language instructor at Miyako in August 2008.
61. "National" is for the formation of Japanese language classes, and "local" is for offering heritage language teaching/ethnic club activities.
62. In papers I presented in 2003 and 2007, I added "international influence" as another factor that contributed to the making of space for this type of education, e.g., Japan's adaptation of the UN-advocated concept of "human rights" and U.S.–style multicultural education. See "Learning the National Language, Performing Ethnic Cultures: Cultural Politics of Multicultural Education in Osaka, Japan." Paper presented at the Canadian Anthropology Society and the American Ethnological Society Conference, Toronto, Canada, in 2007. See note 44 for the paper presented in 2003.
63. Teachers believed that the phrase was from the Ministry of Education; however, the Ministry has not acknowledged education for foreign children other than language instruction, as previously discussed.
64. Mori 1990; Minzokusabetsu to tatakau Ōsaka renraku kyōgikai 1992.
65. See Okubo 2005, chap. 4.
66. In a homeroom class of twenty-two children, two were Vietnamese and at least two were resident Koreans, along with one half-Japanese and half-Korean student. Regarding the number of the children from Korean background, the homeroom teacher said she could not ask each student and family; they needed to inform her themselves. From my field notes in December 1998.
67. From my field notes, January 2000. See Fukuoka and Kim (1997), Kuraishi (2007), and Lim (2009) for discussions on names for resident Koreans. In particular, Lim (2009) argues that names are the only markers that signal those of Korean origin for Japan-born Koreans educated in the Japanese school system.
68. Teachers and staff members of the Korean education center in the neighborhood told me that some of the Vietnamese and resident Korean students switched back to their Japanese names when they entered high school or the job market, despite their pledge to use their ethnic names. A 19 November article in Chosun Ilbo reports that 25.4 percent of those who are affiliated with Mindan (Korean Residents Union in Japan) use "only their Korean names." Although this is higher than the 13.4 percent figure from the 2000 survey, the figure shows that the use of ethnic names is still not common among foreign residents in Japan. As those who are affiliated with the organization are more likely to use their ethnic names than ordinary resident Koreans, the percentage of those who use their Korean names against resident Koreans as a whole is assumed to be lower than 25.4 percent. http://www.chosunonline.com/news/200911190000 44 (accessed 22 November 2009).
69. Five more Vietnamese students were using their Japanese names in 2008. In addition, one person said she would start using her Japanese name after becoming a Japanese national. Interview conducted in August 2008 and from my field notes in August 2008.
70. From my field notes, November 1998.
71. Suzuki 2010.
72. Morris-Suzuki 1998; Nukaga 2003; Chapman 2006.
73. As explained above, only two to four out of approximately sixty resident Korean children participated in the ethnic club activities designed for Koreans.
74. Yamasaki 2010; Doerr and Lee 2010.
75. This practice goes together with Japanese teachers' tendency to overlook students' social backgrounds and to view each child as an individual (kojinka). In my field site, the institutional framework categorized children as "Japanese," "Chinese," or "Vietnamese." (Koreans and the Buraku were also so categorized to a certain extent). Children, however, were viewed apart from the specific individual social background of each category. Shimizu (2002) argues that Japanese teachers tend

not to consider social differences but rather to consider differences in academic performance by de-contextualizing, treating all children as equal, and reducing all phenomena to the capability or effort of the individual (2002, 87).
76. Hall 2006, 220.
77. Lie 2001, 81, 138–41, 170–72.
78. Hall 2006, 215.
79. Interview conducted in July 2008.
80. Farrer's study of a subculture of Chinese immigrants in Tokyo shows as well that the sociality of a space like Tomoni's — a sort of ethnic enclosure — facilitates the empowerment of individual participants. See Farrer 2004.
81. See Uchibori 1989.
82. Takamori 2010.
83. Sakai 2005 (1996).

Chapter 4 – Doerr and Lee

1. See Doerr's introduction in Doerr 2010, 53–62.
2. Fishman 2001, 95. See also, Cho 2000; Moses 2000.
3. Wright and Taylor 1995.
4. Huebner 1999, 9.
5. He 2006; Hornberger and Wang 2008.
6. As Doerr discusses in her introduction to "Heritage, Nationhood, and Language" (Doerr 2010), calling minority language education "heritage" language education is a recent phenomenon and is specific to the North American context. See Wiley and Valdés 2000. For research on heritage language schools, see Peyton et al. 2001; Silver 2003.
7. Kirshenblatt-Gimblett 2006.
8. Breglia 2006.
9. Bourdieu and Passeron 1977.
10. Varenne and McDermott 1999.
11. Bourdieu 1984.
12. Kincheloe and Steinberg 1997.
13. Doerr 2009 (Meaningful); Wells and Serna 1996.
14. Lee 1996; Milroy and Milroy 1991; Yasuda 2003.
15. Anderson 1991; Baumann and Biggs 2000.
16. Doerr, ed. 2009 ; Pavlenko 2002; Pavlenko and Blackledge 2004.
17. Apple 2000; Bigler 1999; Freedman 1998; Giroux 2001.
18. Doerr 2009; Varenne and McDermott 1999.
19. For diverse ways to inherit other languages, see Ernst-Slavit 1997; He and Yun, eds. 2008.
20. Althusser 1971.
21. Butler (1993: 2) uses performativity "not as the act by which a subject brings into being what she/he names, but rather, as that reiterative power of discourse to produce the phenomena that it regulates and constrains."
22. Butler 1993, 2–13.
23. Smith 1988.
24. Most heritage language schools are run by local communities in the United States without much formal involvement of the government of the immigrants' "homeland" (Fishman 2001).
25. For example, the establishment of the Washington Japanese Heritage Center in 2004, separate from Washington Hoshūkō. See www.keisho.org/ (accessed 15 May 2009).
26. Sato 1997.
27. Hoshūkō sometimes include a preschool, a kindergarten, and a high school.
28. MEXT 2008.
29. This is unlike the cases in Bolivia (Suzuki 2010) and Peru (Yamasaki 2010).
30. Douglas 2005; Chinen 2004.
31. Yasuda 2003, 22 (Doerr's translation).

32. Not following the guidelines occasionally creates struggles for legitimacy on the part of keishōgo program (Doerr and Lee 2009).
33. For a detailed discussion, see Doerr and Lee 2009.
34. Valdés 2001, 38.
35. Doerr and Lee work in progress.
36. For another case see Okubo 2010.
37. Occasionally, English glossary lists were provided for new vocabulary in Level 4.
38. These are conventional categories used at hoshūkō throughout the United States. See Sato and Kataoka 2008.
39. What constitutes one's "first language" or "mother tongue" cannot be readily assumed. Tove Skutnabb-Kangas and Robert Phillipson (1989) suggest that there are four possible definitions of "mother tongue": (1) the language(s) one learns first; (2) the language(s) one knows best; (3) the language(s) one uses most; and (4) the language(s) one identifies with. Thus, one person may have different languages as one's "mother tongues," depending on which definition is used. It is this kind of marking that we examine in this article.
40. Although there is another group of students who study Japanese as a foreign language, they are beyond the scope of our research.
41. See also Doerr and Lee 2009.
42. Doerr interviewed nine students and six parents in the hoshūkō, and six students and one parent in the Jackson Course. Lee interviewed one student and three parents in the hoshūkō and five parents in the Jackson Course. Because Lee is the administrator of Jackson Course and is familiar with these parents, Lee interviewed them in the hope of their opening up to the interviewer while being aware that power relationships between the administrator and parent as well as Lee's explicit support for the Jackson Course could affect the interview results.
43. For a detailed analysis, see Doerr and Lee 2009.
44. Public education throughout Japan is carried out in standard Japanese. However, casual conversations between teachers and students as well as among students are usually in the local dialect. As mentioned in the main text, Yaichi's friends ridiculed him for putting "ne" at the end of the sentence, a practice common in standard Japanese but feminine-sounding in the Osaka dialect. Their ridicule evokes a hierarchy of the Osaka dialect and Tokyo dialect (read standard Japanese). That is, in his hometown in Osaka, a normative regime of regional difference positions the local dialect (in this case, Osaka dialect) as the most desirable. The normativity of standard Japanese remains in the government-related domain, such as in government-certified textbooks, where standard Japanese is the default.
45. The hierarchies between the standard and nonstandard forms in heritage language educations have been critically discussed in Spanish-as-a-Heritage-Language education (Martinez 2003; Valdés 1981), but not extensively in Japanese-as-a-Heritage-Language education.
46. Kumiko is considered as eijū because she has no plans to live in Japan. However, because she was born and raised in Japan until the age of six and her biological father is Japanese, her situation is different from the typical eijū students, who were born in the United States and often have one parent who is not Japanese.
47. Kumiko goes to Japan every year from a week to a month during her American school's summer break and attends school there (Japanese schools do not break for summer until late July).
48. Jake's mother said in her interview that she is Japanese and her husband is American.
49. The seventh grade teacher was born and raised in Japan, but came to the United States with her Japanese husband in the early 1980s. She had no concrete plan to go back to Japan to live.
50. Ohnuki-Tirney 1993.
51. For more conscious manipulation of different ways to link to "Japanese-ness," see Takamori 2010.
52. Sasha has also been going to Chinese language school on Friday nights (for about eight years), but she said she finds Chinese more difficult than Japanese.

53. This teacher was born and raised in Japan and moved to Jackson in 2007. His wife is American. The teacher had taught in a middle school in Japan for over twenty years. The Japanese government had sent him to a hoshūkō in a different region in the United States for three years. This was his first year teaching in the Jackson Course.

Chapter 5 – Takamori

1. See Doerr 2010 for a discussion of concepts and theories of "heritage language."
2. Edwards 1985 is a notable exception. He argues that language shift does not necessarily indicate a loss of identity.
3. For critiques of the "minority" concept, see Deleuze and Guattari 1987; Lionnet and Shih 2005; and Wilkinson 2000.
4. The terms nikkei and nikkeijin refer to people of Japanese ancestry born outside Japan.
5. Waters and Jiménez 2005.
6. Portes and Schauffler 1994, 643.
7. See Lowe 1996 on citizenship and immigration acts.
8. Morimoto 1997.
9. Waters and Jiménez 2005, 110.
10. Lopez 1982.
11. Lovejoy has also noted that the cultural climate and anti-Japanese sentiment of the postwar period in the United States fostered the stigmatization of Japanese identification. See Lovejoy 1986, 29–30.
12. Brazilian nikkei residents, comprising the largest foreign population in Japan at over 300,000, have been working as laborers in the manufacturing sector since the late 1980s. See Lesser 2003; Roth 2002; and Tsuda 2003.
13. By "younger," I refer not to generation, but to those under the age of about thirty-five.
14. Generational terminology in Japanese diaspora populations is an important way in which people identify themselves. Issei refers to the immigrant generation. Nisei refers to those born outside of Japan to Japanese parents. Sansei refers to the third generation or the children born to nisei parents. Among my informants in Japanese, there were also yonsei (fourth generation) and gosei (fifth generation) Japanese Americans. Additionally, hapa, a term originally appropriated from Hawaiian, was used by those who identify as mixed race.
15. Reyes and Lo 2008 is the first edited collection to focus on Asian Pacific Americans and questions of language and identity. Shankar (2008) gives an account of language use among Desi teenagers in California and their use of language to mark gender, style, race, and class. He and Yun (2008) focus on Chinese heritage language. Sridhar (1988) analyzes the relationship between language maintenance and class among Indian Americans in New York. Hinton (2001) gives a useful overview of Asian Pacific American narratives about heritage language, but does not extensively theorize the relationship of language loss to class mobility.
16. Edwards 1985.
17. Here I am specifically discussing Hirahara 2004 and Hirahara 2005.
18. Lopez 1976.
19. Turner 1993, 412.
20. San Juan 2002.
21. Literally, "new nisei." Shin nisei refers to niseis whose parents immigrated to the United States after the 1965 immigration reforms.
22. McGray 2002.
23. Lopez 1982, 53.
24. Irvine 1998, 52.
25. The formation of Japanese diasporas has never been a one-way process, even from the start. Kibeis, for example, are those Japanese Americans who were born in the United States but raised or educated in Japan. Kikokushijo is a term that refers to those who are born in Japan, spent some time as children or youths abroad, but then subsequently returned to Japan.

26. For further discussion and analyses of Japanese ideologies of blood, culture, and nation, see Robertson 2002; Robertson 2005; Weiner 1994; Weiner 2009 (1997); and Yoshino 1997.
27. Robertson 2005; Weiner 2009.
28. Robertson 2005, 329.
29. All names of informants are pseudonyms.
30. Robertson forthcoming.
31. Worth noting is that English language ability (and identification as "American") is a significant factor within political economic conditions in determining differences in class mobility and cultural capital between Latin American and North American nikkeis in Japan.
32. Garrett and Baquedano-López 2002, 350.
33. For discussion and analyses of nihonjinron, see Befu 2001; Dale 1986; Miller 1982; Mouer and Sugimoto 1986; Sugimoto 1999.
34. Public discourse and academic knowledge in Japan about nikkeijins have of course broadened in the last decade or two, particularly around South American "returnee" laborers and aging Filipino Japanese reclaiming Japanese citizenship. However, outside certain specialized social circles and institutional/academic venues, knowledge of North American nikkeijins is still relatively limited.
35. Kondo 1990, 11.
36. Krashen 1998.
37. Dolar 1991, 19.
38. For an analysis of the relationship between modernity and the uncanny in Japan, see Ivy 1995.
39. Hamabata 1991.
40. Sakai 1997.
41. Sakai 2005, 2.
42. Safran 2005, 4.
43. Manalansan 2003.

Chapter 6 – Miller

1. Ayukawa 2000.
2. Ibid., 70.
3. Doerr and Lee 2010.
4. Moerman 1965.
5. Ibid.,1219.
6. Doerr and Lee 2010.
7. Yamasaki 2010.
8. In a study of Americans learning Russian during study abroad, we found that students were not taking advantage of the rich linguistic context afforded by living in Moscow. Instead, they carried a model of classroom Russian with them into public life and evaluated native-speaking Russians who did not adhere to this model as deficient speakers. See Miller and Ginsberg 1995.
9. Iino 1996.
10. Although not investigated in the articles in this thematic collection, there is also a relationship between heritage language print media and ethnic maintenance. One interesting case is that of Chicago Shimpō (Shikago Shimpō), a Japanese language newspaper published since 1945. For decades this was a Nisei paper that carried local events in both Nisei vernacular written Japanese and English. However, a native-speaking Japanese has assumed its editorship and ownership, and now Tokyo dialect coverage celebrates an imagined homogeneous Cool Japan. There are few remnants of the paper's former identity as a "heritage" Nisei newspaper. For more on Chicago Shimpō, see Miller 2003.
11. Suzuki 2010.
12. From the Japanese Chamber of Commerce in Chicago website: www.jccc-chi.org/en/futabakai. html (accessed 15 September 2008).
13. Goodman 1990.

14. Doerr and Lee 2010.
15. Okubo 2010.
16. For the situation in Brazil, see Adachi 2001.
17. Takamori 2010.
18. Ryang 2008, xxxix.

Chapter 7 – Van Vleet

1. Gal 1989, 348.
2. Ibid., 353.
3. Suzuki 2010.
4. Yamasaki 2010.
5. Mannheim 1991. At the time of the European invasion, hundreds of languages were spoken, mostly by people who were at least bilingual, in a territory that extended from southern Colombia to northern Chile. Quechua was the administrative language of the Inca in the mid 1400s, but for the Inca state no ideology of "one nation, one language" existed.
6. Gal 1989, 353–54.
7. As García (2004, 350) notes, during the colonial period, Spanish administrators and elite used Quechua as the language of proselytizing and administration; they preferred learning Quechua to allowing indigenous people to learn Spanish.
8. Suzuki 2010, 82; on racial formation in the Andes see also Weismantel 2001; Canessa 2005.
9. Suzuki 2010, 84.
10. Ibid., 65.
11. Ibid., 73.
12. Yamasaki 2010.
13. Ibid., 90.
14. Ibid., 95.
15. Ibid., 90.
16. Okubo 2010.
17. García 2005; Gustafson 2009.
18. Bucholtz and Hall 2005, 594.
19. Ibid.
20. Okubo 2010.
21. Ibid., 129.
22. Ibid., 128.
23. Ibid., 130–31.
24. Okubo 2010, 128–29. For additional examples, see Hill (1998) on indexicality and discourses of race in "mock Spanish" and Inoue (2002) on "women's language," idexicality, and modernity in nineteen- and twentieth-century Japan.
25. Takamori 2010, 205–06.
26. Ibid., 205.
27. Ibid., 205–06.
28. Yamasaki 2010, 98.
29. Takamori 2010, 208.
30. Ibid.
31. Takamori 2010, 202–03, 209. Blood is a metaphor for essential characteristics in Japan and the United States (as well as in the Andes), although the histories of use and the valences of meaning do not completely overlap. On Japan, see Robertson 2002.
32. Takamori 2010, 197–98.
33. Ibid., 201.
34. Ibid., 203.
35. Doerr and Lee 2010.
36. Ibid., 193–94.
37. Ibid., 200.
38. Yamasaki 2010, 101.

39. Ibid., 103.
40. Yamaguchi 2010, 92.
41. Escheverria 2003.
42. Ibid., 267.
43. Ibid., 368.
44. Yamasaki 2010, 105.
45. Hornberger 2000, 175; italics in original.

Chapter 8 – Meek

1. Takamori 2010, 234.
2. Deloria 2004.
3. Doerr and Lee 2010; Keane 2003.
4. An interesting sentiment underscoring this Canadian publication is the distinguishing of a Canadian approach from a U.S. approach. Posed as a series of questions, the CAE creates this framing by juxtaposing the concept of "multiculturalism" and that of "melting pot"; "On the social and political levels, the debate continues on the advisability of maintaining multiculturalism: should Canada encourage its recent arrival to maintain their own identity, language and culture? is there value in diversity? or should we adopt the way of the United States, encouraging all to blend into the "melting pot"?" Canadian Education Association 1991, 1.
5. Ibid., 3.
6. Ibid.
7. Cummins 1983, 7.
8. Fishman 1999; Peyton et al. 2001.
9. Miller 2010.
10. Takamori 2010; Doerr 2010.
11. A subtle distinction exists between the notion of "minority language" and "heritage language." For example, Cummins (1983) notes that "the term "minority language program" is used to include both "bilingual programs" where the minority language is used as a medium of instruction and "heritage language programs" where the minority languages are taught as a subject of instruction. More recently, scholars have shifted away from referring to languages as "minority" because of the negative connotations associated with the term and its enumerative ambiguity (that is, a "minority" language may not be in the minority within particular communities or social networks).
12. See Peyton et al. 2001.
13. Available at http://www.cal.org/heritage/index.html (accessed 1 March 2010).
14. Fishman 2001.
15. Some overlap may exist between the immigrant heritage language category and the colonial heritage language category (e.g., Spanish).
16. Schieffelin and Ochs 1986.
17. Doerr and Lee 2010, 207.
18. Kulick 1992, 1993.
19. Takamori 2010, 227.
20. On modernity, see Appadurai 1996 (Modernity), Deloria 2004, Latour 1993; on gaps and tears, see Bauman 2005, Irvine 2005; on the concept of social and sociolinguistic disjuncture, see Meek 2010.
21. Takamori 2010, 227, 229–30.
22. Bailey 2001.
23. Takamori 2010, 234.

References

Adachi, Nobuko. 2001. Japanese Brazilians: The Japanese language community in Brazil. *Studies in Linguistic Sciences* 31 (1): 161–78.

Al Sayyad, Nezar, ed. 2001. *Consuming tradition, manufacturing heritage: Global norms and urban forms in the age of tourism*. London and New York: Routledge.

Allen, Matthew. 2003. Wolves at the back door: Remembering the Kumejima massacres. In Laura Hein and Mark Selden, eds. *Islands of discontent: Okinawan responses to Japanese and American power*. Lanham, Md.: Rowman and Littlefield. 39–64.

Althusser, Louis. 1971. *Lenin and philosophy and other essays*. New York: Monthly Review Press.

Amemiya, Kozy K. 1999. The Bolivian connection: U.S. bases and Okinawan emigration. In Chalmers Johnson, ed. *Okinawa: Cold war island*. Cardiff, Calif.: Japan Policy Research Institute. 23–70.

Anbo, Hideo, Hironori Ishii, and Hideshi Ohashi. 1998. Boribia ni okeru Nikkeijin no dōka no shosō 1: Nōgyō ijūsha no ba'ai [Aspects of Japanese-Bolivians' assimilation 1: A case of agricultural immigrants]. In Hideshi Ohashi, ed. *Nanbei Boribia no Okinawa mura: Imin no shakai-shinrigaku-teki kenkyū* [Okinawan village in Bolivia, South America: A social psychological study of immigrants]. Sendai, Japan: Shinrigaku Kenkyū-shitsu, Bungaku-bu, Tōhoku Daigaku (Department of Psychology, Faculty of Arts and Letters, Tohoku University). 225–59.

Anderson, Benedict. 1991. *Imagined communities*. London: Verso.

Aoyama City. 2001. *Dōwa mondai no kaiketsu ni muketa jittaitō chōsa: Seikatsu jittai chōsa hōkokusho* [Study on the actual conditions to solve the Buraku issue: Report on the study of life situation]. Aoyama City, Osaka Prefecture.

———. 2003. *Kokusaika sesaku suishin kihon shishin* [Basic guidelines for promoting internationalization policies]. Aoyama City, Osaka Prefecture.

———. 2004. *Kokusaika sesaku suishin keikaku* [Plans for promoting internationalization policies]. Aoyama City, Osaka Prefecture.

Appadurai, Arjun. 1990. Disjuncture and difference in the global cultural economy. *Public Culture* 2 (2): 1–24.

———. 1996. *Modernity at large: Cultural dimensions of globalization*. Minneapolis: University of Minnesota Press.

———. 1996. Sovereignty without territoriality: Notes for a postnational geography. In Patricia Yaeger, ed. *The geography of identity*. Ann Arbor: University of Michigan Press.

Apple, Michael. 2000. 2d ed. *Official knowledge: Democratic education in a conservative age*. New York: Routledge.

Arakaki, Robert K. 2002. Theorizing on the Okinawan diaspora. In Robert Y. Nakasone, ed. *Okinawan Diaspora*. Honolulu: University of Hawai'i Press. 26–43.

Araki, Raúl. 2002. An approach to the formation of Nikkei identity in Peru: Issei and Nisei. In L. R. Hirabayashi et al., eds. *New worlds, new lives: Globalization and people of Japanese descent in the Americas and from Latin America in Japan*. Stanford: Stanford University Press. 76–89.

Araragi, Shinzo, ed. 2000. *"Chūgoku kikokusha" no seikatsu sekai* [The social world of "Chinese returnees"]. Kyoto: Kōrosha.

Axel, Brian Keith. 2001. *The nation's tortured body: Violence, representation, and the formation of a Sikh "diaspora."* Durham, N.C.: Duke University Press.

Ayukawa, Michiko Midge. 2000. Japanese language: Reflection, rediscovery, and reclamation. *Pan-Japan: The International Journal of Japanese Diaspora* 1 (2): 62–74.

Bailey, Benjamin. 2001. The language of multiple identities among Dominican Americans. *Journal of Linguistic Anthropology* 10 (2): 190–223.

Baker, Colin. 2006. 4th ed. *Foundations of bilingual education and bilingualism*. Clevedon, Avon (UK): Multilingual Matters.

Balibar, Etienne. 1988. The nation form: History and ideology. In Etienne Balibar and Immanuel Wallerstein, eds. *Race, nation, class: Ambiguous identities*. London: Verso. 86–106.

———. 1994. *Masses, classes, ideas: Studies on politics and philosophy before and after Marx*. New York: Routledge.

Banks, James. 1995. Multicultural education: Historical development, dimensions, and practice. In Banks and Banks, eds. 1995, 3–24. (Originally published in 1993 in *Review of Research in Education* 19: 3–49.)

Banks, James, and Cherry A. McGee Banks, eds. 1995. *Handbook of research on multicultural education*. New York: Macmillan.

Barrell, Tony, and Rick Tanaka. 1997. *Okinawa dreams OK*. Berlin: Die Gestalten Verlag.

Basu, Paul. 2007. *Highland homecomings: Genealogy and heritage tourism in the Scottish diaspora*. London: Routledge.

Bauman, Richard. 2005. Commentary. Indirect indexicality, identity performance: Dialogic observations. *Journal of Linguistic Anthropology* 15 (1): 145–50.

Bauman, Richard, and Charles L. Briggs. 2000. Language philosophy as language ideology: John Locke and Johann Gottfried Herder. In Paul V. Kroskrity, ed. *Regimes of language: Ideologies, polities, and identities*. Santa Fe, N.M.: School of American Research Press. 139–204.

Befu, Harumi. 2001. *Hegemony of homogeneity: An anthropological analysis of "Nihonjinron*. Melbourne: Trans Pacific Press.

Bhabha, Homi K. 1994. *The location of culture*. New York: Routledge.

Bigler, Ellen. 1999. *American Conversations*. Philadelphia: Temple University Press.

Bourdieu, Pierre. 1984. *Distinction: A social critique of the judgment of taste*. Cambridge, Mass.: Harvard University Press.

Bourdieu, Pierre. 1991 (1977). *Language and symbolic power*. Cambridge, Mass.: Harvard University Press.

Bourdieu, Pierre, and Jean-Claude Passeron. 1977 (1990). *Reproduction in education, society, and culture.* London: Sage.
Breglia, Lisa. 2006. *Monumental ambivalence: The politics of heritage.* Austin: University of Texas Press.
Brutt-Griffler, Janina, and Sinfree Makoni. 2005. The use of heritage language: An African perspective. *The Modern Language Journal* 89 (4): 609–12.
Bucholtz, Mary, and Kira Hall. 2005. Identity and interaction: A sociocultural linguistic approach. *Discourse Studies* 7 (4-5): 585–614.
Buraku kaihō dōmei Ōsaka-fu rengōkai. 1982. *Hisabetsu buraku ni ikiru chōsenjin* [Koreans living in the Buraku community]. Osaka: Kaihō shinbunsha.
Butler, Judith. 1993. *Bodies that matter.* New York: Routledge.
Canadian Education Association. 1991. Heritage language programs in Canadian school boards. Toronto: Canadian Education Association.
Canagarajah, A. Suresh. 1999. *Resisting linguistic imperialism in English teaching.* Oxford: Oxford University Press.
Canessa, Andrew, ed. 2005. *Natives making nation: Gender, indigeneity, and the state in the Andes.* Tuscon: University of Arizona Press.
Carreira, Maria. 2004. Seeking explanatory adequacy: A dual approach to understanding the term "heritage learner." *Heritage Language Journal* 2 (1): 1-25. On-line at www.heritagelanguages.org (accessed 10 November 2007).
Castles, Stephen, and Mark J. Miller. 2003 (1993). *The age of migration: International population movements in the modern world.* 3rd ed. Hampshire (UK) and New York: Palgrave Macmillan.
Chambers, Erve. 2005. Whose heritage is it? History, culture and inheritance. *Anthropology News* (April 2005): 7-8.
Chapman, David. 2006. Discourses of multicultural coexistence (*tabunka kyōsei*) and the "old-comer" Korean residents of Japan. *Asian Ethnicity* 7 (1): 89–102.
Chinen, Kiyomi. 2004. *Heritage language development: Understanding the roles of ethnic identity, attitudes, motivation, schooling, family support and community factors.* PhD diss., Carnegie Mellon University.
Cho, Grace. 2000. The role of heritage language in social interactions and relationships: Reflections from a language minority group. *Bilingual Research Journal* 24 (4): 333–48.
Christy, Alan S. 1997. The making of imperial subjects in Okinawa. In Tani E. Barlow, ed. *Formations of colonial modernity in East Asia.* Durham, N.C.: Duke University Press. 141–69.
Comaroff, John L., and Jean Comaroff. 2004. Criminal justice, cultural justice: The limits of liberalism and the pragmatics of difference in the new South Africa." *American Ethnologist* 31 (2): 188–204.
Cook, Vivian. 1999. Going beyond the native speaker in language teaching. *TESOL Quarterly* 33 (2): 185–209.
Corsane, Gerard. 2005. Issues in heritage, museums and galleries. In Gerard Corsane, ed. *Heritage, museums, and galleries: An introductory reader.* Oxon (UK) and New York: Routledge. 1–12.
Crowley, Tony. 1989. *Standard English and the politics of language.* Urbana: University of Illinois Press.
Cummins, Jim. 1983. Heritage language education: A literature review. Toronto: Ontario Institute for Studies in Education, The Minister of Education.

———. 1995. Heritage language teaching in Canadian schools. In O. Garcia and C. Baker, eds. *Policy and practice in bilingual education: A reader extending the foundations*. Clevedon, Avon (UK): Multilingual Matters. 134–38.

———. 2001 (1996). *Negotiating identities: Education for empowerment in a diverse society*. Los Angeles: California Association for Bilingual Education.

———. 2005. A proposal for action: Strategies for recognizing heritage language competence as a learning resource within the mainstream classroom. *The Modern Language Journal* 89 (4): 585–92.

Dale, Peter N. 1986. *The myth of Japanese uniqueness*. New York: St. Martin's Press.

De Bot, Kees, and Durk Gorter. 2005. European perspective on heritage languages. *The Modern Language Journal* 89 (4): 612–16.

Deleuze, Gilles, and Felix Guattari. 1987. Trans. Brian Massumi. *A thousand plateaus: Capitalism and schizophrenia*. Minneapolis: University of Minnesota Press.

Deloria, Philip J. 2004. *Indians in unexpected places*. Lawrence: University Press of Kansas.

Delpit, Lisa. 1995. *Other people's children: Cultural conflict in the classroom*. New York: The New Press.

Deusen-Scholl, Nelleke van. 2003. Toward a definition of heritage language: Sociopolitical and pedagogical considerations. *Journal of Language, Identity, and Education* 2 (3): 211–30.

Doerr, Neriko. 2009. *Meaningful inconsistencies: Bicultural nationhood, the free market, and schooling in Aotearoa/New Zealand*. New York: Berghahn Books.

———. 2010. Introduction. Heritage, nationhood, and language: Migrants with Japan connections. *Critical Asian Studies* 42 (1): 53–62.

———, ed. 2009. *The native speaker concept: Ethnographic investigations of native speaker effects*. Berlin: Mouton de Gruyter.

Doerr, Neriko, and Kiri Lee. 2009. Contesting heritage: Language, legitimacy, and schooling at a weekend Japanese language school in the United States. *Language and Education* 23 (5): 425–41.

———. 2010. Inheriting "Japanese-ness" diversely: Heritage practices at a weekend Japanese language school in the United States. *Critical Asian Studies* 42 (2): 191–216.

———. Inheriting "Japanese" diversely: Heritage practices at a weekend Japanese language school in the United States. *Critical Asian Studies* 41 (2): June 2010.

Dolar, Mladen. 1991. "I shall be with you on your wedding night": Lacan and the uncanny. *October* 58: 5–23.

Douglas, Masako. 2005*. Pedagogical theories and approaches to teach young learners of Japanese as a heritage language. *Heritage Language Journal* 3 (1): 62–82.

Douglas, Masako. 2006*. Pedagogical theories and approaches to teach young learners of Japanese as a heritage language. *Heritage Language Journal* 3 (1): 60–82.

Edwards, John. 1985. *Language, society and identity*. Oxford and New York: Blackwell.

Eidson, John R. 2005. Between heritage and countermemory: Varieties of historical representation in a West Germany community. *American Ethnologist* 32 (4): 556–75.

Eldering, Lotty. 1996. Multiculturalism and multicultural education in an international perspective. *Anthropology and Education Quarterly* 27 (3): 315-30.

Eller, Jack David. 1997. Anti-anti-multiculturalism. *American Anthropologist* 99 (2): 249–56.

Ernst-Slavit, Gisela. 1997. Different words, different worlds: Language use, power, and authorized language in a bilingual classroom. *Linguistics and Education* 9, 25–48.

Escheverria, Begoña. 2003. Schooling, language, and ethnic identity in the Basque autonomous community. *Anthropology and Education Quarterly* 34 (4): 351–72.

Farrer, Gracia Liu. 2004. The Chinese social dance party in Tokyo: Identity and status in an immigrant leisure subculture. *Journal of Contemporary Ethnography* 33 (6): 651-74.

Field, Norma. 1993. *In the realm of a dying emperor: Japan at century's end*. New York: Vintage.

Firth, Alan, and Johannes Wagner. 2007a. On discourse, communication, and (some) fundamental concepts in SLA research. *The Modern Language Journal* 91: 757–72. Republished from *The Modern Language Journal* 81 (1997): 285–300.

———. 2007b. Second/foreign language learning as a social accomplishment: Elaborations on a reconceptualized SLA. *The Modern Language Journal* 91: 800–19.

Fishman, Joshua A. 1991*. *Reversing language shift: Theoretical and empirical foundations of assistance to threatened languages*. Clevedon, Avon (UK): Multilingual Matters.

———. 1991*. *Reversing language shift: Theory and practice of assistance to threatened languages*. Clevedon: Multilingual Matters.

———. 2001. 300-plus years of heritage language education in the United States. In Joy K. Peyton et al., eds. *Heritage Languages in America: Preserving a National Resource*. McHenry, Ill., and Washington D.C.: Delta Systems and Center for Applied Linguistics. 87–97.

———, ed. 1999. *Handbook of language and ethnic identity*. Oxford: Oxford University Press.

Fiske, John. 1991 (1989). *Understanding popular culture*. London: Routledge.

Fukumoto, Mary.1997. *Hacia un nuevo sol: Japoneses y sus descendientes en el Perú*. Lima : Associación Peruano Japonesa del Perú.

Fukuoka, Yasunori, and Myung-Soo Kim. 1997. *Zainichi kankoku seinen no seikatsu to ishiki* [Lives and consciousness of resident Korean youths]. Tokyo: Tōkyō daigaku shuppankai.

Gal, Susan. 1989. Language and political economy. *Annual Review of Anthropology* 18: 345–67.

García, María Elena. 2004. Rethinking bilingual education in Peru: Intercultural politics, state policy, and indigenous rights. *Bilingual Education and Bilingualism* 7 (5): 348–67.

———. 2005. *Making indigenous citizens: Identities, education, and multicultural development in Peru*. Stanford, Calif.: Stanford University Press.

Garrett, Paul B., and Patricia Baquedano-López. 2002. Language socialization: Reproduction and continuity, transformation and change. *Annual Review of Anthropology* 31: 339–61.

Gillis, John, ed. 1994. *Commemorations: The politics of national identity*. Princeton, N.J.: Princeton University Press.

Giroux, Henry. A. 2001. Rev. and expanded ed. *Theory and resistance in education: Towards a pedagogy for the opposition*. Westport, Conn.: Bergin and Garvey.

Goldberg, David Theo. 1994. Introduction: Multicultural Conditions. In David Theo Goldberg, ed. *Multiculturalism: A critical reader*. Oxford, U.K. and Cambridge, Mass.: Blackwell. 1–41.

Goodman, Roger. 1990. Japan's "international youth": The emergence of a new class of schoolchildren. Oxford: Oxford University Press.

Graburn, Nelson H.H. 2001. Learning to consume: What is heritage and when is it traditional? In Al Sayyad 2001, 68–89.

Graburn, Nelson H.H., John Ertl, and R. Kenji Tierney, eds. 2008. *Multiculturalism in the new Japan: Crossing the boundaries within*. New York and Oxford: Berghahn Books.

Graham, Brian, John Ashworth Gregory, and John E. Tunbridge, 2005. The uses and abuses of heritage. In Gerard Corsane, ed. *Heritage, museums, and galleries: An introductory reader*. Oxon (UK) and New York: Routledge. 26–37.

Gushiken, Kōtei. 1995. *Hōjin zaisan no hogo ni tsuite* [Regarding the protection of the property of Japanese nationals]. Colonia Okinawa, Santa Cruz, Bolivia: Okinawa Nihon-Boribia Kyōkai.

Gustafson, Bret. 2009. *New languages of the state: Indigenous resurgence and the politics of knowledge in Bolivia*. Durham, N.C.: Duke University Press.

Hall, Stuart. 2006. Conclusion: The multicultural question. In Hesse 2006, 209–41.

Hamabata, Matthew. 1991. *Crested kimono: Power and love in a Japanese business family*. Ithaca, N.Y.: Cornell University Press.

Hamlish, Tamara. 2000. Global culture, modern heritage: Re-membering the Chinese imperial collections. In Susan A. Crane, ed. *Museums and memory*. Stanford: Stanford University Press.

Handler, Richard. 1985. On having a culture: Nationalism and the preservation of Quebec's patrimoine. In George W. Stocking Jr., ed. *Objects and others: Essays on museums and material culture*. Madison: University of Wisconsin Press. 192–217.

Hannerz, Ulf. 1992. *Cultural complexity: Studies in the social organization of meaning*. New York: Columbia University Press.

He, Agnes Weiyun. 2006. Toward an identity theory of the development of Chinese as a heritage language. *Heritage Language Journal* 4 (1): 1–28.

He, Agnes Weiyun, and Yun Xiao, eds. 2008. *Chinese as a heritage language: Fostering world citizenry*. Honolulu: University of Hawai'i Press.

Hein, Laura, and Mark Selden. 2003a. Culture, power, and identity in contemporary Okinawa. In Hein and Selden, eds. 2003b. 1–35.

———, eds. 2003b. *Islands of discontent: Okinawan responses to Japanese and American power*. Lanham, Md.: Rowman and Littlefield.

Heller, Monica. 2001. Legitimate language in a multilingual school. In M. Heller and M. Martin-Jones, eds. *Voices of authority: Education and linguistic differences*. Westport, Conn.: Ablex Publishing. 381–402.

Henze, Rosemary, and Davis, Kathryn A. 1999. Authenticity and identity: Lessons from indigenous language education. *Anthropology and Education Quarterly* 30 (1): 3–21.

Hesse, Barnor, ed. 2006. *Un/Settled multiculturalisms: Diasporas, entanglements, "transruptions."* London and New York: Zed Books.

Higa, Hiroshi. 2000. Okinawa ijūchi no kensetsu to hatten [Foundation and development of Colonia Okinawa]. In Boribia Nihonjin Ijū 100-shūnen-shi Hensan Iinkai (Editorial Committee of A Commemorative Book of Centennial of Japanese Immigration). *Boribia ni ikiru: Nihonjin ijū 100 shūnen kinen-shi* [Living in Bolivia: A commemorative book of centennial of Japanese immigration]. Santa Cruz de la Sierra, Bolivia: Federación Nacional de Asociaciónes Boliviano-Japonesas. 233–60.

Hill, Jane. 1998. Language, race, and white public space. *American Anthropologist* 100 (3): 680–89.

Hinton, Leanne. 2001. Involuntary language loss among immigrants. *Georgetown University Roundtable in Language and Linguistics*. 1999: 203–52.

Hirahara, Naomi. 2004. *The summer of the big bachi*. New York: Bantam Dell.

———. 2005. *Gasa gasa girl*. New York: Bantam Dell.

Hook, Glenn D., and Richard Siddle, eds. 2003. *Okinawa: Structure and subjectivity*. London: RoutledgeCurzon.

Hornberger, Nancy H. 1988. Language ideology in Quechua communities of Puno, Peru. *Anthropological Linguistics* 30 (2): 214–35.

——— 2000. Bilingual education policy and practice in the Andes: Ideological paradox and intercultural possibility. *Anthropology and Education Quarterly* 31 (2): 173–201.

Hornberger, Nancy H., and Shuhan C. Wang. 2008. Who are our heritage language learners? Identity and biliteracy in heritage language education in the United States. In Donna M. Brinton, Olga Kagan, and Susan Bauckus, eds. *Heritage language education: A new field emerging*. New York: Routledge. 3–38.

Horvath, Barbara M., and Paul Vaughan. 1991. *Community languages: A handbook*. Clevedon, Avon (UK): Multilingual Matters.

Huebner, Thomas. 1999. Sociopolitical perspectives on language policy, politics and praxis. In Thomas Huebner and Kathryn A. Davis eds., *Sociopolitical perspectives on language policy and planning in the USA*. Amsterdam/Philadelphia: John Benjamins Publishing Company. 1–15.

Ige, Philip K. 1981. An Okinawan nisei in Hawai'i. In United Okinawan Association of Hawai'i, Ethnic Studies Oral History Project, ed. *Uchinanchu: A history of Okinawans in Hawai'i*. Honolulu: Ethnic Studies Program, University of Hawai'i at Manoa. 149–60.

Iino, Masakazu. 1996. Excellent foreigner! Gaijinization of Japanese language and culture in contact situations. An ethnographic study of dinner table conversations between Japanese host families and American students. PhD diss., Graduate School of Education, University of Pennsylvania.

Inoue, Miyako. 2002. Gender, language, and modernity: Toward an effective history of Japanese women's language. *American Ethnologist* 29 (2): 392–422.

Irvine, Judith T. 1998. Ideologies of honorific language. In Bambi B. Schieffelin, Kathryn A. Woolard, and Paul V. Kroskrity, eds. *Language ideologies: Practice and theory*. New York and Oxford: Oxford University Press.

——— 2005. Commentary: Knots and tears in the interdiscursive fabric. *Journal of Linguistic Anthropology* 15 (1): 72–80.

Irvine, Judith T., and Susan Gal. 2000. Language ideology and linguistic differentiation. In Paul V. Kroskrity, ed. *Regimes of language: Ideologies, polities, and identities*. Santa Fe, N.M.: School of American Research Press. 35–83.

Ishikawa, Tomonori. 1973. Dai-ni-ji sekai taisen mae no Okinawa-ken kara no dekasegi ni tsuite [Sojourning from Okinawa Prefecture before World War II]. *Jinbun Chiri* 25: 456–77.

Ivy, Marilyn. 1995. *Discourses of the vanishing: Modernity, phantasm, Japan*. Chicago and London: University of Chicago Press.

Japanese Ministry of Justice. 2006. Statistics on registration of foreign residents. Available on-line at http://www.moj.go.jp/PRESS/040611-1/040611-1.html (accessed 6 March 2006).

Jo, Hye-young. 2001. Heritage language learning and ethnic identity: Korean Americans' struggle with language authorities. *Language, Culture and Curriculum* 14 (1): 26–41.

Johnson, Chalmers, ed. 1999. *Okinawa: Cold war island*. Cardiff, Calif.: Japan Policy Research Institute.

Kaji, Itaru. 2008. Ōsaka-fu ni okeru nyūkamā to kōkō nyūshi [Newcomers in Osaka Prefecture and high school entrance examination]. In Shimizu 2008, 75–89.

Kajita, Takamichi, Kiyoto Tanno, and Naoto Higuchi. 2005. *Kao no mienai teijūka: Nikkei Burajirujin to kokka, shijō, imin nettowāku* [Settlement without visible faces: Japanese-Brazilians, state, market, and immigration network]. Nagoya: Nagoya daigaku shuppankai.

Kaneshiro, Edith M. 2002. "The other Japanese": Okinawan immigrants to the Philippines, 1903–1941. In Robert Y. Nakasone, ed. *Okinawan diaspora*. Honolulu: University of Hawai'i Press. 71–89.

Kato, Chikako. 2008. Joron: "Tabunka kyōsei" e no dōtei to shinjiyūshugi no jidai [Introduction: A journey to "multiculturalism and coexistence" and the era of neoliberalism]. In Paku, Ueno, Ito, and Cho 2008, 11-31.

Kawakami, Ikuo. 2001. *Ekkyōsuru kazoku: Zainichi Betonamukei jyūmin no seikatsu sekai* [Families crossing borders: Social world of Vietnamese residents in Japan]. Tokyo: Akashi Shoten.

Keane, Webb. 2003. Semiotics and the social analysis of material things. *Language and Communication* 23: 409–25.

Kerr, George H. 1958. *Okinawa: The history of an island people*. Rutland, Vt.: Tuttle.

Kimura, Yukiko. 1981. Social-historical background of the Okinawans in Hawai'i. In Okinawan Association of Hawai'i, Ethnic Studies Oral History Project, ed. *Uchinanchu: A history of Okinawans in Hawai'i*. Honolulu: Ethnic Studies Program, University of Hawai'i at Manoa. 51–71.

Kincheloe, Joe L. 2002. Foreward: Exploring a transformative multiculturalism — Justice in a zeitgeist of despair. In Carol Korn and Alberto Bursztyn, eds. *Rethinking multicultural education: Case studies in cultural transition*. Westport, Conn., and London: Bergin and Garvey, 2002. ix-xxv.

Kincheloe, Joe L., and Shirley R. Steinberg. 1997. *Changing multiculturalism*. Buckingham (UK): Open University Press.

King, Kendall A. 2000. Language ideologies and heritage language education. *International Journal of Bilingual Education and Bilingualism* 3 (3): 167–84.

Kirshenblatt-Gimblett, Barbara. 2006. World heritage and cultural economics. In Ivan Karp, Corinne A. Kratz, Lynn Szwaja, and Tomas Ybarra-Frausto, eds. *Museum frictions: Public cultures/global transformations*. Durham, N.C.: Duke University Press. 161–202.

Kitayama, Natsuki. 2004. Zainichi Betonamujin [Vietnamese residents in Japan]. In National Museum of Ethnology, ed. 2004, 100–4.

Komai, Hiroshi. 2006. Tabunka kyōsei shakai o dō kensetsu suruka [How to construct a society for multiculturalism and coexistence]. In Hiroshi Komai, *Gurōbaruka jidai no Nihongata tabunka kyōsei shakai* [A Japanese-style multicultural society for coexistence in a globalized era]. Tokyo: Akashi Shoten. 128–42.

Kondo, Dorrine K. 1990. *Crafting selves: Power, gender, and discourses of identity in a Japanese workplace*. Chicago and London: University of Chicago Press.

Korn, Carol. 2002. Introduction: Cultural transitions and curricular transformations. In Carol Korn and Alberto Bursztyn, eds. *Rethinking multicultural education: Case studies in cultural transition*. Westport, Conn., and London: Bergin and Garvey. 1–11.

Krashen, Stephen D. 1998. Language shyness and heritage language development. In Stephen D. Krashen, Lucy Tze and Jeff McQuillan, eds. *Heritage language development*. Culver City, Calif.: Language Education Associates. 41–49.

Kreamer, Christine Mullen. 2006. Shared heritage, contested terrain: Cultural negotiation and Ghana's Cape Coast Castle Museum exhibition, "Crossroads of people, crossroads of trade." In Ivan Karp, Corinne A. Kratz, Lynn Szwaja, and Tomas Ybarra-Frausto, eds. *Museum frictions: Public cultures/global transformations*. Durham, N.C.: Duke University Press. 435–68.

Kroskrity, Paul V. 2000. Regimenting languages: Language ideological perspective. In Paul V. Kroskrity, ed. *Regimes of language: Ideologies, polities, and identities*. Santa Fe, N.M.: School of American Research Press. 1–34.

Kulick, Don. 1992. *Language shift and cultural reproduction: Socialization, self, and syncretism in a Papua New Guinea village*. Cambridge: Cambridge University Press.

———. 1993. Growing up monolingual in a multilingual community: How language socialization patterns are leading to language shift in Gapun (Papua New Guinea). In Kenneth Hyltenstam and Åke Viberg, eds. *Progression and regression in language: Sociocultural, neuropsychological and linguistic perspectives*. Cambridge: Cambridge University Press. 94–121.

Kunimoto, Iyo. 1989. Boribia Nikkei shakai no genjō to mondai [Current situations of Nikkei Bolivian society and its problems]. *Kikan Kaigai Nikkeijin* 24 (May).

Kuraishi, Ichiro. 2007. Uchigawa kara kirisaku: "Zainichi" ni okeru namae/nanori mondai saikō [Ripping from inside: Reconsideration of the name issue for "Resident Koreans"]. In Ichiro Kuraishi, *Sabetsu to nichijō no keiken shakaigaku: Kaidoku suru "watashi" no kenkyūshi* [Empirical sociology of discrimination and everyday life: Research notes on "I" as a decoder]. Tokyo: Seikatsu shoin. 359–72.

Kymlicka, Will. 1995. *Multicultural citizenship: A liberal theory of minority rights*. Oxford: Clarendon Press.

Lan, Pei-Chia. 2003. They have more money but we speak better English: Transnational encounters between Filipina domestics and Taiwanese employers. *Identities* 10 (2): 132–61.

———. 2006. *Global Cinderellas: Migrant domestics and newly rich employers in Taiwan.* Durham, N.C.: Duke University Press.

Latour, Bruno. 1993. *We have never been modern.* Trans. Catherine Porter. Cambridge: Harvard University Press.

Lee, Yeounsuk. 1996. *"Kokugo" toiu shiso: Kindai Nihon no gengo ninshiki* [Philosophy called "national language": Language cognition of modern Japan]. Tokyo: Iwanami Shoten

Lee, Yuonsk.{check name} 1996. *Thought called "kokugo": Cognition of language in modern Japan* [Kokugo toiu Shisou: Kindai Nihon no gengo ninshiki]. Tokyo: Iwanami Shoten.

Lesser, Jeffrey, ed. 2003. *Searching for home abroad: Japanese Brazilians and transnationalism.* Durham: Duke University Press.

Leung, Constant, Roxy Harris, and Ben Rampton. 1997. The idealized native speaker, reified ethnicities, and classroom realities. *TESOL Quarterly* 31 (3): 543–60.

Li, Guofang. 2006. Biliteracy and trilingual practices in the home context: Case studies of Chinese-Canadian children. *Journal of Early Childhood Literacy* 6 (3): 355–81.

Lie, John. 2001. *Multiethnic Japan.* Cambridge: Harvard University Press.

Lim, Youngmi. 2009. Reinventing Korean roots and Zainichi routes: The invisible diaspora among naturalized Japanese of Korean descent. In Ryang and Lie, eds. 2009, 81–106.

Linger, Daniel Touro. 2001. *No one home: Brazilian selves remade in Japan.* Stanford: Stanford University Press.

Lionnet, Françoise, and Shu-mei Shih, eds. 2005. *Minor transnationalism.* Durham, N.C., and London: Duke University Press.

Lopez, David E. 1976. The social consequences of Chicano home/school bilingualism. *Social Problems* 24 (2): 234–46.

———. 1982. Vol. 4. *Language maintenance and shift in the United States today.* Los Alamitos, Calif.: National Center for Bilingual Research.

Lovejoy, Leo. 1986. *Explorations in Japanese sociolinguistics.* Amsterdam and Philadelphia: John Benjamins Publishing.

Lowe, Lisa. 1996. *Immigrant acts: On Asian American cultural politics.* Durham, N.C.: Duke University Press.

Lowenthal, David. 1994. Identity, heritage, and history. In Gillis, ed. 1994, 41–57.

Lumley, Robert. 2005. The debate on heritage reviewed. In Gerard Corsane, ed. *Heritage, museums and galleries: An introductory reader.* London: Routledge. 15–25.

Luykx, Aurolyn. 2003. Whose language is it anyway? Historical fetishism and the construction of expertise in Bolivian language planning. *Current Issues in Comparative Education.* 5 (2): 92–102.

Lynch, Andrew. 2003. The relationship between second and heritage language acquisition: Notes on research and theory building. *Heritage Language Journal* 1 (1): unpaged.

Manalansan, Martin. 2003. *Global divas: Filipino gay men in the diaspora.* Durham, N.C.: Duke University Press.

Mannheim, Bruce. 1991. *The language of the Inka since the European invasion.* Austin: University of Texas Press.

Martinez, Glenn A. 2003. Classroom based dialect awareness in heritage language instruction: A critical applied linguistics approach. *Heritage Language Journal* 1 (1): http://www.heritage languages.org/ (accessed 11 February 2010).

Mashiko, Hidenori. 2003. *Ideologii to shite no "Nihon": "Kokugo," "Nihonshi" no chishiki shakaigaku* ["Japan" as an ideology: Sociology of knowledge of "national language," "Japanese history"]. Sangensha: Tokyo.

Masuda, Yoshio, and Toshio Yanagida. 1999. *Peru: Taiheiyō to Andes no Kuni* (Peru: A Pacific and Andean Country. Tokyo: Chuo Koron Shinsha

May, Stephen. 2001. *Language and minority rights: Ethnicity, nationalism and the politics of language.* Harlow: Pearson Education.

McGray, Douglas. 2002. Japan's gross national cool. *Foreign Policy.* May/June. 44–54.

Meek, Barbra. 2010. *We are our language: An ethnography of language revitalization in the Yukon Territory, Canada.* Tucson: University of Arizona Press.

MEXT 2008. *Kaigai-de manabu nihon-no kodomotachi: Wagakuni-no genjō* [Japanese children overseas: Present situation in our country]. Tokyo: MEXT. January.

Miller, Andrew R. 1982. *Japan's modern myth: The language and beyond.* New York: Weatherhill.

Miller, Laura. 2003. Consuming Japanese print media in Chicago. In Marcia Farr, ed. *Ethnolinguistic Chicago: Language and literacy in Chicago's neighborhoods.* Mahwah, N.J.: Lawrence Erlbaum.

———. 2010. Japan-related linguistic intervention. *Critical Asian Studies* 42 (2): 239–46.

Miller, Laura, and Ralph Ginsberg. 1995. Folklinguistic theories of language learning. In Barbara F. Freed, ed. *Second language acquisition in a study abroad context.* Amsterdam: John Benjamins.

Milroy, James, and Lesley Milroy. {check note}1991 (1985). *Authority in language: Investigating language prescription and standardization.* London: Routledge.

Milroy, James, and Lesley Milroy. 1999 (1985). *Authority in language: Investigating standard English.* New York: Routledge.

Ministry of Internal Affairs and Communications (MIC). 2006. *Tabunka kyōsei no suishin ni kansuru kenkyūkai hōkokusho: Chiiki ni okeru tabunka kyōsei no suishin ni mukete* [Study Group on the Promotion of Multiculturalism and Coexistence's report: Toward the promotion of multiculturalism and coexistence in local society]. Available online at http://www.soumu.go.jp/kokusai/pdf/sonota_b5.pdf (accessed 9 October 2007).

Minzoku sabetsu to tatakau Ōsaka renraku kyōgikai. 1992. *Hansabetsu to jinken no minzoku kyōiku o* [Ethnic education for anti-descrimination and human rights]. Osaka: Minzoku sabetsu to tatakau Ōsaka renraku kyōgikai.

Miyagi, Eishō. 1968. *Okinawa no rekishi* [History of Okinawa]. Tokyo: Nihon Hōsō Kyōkai.

Miyajima, Takashi, and Hiromasa Kano, eds. 2002. *Henyōsuru Nihonshakai to bunka* [Changes in Japanese Culture and Society]. Tokyo: Tōkyō daigaku shuppankai.

Moerman, Michael. 1965. Ethnic identity in a complex civilization: Who are the Lue? *American Anthropologist* 67 (5): 1215–30.

Molasky, Michael. 2003. Medoruma Shun: The writer as public intellectual in Okinawa today. In Hein and Selden 2003b. 161–91.

Moore, Donald S., Jake Kosek, and Anand Pandian. 2003. Introduction. The cultural politics of race and nature: Terrains of power and practices. In Donald S. Moore, Jake Kosek, and Anand Pandian, eds. *Race, nature, and the politics of difference.* Durham and London: Duke University Press, 2003. 1–70.

Mori, Kōichi. 1998. Dai-ichi Okinawa ijūchi ni okeru kyōiku to gakkou no rekishiteki tenkai [Historical development of education and schools in Colonia Okinawa Uno]. In Hideshi Ohashi, ed. *Nanbei Boribia no Okinawa mura: Imin no shakai-shinrigaku-teki kenkyū* [Okinawan village in Bolivia, South America: A social psychological study of immigrants]. Sendai, Japan: Shinrigaku Kenkyū-shitsu, Bungaku-bu, Tōhoku Daigaku (Department of Psychology, Faculty of Arts and Letters, Tohoku University). 101–16.

Mori, Minoru. 1990. Shakaiteki tachiba no jikaku to gakkō: Buraku mondai kara no shiten [Awareness of social location and schools: From a perspective of Buraku issues]. In Nagao, Akio, and Hiroshi Ikeda, eds. 1990, 193-217.

Morimoto, Amelia. 2002. Peruvian Nikkei: A Sociopolitical portrait. In L.R. Hirabayashi et al., eds. *New worlds, new lives: Globalization and people of Japanese descent in the Americas and from Latin America in Japan.* Stanford: Stanford University Press. 141–58.

Morimoto, Toyotomi. 1997. *Japanese Americans and cultural continuity: Maintaining language and heritage.* New York and London: Garland Publishing.

Morris-Suzuki, Tessa. 1998. *Re-inventing Japan: Time, space, nation.* Armonk, N.Y.: M.E. Sharpe.

Moscardo, Gianna. 1996. Mindful visitors: Heritage and tourism. *Annals of Tourism Research* 23 (2): 376–97.

Moses, Michele S. 2000. Why bilingual education policy is needed: A philosophical response to the critics. *Bilingual Research Journal* 24 (4): 334–54.

Mouer, Ross and Yoshio Sugimoto. 1986. *Images of Japanese society.* London: Routledge.

Mukai, Kiyoshi. 1992. Sotetsu jigoku [Sotetsu palm hell]. In Ryukyu Shimpō-sha, ed. *Shin Ryūkyū-shi* [New Ryūkyū history]. Naha, Japan: Ryukyu Shimpō-sha. 191–213.

Nagao, Akio, and Hiroshi Ikeda, eds. 1990. *Gakkō bunka: Shinsō e no paasupekutibu* [School culture: A perspective to its underlying stratum]. Tokyo: Tō shindō.

Nakajima, Kazuko. 2003. Mondai teiki JHL no wakugumi to kadai – JSL/JFL to dō chigauka [Proposal: The framework of JHL and agenda – the difference of JSL/JFL]. Bogo, keishōgo, bairingaru kyōiku kenkyūkai. Available online at http://www.mhb.jp/2003/08/jhljsljfl.html (accessed 29 April 2008).

Nakasone, Robert Y. 2002. An impossible possibility. In Robert Y. Nakasone, ed. *Okinawan diaspora.* Honolulu: University of Hawai'i Press. 3–25.

Nakayama, Mitsuru, et al. 1986. *Nanbei ni okeru Okinawa-ken shusshin imin ni kansuru chirigaku-teki kenkyū II: Boribia, Burajiru* [Geographic research on the Okinawan immigrants in South America. Part II: Bolivia, Brazil]. Naha, Japan: Ryūkyū Daigaku Houbun Gakubu Chirigaku Kyōshitsu (Division of Geography, Faculty of Law and Letters, the University of the Ryukyus).

National Museum of Ethnology, ed. 2004. *Taminzoku Nihon: Zanichi gaikokujin no kurashi* [Multiethnic Japan: Life and history of immigrants]. Osaka: National Museum of Ethnology.

Neary, Ian. 1997. Burakumin in contemporary Japan. In Weiner, ed. 1997, 50–78.

Nichibo Kyōkai (Okinawa Nihon-Boribia Kyōkai). 1985. Okinawa-ken kyoikuchō Yonemura Yukimasa-shi, kyōku iinkai shidou shuji Shimada Kenmatsu-shi tono kyōiku kondan-kai [A roundtable discussion on education with Mr. Yonemura Yukimasa, education minister, and Mr. Shimada Kenmatsu, Education Committee chair of Okinawa Prefecture]. Colonia Okinawa, Santa Cruz, Bolivia: Okinawa Nihon-Boribia Kyōkai.

———. 1998. 1998 Nen-do yosan-sho [1998 annual budget]. Colonia Okinawa, Santa Cruz, Bolivia: Okinawa Nihon-Boribia Kyōkai.

Nippert-Eng, Christena. 1996. *Home and work: Negotiating boundaries through everyday life.* Chicago: University of Chicago Press.

Nukaga, Misako. 2003. Japanese education in an era of internationalization: A case study of an emerging multicultural coexistence model. *International Journal of Japanese Sociology* 12 (1): 79–94.

Nuryanti, Wiendu. 1996. Heritage and postmodern tourism. *Annals of Tourism Research* 23 (2): 249–60.

Ogawa, Yuki. 2008. Zainichi, "shinjūmin" no chikara ni – gakkō no fuan, aidentitī no yure. "Onaji kurushimi, nidoto." [Resident Koreans want to give assistance to "new residents": Anxiety at school, identity struggles, "No more same pain"]. *Asahi Shimbun,* 19 March.

Oguma, Eiji. 1995. *Tannitsu minzoku shinwa no kigen* [The origin of the myth of homogeneous nation]. Tokyo: Shinyōsha.

———. 1998. *"Nihonjin" no kyōkai: Okinawa, Ainu, Taiwan, Chōsen shokuminchi-shihai kara fukki undō made* [The boundaries of the "Japanese": From colonial rule of Okinawa, Ainu, Taiwan, Korea to reversion movements]. Tokyo: Shin'yō-sha.

Ohnuki-Tierney, Emiko. 1993. *Rice as self: Japanese identities through time.* Princeton, N.J.: Princeton University Press.

Okinawa Daiichi Nichibo-kou. 1998. *1998 nen-do shūshi yosan-sho* [Annual budget plan for 1998]. Colonia Okinawa, Santa Cruz, Bolivia: Okinawa Daiichi Nichibo Gakkou (CBJ).

———. 2001. Kyōku keikaku [Education plan]. Colonia Okinawa, Santa Cruz, Bolivia: Okinawa Daiichi Nichibo Gakkou.

Okubo, Yuko. 2005. "Visible" minorities and "invisible" minorities: An ethnographic study of multicultural education and the production of ethnic "others" in Japan. PhD diss. (University of California, Berkeley).

Okubo, Yuko. 2010. Heritage: Owned or assigned? The cultural politics of teaching heritage language in Osaka, Japan. *Critical Asian Studies* 42 (1): 111–38.

Olwig, Karen Fog. 1999. The burden of heritage: Claiming a place for a West Indian culture. *American Ethnologist* 26 (2): 370–88.

Oshiro, Masayasu. 1992. *Ryūkyū seifu* [Ryūkyū government]. Naha, Japan: Hirugi-sha.
Osterweil, Marc J. 1998. The economic and social conditions of Jewish and Arab immigrants in Bolivia, 1890–1980. In Ignacio Klich and Jeffrey Lesser, eds. *Arab and Jewish immigrants in Latin America*. London: Frank Cass. 146–66.
Ota, Haruo. 2000. *Nyuukamaa no kodomo to Nihon no gakkō* [Newcomer children and Japanese schools]. Tokyo: Kokusai shoin.
Ota, Masahide. 1999. Re-examining the history of the battle of Okinawa. In Johnson 1999. 13–37.
Paku, Chonsoku, Chizuko Ueno, Akira Ito, and Kyonhi Cho. 2008. *Nihon ni okeru tabunka kyōsei towa nanika: "Zainichi" no keiken kara* [What is multiculturalism and coexistence in Japan? From the experience of "Zainichi"]. Tokyo: Shinyōsha.
Pavlenko, Aneta. 2002. "We have room for but one language here": Language and national identity in the US at the turn of the twentieth century. *Multilingua: Journal of Cross-Cultural and Interlanguage Communication* 21, 163–96.
Pavlenko, Aneta, and Adrian Blackledge. 2004. *Negotiation of identities in multilingual contexts*. Clevedon (UK): Multilingual Matters.
Peattie, Mark R. 1988. *Nan'yō: The rise and fall of the Japanese in Micronesia, 1885–1945*. Honolulu: University of Hawai'i Press.
Peyton, Joy Kreeft, Donald A. Ranard, and Scott McGinnis. 2001*. Charting a new course: Heritage language education in the United States. In Peyton et al., eds., 2001. 3–26.
Peyton, Joy Kreeft, Donald A. Ranard, and Scott McGinnis, eds. 2001*. *Heritage language in America: Preserving a national resource*. McHenry, Ill.: Center for Applied Linguistics and Delta Systems.
Phillipson, Robert, Mart Rannut, and Tove Skutnabb-Kangas. 1995. Introduction. In Tove Skutnabb-Kangas and Robert Phillipson, eds. *Linguistic human rights: Overcoming linguistic discrimination*. Berlin: Mouton de Gruyter. 1–24.
Portes, Alejandro, and Richard Schauffler. 1994. Language and the second generation: Bilingualism yesterday and today. *International Migration Review* 28 (4): 640–61.
Povinelli, Elizabeth. 2002. *The cunning of recognition: Indigenous alterities and the making of Australian multiculturalism*. Durham, N.C., and London: Duke University Press.
Prentice, Richard. 2005. Heritage: A key sector in the "new" tourism. In Gerard Corsane, ed. *Heritage, museums, and galleries: An introductory reader*. London: Routledge. 243–56.
Rabson, Steve. 2003. Memories of Okinawa: Life and times in the greater Osaka diaspora. In Hein and Selden 2003b. 99–134.
Reyes, Angela, and Adrienne Lo, eds. 2008. *Beyond yellow: Toward a linguistic anthropology of Asian Pacific America*. Oxford and New York: Oxford University Press.
Richter, Linda K. 2005. The politics of heritage tourism development: Emerging issues for the new millenium. In Gerard Corsane, ed. *Heritage, museums, and galleries: An introductory reader*. London: Routledge. 257–71.
Robertson, Jennifer. 2002. Blood talks: Eugenic modernity and the creation of new Japanese. *History and Anthropology* 13 (2): 191–216.

———. 2005. Biopower: Blood, kinship, and eugenic marriage. In Jennifer Robertson, ed. *A companion to the anthropology of Japan*. Malden: Blackwell. 329–54

———. Forthcoming. Blood – in all its senses – as a cultural resource. In Shinji Yamashita and Jeremy Eades, eds. *Cultural resources*. Asian Anthropologies Series. Oxford: Berghahn Press.

Roth, Joshua H. 2002. *Brokered homeland: Japanese Brazilian migrants in Japan*. Ithaca, N.Y.: Cornell University Press.

Ryang, Sonia. 2008. *Writing selves in diaspora: Ethnography of autobiographies of Korean women in Japan and the United States*. Lanham, Md.: Lexington Books.

Ryang, Sonia, and John Lie, eds. 2009. *Diaspora without homeland: Being Korean in Japan*. Berkeley, Los Angeles, and London: University of California Press.

Safran, William. 2005. Introduction: The political aspects of language. In William Safran and Jean Al. Laponce, eds. *Language, ethnic identity, and the state*. London and New York: Routledge.

Sakai, Naoki. 1997. *Translation and subjectivity: On Japan and cultural nationalism*. Minneapolis: University of Minnesota Press.

———. 2005*. Introduction: Nationality and the politics of the "mother tongue." In Naoki Sakai, Brett de Bary, and Toshio Iyotani, eds. *Deconstructing nationality*. Ithaca, N.Y.: Cornell University Press, 2005. (First published in Japanese in 1996.) 1–38.

Sakihara, Mitsugu. 1981. History of Okinawa. In United Okinawan Association of Hawai'i, Ethnic Studies Oral History Project, ed. *Uchinanchu: A history of Okinawans in Hawai'i*. Honolulu: Ethnic Studies Program, University of Hawai'i at Manoa. 3–22.

San Juan, Epifanio, Jr. 2002. *Racism and cultural studies: Critiques of multiculturalist ideologies and the politics of difference*. Durham, N.C.: Duke University Press.

Sato, Gunei. 1997. *Kaigai/kikoku shijyo kyoiku no saikochiku-ibunkakan kyoikugaku no shiten kara* [Reconstruction of education of overseas/returnee children: From the perspective of cross-cultural education]. Tokyo: Tamagawa University Press.

Sato, Gunei, and Kataoka Hiroko. 2008. *Amerika de Sodatsu Nihon no Kodomotachi* [Japanese children growing up in America]. Tokyo: Akashi Shoten.

Schieffelin, Bambi, and Elinor Ochs, eds. 1986. *Language socialization across cultures*. Cambridge: Cambridge University Press.

Shankar, Shalini. 2008. Speaking like a model minority: "FOB" styles, gender, and racial meanings among Desi teens in Silicon Valley. *Journal of Linguistic Anthropology* 18 (2): 268–89.

Shimizu, Kokichi. 2002. Gakkō sekai no tabunkaka: Nihon no gakkō wa dō kawaruka [School world becoming multicultural: How will Japanese schools change?]. In Miyajima and Kano, eds. 2002, 69–92.

Shimizu, Kokichi. ed. 2008. *Kōkō o ikiru nyuukamaa: Ōsaka furitsu kōkō ni miru kyōiku shien* [Newcomers in high school: Educational assistance of Osaka prefectural high schools]. Tokyo: Akashi Shoten.

Silver, Peter C. 2003. *Our spiritual center: Language ideology and personhood at a Chinese community heritage language school*. PhD diss., University of Massachusetts–Amherst.

Silverstein, Michael. 1979. Language structure and linguistic ideology. In P.R. Clynem et al., eds. *The elements: A parasession on linguistic units and levels*. Chicago: Chicago Linguistic Society. 219–59.

———. 2003. The when's and where's — as well as how's — of ethnolinguistic recognition. *Public Culture* 15 (3): 531–57.

Skutnabb-Kangas, Tove, and Robert Phillipson. 1989. "Mother tongue": The theoretical and sociopolitical construction of a concept. In Ulrich Ammon, ed. *Status and function of languages and language varieties*. Berlin: Walter de Gruyter. 450–77.

Smith, Laurajane. 2006. *Uses of heritage*. London: Routledge.

Smith, Paul. 1988. *Discerning the subject*. Minneapolis: University of Minnesota Press.

Sridhar, Kamal K. 1988. Language maintenance and language shift among Asian-Indians: Kannadigas in the New York area. *International Journal of the Sociology of Language*. 69: 73–88.

Stephenson, Marcia. 1999. *Gender and modernity in Andean Bolivia*. Austin, Tx.: University of Texas Press.

Stone, Peter. 2005. Presenting the past: A framework for discussion. In Gerard Corsane, ed. *Heritage, museums, and galleries: An introductory reader*. London: Routledge. 215–27.

Sugimoto, Yoshio. 1999. Making sense of nihonjinron. *Thesis Eleven* 57 (1): 81–96.

Suzuki, Taku. 2006. Becoming "Japanese" in Bolivia: Okinawan-Bolivian trans(national) formations in Colonia Okinawa. *Identities* 13: 455–81.

———. 2007. Blue-collar *patrones*: Transnational Okinawan-Bolivians in Bolivia and Japan. In A. Asgharzadeh et al., eds. *Diasporic ruptures: Globality, migrancy, and expressions of identity*. Vol. I. Rotterdam, Netherlands: Sense Publishers. 69–90.

———. 2010. Learning to be transnational: Japanese language education for Bolivia's Okinawan diaspora. *Critical Asian Studies* 42 (1): 63–88.

———. Forthcoming. *Embodying belonging: Racializing Okinawan diaspora in Bolivia and Japan*. Honolulu: University of Hawai'i Press.

Tai, Eika. 2006. Korean activism and ethnicity in the changing ethnic landscape of urban Japan. *Asian Studies Review* 30 (1): 41-58.

Takamori, Ayako. 2010. Rethinking Japanese American "heritage" in the homeland. *Critical Asian Studies* 42 (2): 217–38.

Takato, Michiyo. 2008. Okinawa Nikkei diaspora, Kokugo, gakko: Kotoba no ishu konton sei to tan-itsu-ka no minzokushi-teki kousatsu [Okinawa *Nikkei* diaspora, national language, and school: Ethnographical discussion of hybridity of language and unification]. In Shinji Sato and Neriko Doerr, eds. *Bunka, kotoba, kyoiku: Nihongo/Nihon no kyouiku no "hyoujun" wo koete* (Culture, language, education: Beyond the "standard" of education in Japanese/Japan). Tokyo: Akashi-Shoten. 267–92.

———. 2009. "Native speaker" status on border-crossing: Okinawan *Nikkei* diaspora, national language, heterogeneity." In Doerr, ed. 2009.

Takenaka, Ayumi. 2003. The mechanisms of ethnic retention: Later-generation Japanese immigrants in Lima, Peru. *Journal of Ethnic and Migration Studies* 29 (3): 467–83.

Tamanoi, Mariko. 2000. A road to "A redeemed mankind": The politics of memory among the former Japanese peasant settlers in Manchuria. *South Atlantic Quarterly* 99 (1): 163-89.

———. 2003. Between colonial racism and global capitalism: Japanese repatriates from northeast China since 1946. *American Ethnologist* 39 (4): 527-39.

Tanabe, Shigeharu, ed. 1989. *Jinruigakuteki ninshiki no bōken: Ideorogī to purakutisu* [The adventure of anthropological recognition: Ideology and practice]. Tokyo: Dōbunkan.

Tavares, Antonio (Tony) J. 2000. From heritage to international languages: Globalism and Western Canadian trends in heritage language education. *Canadian Ethnic Studies Journal* 3 (1): 1–13.

Taylor, Charles. 1994. The politics of recognition. In David Theo Goldberg, ed. *Multiculturalism: A critical reader.* Oxford: Blackwell. 75–106.

Toda, Yoshiko. 2001. *Nihon no Betonamujin komyuniti: Issei no jidai, soshite ima* [Vietnamese community in Japan: First-generation and now]. Tokyo: Akatsukiin Shokan.

Tomiyama, Ichirō. 1990. *Kindai Nihon shakai to "Okinawa-jin": "Nihon-jin" ni naru to iukoto* [Modern Japanese society and "Okinawans": On becoming "Japanese"]. Tokyo: Nihon Keizai Hyōron-sha.

———. 1997. Colonialism and the sciences of the tropical zone: The academic analysis of difference in "the island peoples." In Tani E. Barlow, ed. *Formations of colonial modernity in East Asia*. Durham, N.C.: Duke University Press. 199–221.

———. 2002. The "Japanese" of Micronesia: Okinawans in the Nan'yō Islands. In Robert Y. Nakasone, ed. *Okinawan diaspora*. Honolulu: University of Hawai'i Press. 57–70.

Tomoni. 2002. *Nyūsu tokubetsu-gō* [News Special Issues].

———. 2005. *"Ibunka rūtsu no kodomotachi no jinzai ikusei jigyō" hōkokusho: Ruutsu-go shūtoku no kanōsei o motomeru torikumi ni tsuite* [Report on "The project to train talented persons of the children with roots on different cultures": A program for pursuing the possibility of learning one's root languages].

Toyama, Henry, and Kiyoshi Ikeda. 1981. The Okinawan-Naichi Relationship. In United Okinawan Association of Hawai'i. Ethnic Studies Oral History Project, ed. *Uchinanchu: A history of Okinawans in Hawai'i.* Honolulu: Ethnic Studies Program, University of Hawai'i at Manoa. 127–42.

Truettner, William H. 2008. Museums and historical amnesia. In Daniel J. Sherman, ed. *Museums and difference*. Bloomington: Indiana University Press. 354–74.

Tsing, Anna. 2005. *Friction: An ethnography of global connection*. Princeton, N.J.: Princeton University Press.

Tsuda, Takeyuki. 2003. *Strangers in the ethnic homeland: Japanese Brazilian return migration in transnational perspective*. New York: Columbia University Press.

Tsujimoto, Masahiro. 1998. Nihon ni okeru Okinawa ijūchi shusshin-sha no tenkai [Trajectories of the migrants from Colonia Okinawa in Japan]. In Hideshi

Ohashi, ed. *Nanbei Boribia no Okinawa mura: Imin no shakai-shinrigaku-teki kenkyū* [Okinawan village in Bolivia, South America: A social psychological study of immigrants]. Sendai, Japan: Shinrigaku Kenkyū-shitsu, Bungaku-bu, Tōhoku Daigaku (Department of Psychology, Faculty of Arts and Letters, Tohoku University). 311–34.

Tsujimoto, Masahiro. 1999. Imin no kyōdōtai hensei ni kansuru shakai-shinrigaku-teki kenkyū: Okinawa-kei Boribia imin no Nanbei to Nihon ni okeru tenkai [A social psychological study on formation of an immigrant community: Trajectories of Okinawan-Bolivians in South America and in Japan]. PhD diss. (Tohoku University).

Tunbridge, J.E., and G.J. Ashworth. 1996. From history to heritage. In J.E. Tunbridge and G.J. Ashworth. *Dissonant heritage: The management of the past as a resource in conflict.* Chichester, New York, Brisbane, Toronto, Singapore: John Wiley and Sons, 1996. 1–19.

Turner, Terence. 1993. Anthropology and multiculturalism: What is anthropology that multiculturalists should be mindful of it? *Cultural Anthropology* 8 (4): 411–29.

Uchibori, Motomitsu. 1989. Minzokuron memorandamu [Notes on the theories on ethnicity]. In Tanabe 1989, 27–43.

Ueunten, Wesley. 2002. Japanese Latin American internment from an Okinawan perspective. In Robert Y. Nakasone, ed. *Okinawan diaspora.* Honolulu: University of Hawai'i Press. 90–111.

Upham, Frank K. 1987. Instrumental violence and the struggle for Buraku Liberation. In Frank K. Upham, *Law and social change in postwar Japan.* Cambridge, Mass., and London: Harvard University Press. 78–123.

Valdés, Guadalupe. 1981. Pedagogical implications of teaching Spanish to the Spanish-speaking in the United States. In Guadalupe Valdés, Anthony G. Lozano, and Rodolfo Garcia-Moya, eds. *Teaching Spanish to the Hispanic bilingual: Issues, aims, and methods.* New York: Teachers College Press. 3–20.

———. 2001. Heritage language students: Profiles and possibilities. In J.K. Peyton et al., eds. *Language in America: Preserving a national resource.* McHenry, Ill.: Center for Applied

Varenne, Hervé, and Ray McDermott. 1999. Successful failure: The school America builds. Boulder, Colo.: Westview Press.

Waters, Mary C., and Tomás R. Jiménez. 2005. Assessing immigrant assimilation: New empirical and theoretical challenges. *Annual Review of Sociology* 31: 105–25.

Weiner, Michael. 1994. *Race and migration in imperial Japan.* New York: Routledge.

———. 2009 (1997). "Self" and "other" in imperial Japan. In Michael Wiener, ed. *Japan's minorities: The illusion of homogeneity.* New York: Routledge. 1–20.

Weiner, Michael, ed. 1997. *Japan's minorities: The illusion of homogeneity.* London and New York: Routledge.

Weismantel, Mary J. 2001. *Cholas and Pishtacos: Stories of race and sex in the Andes.* Chicago: University of Chicago Press.

Wells, Amy Stuart, and Irene Serna. 1996. The politics of culture: Understanding local political resistance to detracking in racially mixed schools. *Harvard Educational Review* 66 (1): 93–118.

Wiley, Terrence, and Guadalupe Valdes{check accent and date}. 2000. Editors' Introduction. Heritage language instruction in the United States: A time for renewal. *Bilingual Research Journal* 24 (4): i–v.

Wiley, Terrence, and Guadalupe Valdes{check accent and date}.. 2001. Editors' introduction: Heritage language instruction in the United States: A time for renewal. *Bilingual Research Journal* 24 (4): i–iv.

Wilkinson, Doris. 2000. Rethinking the concept of "minority": A task for social scientists and practitioners. *Journal of Sociology and Social Welfare* 27 (1): 115–32.

Willis, David Blake, and Stephen Murphy-Shigematsu, eds. 2008. *Transcultural Japan: At the borderlands of race, gender, and identity.* London and New York: Routledge.

Wolf, Eric R. 1994. Perilous ideas: Race, culture, people. *Current Anthropology* 35 (1): 1–7.

Woolard, Kathryn. 1998. Introduction: Language ideology as a field of inquiry. In Bambi Schieffelin, Kathryn Woolard, and Paul Kroskrity, eds. *Language ideologies: Practice and theory.* New York: Oxford University Press. 3–50.

Wright, Stephen C., and Donald M. Taylor. 1995. Identity and the language of the classroom: Investigating the impact of heritage versus second language instruction on personal and collective self-esteem. *Journal of Educational Psychology* 87 (2): 241–52.

Yamasaki, Yuri. 2010. Conflicted attitudes toward heritage: Heritage language learning of returnee adolescents from Japan at a nikkei school in Lima, Peru. *Critical Asian Studies* 42 (1): 89–110.

Yamasaki, Yuri. 2010. Conflicted attitudes toward heritage: Heritage language learning of returnee adolescents from Japan at a nikkei school in Lima, Peru. *Critical Asian Studies* 42 (1): 89–110.

Yamawaki, Chikako. 1996. Katararenai bunka no bekutoru: Okinawa-kei/Nikkei Peru-jin no bunka hen'yō [Vector of unspoken culture: Cultural transformations among Okinawan-/Nikkei Peruvians]. In Toshio Iyotani and Tōru Sugihara, eds. *Nihon shakai to imin* [Japanese society and immigrants]. Tokyo: Akashi Shoten. 201–39.

Yamawaki, Keizo. 2003. Chihō jichitai no gaikokujin shisaku ni kansuru hihanteki kōsatsu [Critical examination of the policies for foreigners of the local governments]. *Meiji Daigaku Shakai Kagaku Kenkyūjo Discussion Paper Series* [Meiji University Institute of Social Sciences Discussion Paper Series] No. J-2003-10.

Yasuda, Toshiaki. 1999. *"Kokugo" to "hōgen" no aida: Gengo kōchiku no seijigaku* [Between "national language" and "dialects": Politics of language construction]. Tokyo: Jinbun Shoin.

———. 2003. *Datsu "Nihongo" e no shiza* [Perspectives towards post–"Japanese language"]. Tokyo: Sangensha.

Yoshino, Kosaku. 1997. The discourse on blood and racial identity in contemporary Japan. In Frank Dikötter, ed. *The construction of racial identities in China and Japan.* Honolulu: University of Hawai'i Press. 199–212.

Zhou, Min, and Carl L. Bankston III. 1998. *Growing up American: How Vietnamese children adapt to life in the United States.* New York: Russell Sage Foundation.

❏

Contributors

Neriko Doerr received a PhD in cultural anthropology from Cornell University. She currently teaches cultural anthropology at Ramapo College (Mahwah, N.J.). Her recent publications include "Meaningful Inconsistencies: Bicultural Nationhood, Free Market, and Schooling in Aotearoa/New Zealand," "The Native Speaker Concept: Ethnographic Investigations of Native Speaker Effects" (as the editor), "Global Structures of Common Difference, Cultural Objectification, and their Subversions: Cultural Politics in an Aotearoa/New Zealand School" (in the journal *Identities: Global Studies in Culture and Power*). nm22@cornell.edu.

Kiri Lee is associate professor of Japanese at Lehigh University (Bethlehem, Penn.). She received her PhD in linguistics from Harvard University in 1993. Her expertise is linguistic pragmatics, and her recent publication in pragmatics is "*Wakaranai* as 'I Don't Know': An Analysis from Territory of Information Theory," in Susumu Kuno, Seiichi Makino, and Susan Strauss, eds. *Aspects of Japanese Linguistics* (Tokyo: Kuroshio Publisher, 2007). 87–107. She is also involved in building a heritage language program at a weekend school in New Jersey, and coauthored with Neriko Musha Doerr "Contesting Heritage: Language, Legitimacy, and Schooling at a Weekend Japanese Language School in the United States," *Language and Education* 23 (5): 425–41. 2009. Email: kjl2@lehigh.edu.

Barbra A. Meek (PhD, University of Arizona, 2001) is associate professor of anthropology and linguistics at the University of Michigan. Her book *We Are Our Language: An Ethnography of Language Revitalization in the Yukon Territory, Canada* is forthcoming from the University of Arizona Press. bameek@umich.edu.

Laura Miller is the Eiichi Shibusawa-Seigo Arai Professor of Japanese Studies at the University of Missouri-St. Louis. She is the author of *Beauty Up: Exploring Contemporary Japanese Body Aesthetics* (University of California Press, 2006) and coeditor of *Manners and Mischief: Gender, Power, and Etiquette in Japan* (University of California Press, forthcoming). millerlau@umsl.edu

Yuko Okubo is an Abe Fellow and associate specialist of the Center for Japanese Studies, University of California, Berkeley. She has published on the cultural politics of minority education in Osaka, Japan. Her publications include "The Localization of Multicultural Education and the Reproduction of 'Native Speaker' Concept in Japan" in *The Native Speaker Concept: Ethnographic Investigations of Native Speaker Effects* (Mouton de Gruyter, 2009), and "'Newcomers' in Public Education: Chinese and Vietnamese Children in a Buraku Community," in *Multiculturalism in the New Japan: Crossing the Boundaries Within* (Berghahn Books, 2008). yukoo@sbcglobal.net.

Taku Suzuki was trained as an anthropologist and is currently Assistant Professor of International Studies at Denison University in Granville, Ohio. He is the author of "Viewing Nations, Narrating Hybridity: Okinawan Diasporic Subjectivity and Japanese Satellite Telecasts in Colonia Okinawa, Bolivia," in *Diaspora: A Journal of Transnational Studies* (2005), "Becoming 'Japanese' in Bolivia: Okinawan-Bolivian Trans(national)formations in Colonia Okinawa," in *Identities: Global Studies in Culture and Power* (2006), and *Embodying Belonging: Racializing Okinawan Diaspora in Bolivia and Japan* (University of Hawai'i Press, forthcoming 2010), among others. takusuzuki71@hotmail.com.

Ayako Takamori is a PhD candidate in socio-cultural anthropology at New York University. Her dissertation, "Native Foreigners: Japanese Americans in Japan," addresses the relationship between Japanese American return migration and constructions of ethnic and national identity. ayako.takamori@nyu.edu.

Krista E. Van Vleet is associate professor of anthropology and director of the Latin American Studies Program at Bowdoin College in Brunswick, Maine. Her research focuses on gender and family in the Andean region and on narrative analysis of everyday interactions. Her most recent book is *Performing Kinship: Narrative, Gender and the Intimacies of Power in the Andes* (Texas, 2008). kvanvlee@bowdoin.edu.

Yuri Yamasaki is a PhD candidate of anthropology and education at Teachers College, Columbia University. She has been conducting research on Japanese descendants in Peru since 2001. Her research interests include youth and popular culture, language education, and language and identity of diasporas. Email: yuryam@gmail.com.

❏

Index

aboriginal or indigenous languages, heritage language and, 118; (in Canada), 117
agentive use of language, 113
Agrarian Reform Law (1953), 19
Ainu, 106
alterity, 98, 101; Japanese Americans and, 102
Althusser, Louis, 65
ancestral root language, 108, 118
Andean region, 109
anime, 91
announcing one's names (*nanori*), 61
assimilation, language shift and, 86; preferences of immigrant and ethic minority children and, 60; pressures and, 101
authentic heritage, assumptions about, 42
authentic language, 104
awareness of social location (*shakaiteki tachiba no jikaku*), 55
Aymara, 110

Balibar, Etienne, 3
Basque, 114
Battle of Okinawa, 11
bi/multilingualism, 4
biculturalism, 91
bilingual and multilingual skills, perceived values of, 31, 107
bilingual education (in the USA), debates about, 91
Bilingual Education Act (USA, 1968), 118
bilingualism, ethnic communities and, 90, 110
blancos (in Bolivia), 23
blood, discourses about, 92, 93; ideology of in Japan, 93
blood, race, nation, and culture, elision of, 92
blood/ethnicity, language and, 89

Bolivia, 110; Okinawan immigrant settlement in, 8, 109
Bolivians of Japanese descent (Boribia Nikkeijin), 14
boundaries (in Japan), ethnic minorities/foreigners and, 62
boundary maintenance practices, 22
boundary work, 8, 18, 21
Bourdieu, Pierre, 3, 41, 65
Brazil, Okinawan émigrés in, 11
Buraku (burakumin), 47, 111
Buraku and Korean communities, relations between, 50
Buraku Liberation League (BLL), 49
Butler, Judith, 65

Canadian Education Association, 117
Canadian languages (official), 117
CEA. *See* Colegio El Agustino
Center for Applied Linguistics (CAL), 119
Center School (*sentaa-kō*) of the Area for the Promotion of Educating and Receiving Foreign Children (*gaikokujin shijo kyōiku ukeire suishin chiiki*), 53
chōki-taizai, 68
childhood language, rejection of, 103
children, as language learners, 113
Chinese residents (in Japan), 111
chūzai, 68
Civil Rights Movement (in USA), 118
class and language, maintenance of, 89
code of speech, 31
codes (language), function of, 32
code-switching, 5, 111, 112
Colegio El Agustino (CEA), 27, 109; preservation of Japanese heritage and, 33
collective ethnic and national identity, heritage and, 43
Colonia Okinawa, 9, 109; Colonia Uno, 12; Colonia Dos, 12; Colonia Trés, 12
Colonia Okinawa, class differences in, 13; ethnic differences in, 13; Japanese

assistance and, 12; Japanese language education in, 9, 20
Colonia Okinawa hospital, Japanese government support for, 18
Colonia-born youth, migration of, 20
colonial heritage languages, 119
community education center (Tomoni, in Miyako), 49
community language, 7
Compulsory Land Expropriation order, 12
conventionalization, 116
Cool Japan, 91
criterion for class placement, language ability and, 35
cultural activism (in the USA), 85
cultural alienation, 85
cultural and linguistic competence, privileging types of, 41
cultural center (*bunka sentaa*), 50
cultural differences, expressions of, 4
cultural politics, definition of, 43
cultural practices, dis-inheriting of, 41
cultural return, heritage education and, 85
cultural tradition, linguistic practice and, 118
culture of power, 5
culture, essentialization of in minority education, 51; homogeneous conceptualizations of, 46
curriculum, Japanese government-prescribed, 84

de Lozada, Sanchez (Bolivian president), 19
de Saussure, Ferdinand, 3
dekasegi (sojourning), 20
dekasegi būmu (*dekasegi* fad), 20
diasporic spaces of belonging, 102
discourses of internationalization, bilingual Japanese Americans and, 92
disjuncture, awareness of, 121; concept of, 120
disjuncture, problematics of, 121
diversity in the classroom, teacher's feelings about, 83
dual heritage, 72

Ecuador, 109, 110

education in Japan, linguistic and cultural diversity and, 44
education of foreign residents (in Osaka), stated goals of, 47
educational practices, community and teachers views about, 57
eijū, 68
eisa dance, 17
empowerment, heritage language education and, 62
ethnic and national identities, in return-migration contexts, 86
ethnic and racial subjectivities, 109
ethnic club programs (after school), boundaries between students in, 61; ethnic identities and, 61, 62; goals and activities, 55; origins of, 54
ethnic cultures, views of in Japan, 59
ethnic group (*minzoku bukai*), 50
ethnic heritage classes (in Japan), 111
ethnic identities, education and the marking of, 57; essentializing of, 56
ethnic identity (aidentiti), teachers' understanding of, 55
ethnic identity, delineation of, 104
ethnic identity, retaining and nurturing of, 55
ethnic minorities and Japanese, boundaries between (in Japan), 44
ethnic socialization, forms of, 105
ethnic/class formations, nature of in Bolivia, 22
ethnically distinct names, uses of, 55, 58
ethnically mixed educational environment (Bolivia), cultural assimilation and, 14
ethnicity, discourses of, 111; indexing of, 112; national language and, 104
ethnocultural language, 118
ethnolinguistic belonging, 118
eugenics, 92
Euserka, 115
expatriate Japanese families (in the USA), 105
extranjeros (foreigners), in Bolivia, 23

family state (*kazoku kokka*), 10–11
first language, 118
food court multiculturalism, 90
foreign children (in Japan), national guidelines for assisting, 53

foreign children (in Miyako), categorization of, 53
foreign residents (in Japan), ratio of, 45
foreigners/foreign residents (in Japan), guidelines regarding, 47
foreign-ness, value of in Bolivia, 22
fūniki (shared and strange aura), 99

gaijin-tarento (foreign celebrity/television personality), 93
gaman (perseverance or endurance), 90
Gasa Gasa Girl, 90
global economic changes, Japanese Americans and, 91
Government of Ryūkyū Islands (GRI), 11, 19
government-sanctioned curriculum guidelines, 67
GRI. *See* Government of Ryūkyū Islands
guidelines for the education of foreign residents (*zainichi gaikokujin kyōiku shishin*), 47

hāhu (half Japanese and half non-Japanese) students, 72, 73
hegemonic structure, production and reproduction of, 43
heritage enterprise, role of individuals in, 42
heritage language and heritage, connection between, 86, 105, 113, 122
heritage language classes (at Tomoni), goals of, 52, 55
heritage language education, cultural identity and, 92; empowerment and, 86, 92, 101; factors affecting, 103, non-institutionalized programs, 39; political and historical forces affecting, 44; positive impacts of, 64, 101; research and, 84; tool of social mobilization or cultural maintenance, 110
heritage language educational programs, 1, 2; antihegemonic nature of, 3, 5; assumptions regarding, 8; attitudes toward, 27; financial benefits of, 21; ideological inconsistencies and tensions and, 27; politics of, 1; research on, 3; role of, 7, 85; role of in Bolivia, 13; school-based, 27
heritage language learner, definition of, 67

heritage language learning, diversity and, 104; involvement of immigrants/ethnic minorities in, 59
heritage language maintenance, deleterious effects of, 90
heritage language proficiency, promotion of, 64
heritage language teaching (*bogo shidō*), 48, 52, 109; aims of, 55; constitutive elements of, 54; effects of, 61, 65, 119; function of as a marker, 44; inheriting Japanese-ness in, 75; Japanese government support for, 66; legitimizing non-Japanese character and, 61; non-school programs and, 61; origins of (in Miyako), 50, 52; unintended effects of, 61; views of immigrant children about, 60
heritage language, acquisition of, 119; ambiguity about, 26; ambivalent feelings about, 59; assumptions regarding, 8;
burdens of, 102; conceptual component of, 117–118, 121; constitution of, 2, 27; defintions of, 7, 44, 86; differences in educational approaches, 67; emotional valence of, 87; immigrant and indigenous languages and, 7; individual's links with, 2; initiatives and programming, 118; leveraging of the term, 119; maintenance of, 87, 90; meaning of (for Peruvian youth), 27; national language and, 8; origins of, 85; politics of, 2, 42; reclaiming of, 108; regimentation and standardization of, 117; transformations of, 42; vulnerability and, 8
heritage learning, home and peer influences on, 40
heritage politics, manifestations of, 5
heritage practices, diversity of, 41; schools as sites of, 64; types of, 40
heritage tourism, 1
heritage, as alienation, 73; as alterity, 79; challenges to the concept of, 27; conceptualization of, 64; definition of, 1, 2, 23, 43; government prescriptions and, 80; local and transnational definitions of, 110; material and symbolic values of, 24; nationalism and, 1; nurturing of as act of social justice, 6;

objectification of, 1; owned or assigned, 59; sites for effective learning of, 40; standardization into, 70
Hirahara, Naomi, 89
homeland, heritage education and, 85, 122
homogenization of society, 60; globalization and, 60
Hontō Island (Okinawa), 11
hoshūkō (weekend supplemental Japanese language schools), 67, 68, 88, 119; diversity of students in, 67, 73, 74

identity, categories of, 111; definition of based on origins, 51; formation of, 60, 73; heritage and, 89
identity struggles (*yuragi*), 51
ideological regimentation, 120
ideology, power of, 121
immigrant heritage languages, 119
immigrant minority groups, heritage language education and, 7
immigrants (in Japan), 44; marginalizing of, 56; origins of, 44; pluralism and, 45
Immigration Control Act (1990 revision), 93
Immigration Control Law (Peru), 26
Imperial Japan, Okinawan immigration and, 10
indentured immigrants (to Peru), reasons for, 25
indexicality, 111
Indian Self-determination and Education Assistance Act (USA, 1975), 118
Indian-ness, conceptualizations of, 116
Indians in Unexpected Places, 116
indigeneity (in Andean region), 109
indigenous heritage languages, 119
indios, stigmitization of in Bolivia, 23
inheriting heritage, 65
institutionalized heritage language education, nature of, 41
Instruction and Advising Guidelines (Kyōiku Shidō Yōryō), 16
instructors, types of (in Bolivia), 15
international cooperation (*kokusai kyōryoku*), 46
international exchange (*kokusai kōryū*), 46, 50

interpellation, 65; heritage language education and, 66
Inuit peoples, 117
isomorphism of language, race, and nation, 94

Jackson Japanese Language School (JJLS), 66, 68
Japan Foundation, 21
Japan International Cooperation Agency (JICA), 12, 15, 18
Japan, homogeneity 47; monoethnic ideology in 60; monoethnicism and, 101; mythologization of, 101; registered foreigners in, 44
Japanese Americans, bilingualism and, 88; English language skills of, 99; heritage language and, 91, 92; internment of, 87; Japanese language and, 67; language and race politics and, 87; language maintenance and, 87, 101; language shift and, 87, 91; living in Japan, 86, 88, 92, 98, 112; opportunities for (in USA), 87; views of Japanese toward, 98
Japanese business community, overseas assignments and, 105
Japanese Canadian, identity of, 103
Japanese Chamber of Commerce in Chicago, 105
Japanese culture and language, ideology of blood and, 93
Japanese diasporas, formation of, 100
Japanese ethnos, 101
Japanese government, subsidies given by, 67, 105
Japanese heritage language education, language revitalization programs and, 122; origins of, 67; perceived benefits of, 18; preference for formal style (in CEA, Lima), 41; styles of, 34; Japanese immigrants (Peru), socioeconomic status of, 25
Japanese labor market, Okinawan-Bolivians entry into, 21
Japanese language acquisition, effects of, 92
Japanese language and culture, efforts to pass on, 41
Japanese language and identity, assumptions about, 93

Index

Japanese language aptitude tests, 39
Japanese language classes (*nihongo kyōshitsu*), 52; factors shaping, 54
Japanese language education, aims of (in CEA, Lima), 31; Japanese government support for, 105; in Nikkei-run schools in Peru, 25; student lack of enthusiasm for (in Lima, CEA), 37
Japanese Language Proficiency Examination (Nihon-go Nōryoku Kentei Shiken), 21
Japanese Language Proficiency Test (JLPT, nihon-go nōryoku shiken), 33
Japanese language proficiency, value of, 39
Japanese language schools (J-schools), 88
Japanese language teachers (in CEA), identity and training of, 29
Japanese Language Teaching Materials Donation Program, 15
Japanese language usage, students rules for (in CEA, Lima), 32
Japanese language, 40; standardization of, 4, 6; wartime prohibition against use of in Peru, 28
Japanese national identity, heritage language education and, 92
Japanese national language, transmission of to Colonia Okinawa, 16
Japanese nation-state, Okinawans and, 9, 17
Japanese popular culture, 39; incorporation into educational programs (in CEA, Lima), 40
Japanese society, heterogeneity of, 111
Japanese vernaculars, 41
Japanese, as a heritage language, 88; lexical use and significance of, 89; non-standard forms of, 38
Japanese, idealized national character of, 15
Japanese-ness, 66, 94, 105; characteristics of, 79; concepts of, 119; constitution of, 78; expressions of, 78; imagining and inheriting (in the USA), 64–65; 73, 77, 83; Japanese Americans and, 98; markers of, 79; negotiation of, 81; role of schools in fostering, 64; types of, 75; views of, 78; ways of relating to, 80
Japanization, 10
JICA. *See* Japan International Cooperation Agency

Kaigai Ijū Jigyōdan (KIJ, Overseas Migration Agency), 12
keishōgo (Japanese-as-a-heritage-language), 67, 68, 113
kokugo (national language/language arts), 4, 67, 113
Korea, Japanization and, 10
Korean American students, heritage language education and (in USA), 26, 38
Korean children (in Miyako), invisibility of, 51
Korean residents (in Japan), 111
kyōsei (co-living), 15
Kyoto-ben, 105

Lan, Pei-Chia, 8
language and identity, relationship between, 101, 104, 114
language ideologies, 4, 26, 91, 101, 102; (in Andrean region), 110; (in Japan), 86; effects of, 101; role of, 26; state power and, 109
language planning, government regimentation of, 121
language revitalization programs (Native Americans), 122
language shift, 86, 117, 120; (among Japanese Americans), reasons for, 88; ethnic affiliation and, 89; mitigation of, 85
language shyness, 100
language socialization, 98, 117, 119, 120; politics and consequences of, 107
language, cultural scholarship on, 109; idealized notions of, 108; language, identity, and power, interrelations among, 109; means of political control, 101; relations of domination and, 109; standardization processes of, 65; valuations of, 109
Lee Yangji (novelist), 107
liberal multiculturalism (in Australia), 46
Lifestyle Reform Movement (seikatsu kaizen undō), 11
Lima, Peru, Nikkei schools in, 28
linguistic birthrights, 92

linguistic choices, factors influencing, 107
linguistic community, standardization and, 4
linguistic diversity, 3, 7
linguistic hegemony, Japanese state promotion of, 115
linguistic heritage, association with Japanese nation-state, 17
linguistic hierarchies, 109–10, 115
linguistic identity positions, construction of, 111
linguistic identity, belonging and, 96
linguistic immersion, forms of, 105
linguistic performance, management of, 122
linguistic practice and social context, links between, 119
linguistic revitalization, hegemonic dimensions of, 110
linguistic variations, valuing of, 26
local language politics, heritage and, 105

"majority," usage of the term, 85
Manchuria, 10
manga (comic books), 39, 40, 72, 91, 105, 114
mass schooling, effects of, 65
meanings of the past, understanding of, 43
Meiji Restoration, 100
Meiji-era practices and values, 100
meta-cultural awareness, 64, 73, 84
meta-linguistic discourses, 87, 94
Micronesia, 10
Micronesia, Okinawan émigrés in, 11
migrant laborers in Japan, from Peru, 26; from South America, 44
Ministry of Education, 53, 59
Ministry of Internal Affairs and Communications (MIC), 45
Ministry of Justice (Japan), 44
minorities, discourses about, 85
minoritized ethnic populations, 87
minoritized identities, meaning and value of term, 86
minority education, effects of, 60; essentializing practices of, 55; goals of, 55
minority language education, 2, 118
minority languages, maintenance of, 4

"minority," usage of the term, 85
minoritized/minority language, 7
Miyazaki Karitasu Shūdōjo-kai (Caritas Sisters of Miyazaki), 13
monoethnicism (*tannitsu minzoku shugi*), 45
monolingualism, 5
mother tongue, constitution of, 2; teaching, 58, 117–18
multicultural education in schools, marginalization and, 62
multicultural education programs (in Miyako), nature of, 54
multicultural education, approaches and modalities of, 46; ambivalent feelings about, 59
Multiculturalism Act (Canada, 1988), 118
multiculturalism, celebration of, 107; coexistence (*tabunka kyōsei*) and, 45; debates about, 91; globalization and, 60; simplistic conceptualization of, 90
multiculturalism (in Japan), 44, 45, 89, 111, 115; forms of, 46; limited nature of, 62
multiculturalist ideologies, 85, 113
multilingualism, celebration of, 107; suspicions about, 4
museum exhibitions, representations of heritage in, 1

Naichi-jin, 10
Naichi-jin, status of Okinawans and, 11
naming (*nazuke*), by outsiders, 61
nation, definition of, 3
national belonging, factors influencing students' sense of, 68
national identity, construction and maintenance of, 86
nationalism, Japanese ideologies of, 113
nationality, categorizing according to, 65
Native Americans, 105, 116
native language, attitudes toward, 105; constitution of, 2
native speaker status, 120
native speaker, homogeneous language and, 2
navigation of identities, language use and, 112
neoliberalization, 91
Nichibo Kyōkai, 13, 14; Japanese support for, 18

nihon-gaeri (returnee students), 33
nihonjinron, 98, 100
Nikkei (in Japan), 88, 93; (in Peru), effects on schools of emigration to Japan, 29; (in Peru), emigration to Japan, 29, 41
Nikkei identity, maintenance of through education, 29
Nikkei institutions (Peru), schools and, 28
Nikkei parents (Peru), educational preferences of, 30
Nikkei Peruvian youth, languages used by, 25
Nikkei Peruvians, 25, 112; collective identity of, 25; institutions established by, 25; migration patterns of, 26
Nikkei returneees to Peru, 41
Nikkei schools (Peru), heritage language education programs in, 41; Japanese language education programs in, 41
Nikkei, Okinawan-Bolivian children's subjectivity and, 15
Nikkeijin accent, 96
Nikkeijin visa, 93
Nikkei-run schools (Peru), language education in, 28
Nikkeis (in Japan), 86
Nisei (second generation), 88
non-Buraku Japanese, 47
non-Nikkei Bolivians, 13, 109
non-Nikkei majority (Peru), 25
non-Nikkei students (in CEA, Lima), 29

Ohnuki-Tirney, Emiko, 77
Okinawa Nihon Boribia Kyōkai (Japan-Bolivia Association of Okinawa), 13
Okinawa Uno Japanese-Bolivian school (Colegio Particular Mixto Centro Boliviano Japones Okinawa Numero Uno (CBJ), 14
Okinawa, emigration from, 9; Imperial Japan and, 9, 10, 17; reversion to Japan of, 12; U.S. military occupation of, 9, 11
Okinawan, community in Peru, 105; diaspora, 7, 9; diasporic community, in Bolivia, 23; emigration, promotion of, 12; identity, 105; immigrants in Bolivia, 2; languages, origins of, 9; traditional arts, 17

Okinawan settlers in Bolivia, citizenship of, 12; economic prosperity of, 18
Okinawan-Bolivian children, heritage language and, 16
Okinawan-Bolivians, 13; dependence on Japanese state, 20; relations with non-Nikkei Bolivians, 21; student performance of, 14
Okinawan-Bolivians' economic assets, Japanese government protection of, 19
Okinawans, emigration destinations, 10; reasons for emigration, 10
one nation/one language, 4, 115
Orientalist discourses, 100
Osaka, 43; dialect, 70, 71, 114; ethnic diversity in, 47; immigrant children in, 44
overseas emigration (Okinawa), effects of, 10; extent of, 10

Passeron, Jean-Claude, 65
patrones Japonesas (Japanese farm owners), 13, 22
performativity, 65, 73, 86
personal identity, heritage and, 43
Peru, 110; Japanese immigrants in, 25, 109; Okinawan émigrés in, 11
political economy of language, 110
politics of difference, 4
politics of heritage, legitimization of power and distinction and, 44
pop culture, 91
private and public language, 107

Quechua, 109, 110

racial and ethnic discourses, situatedness of, 111
racial identification, systems of, 112
racism (institutionalized), 90
radio taiso (warm-up exercises), 28
recurrent migration, 26
rediscovery of heritage, political meanings attached to, 62
regime of translation, 100
regimentation, re-imagining processes of, 116
regimes of difference, 65, 66, 74, 80, 82–83; naturalization and materialization of, 65

resident Koreans (in Japan), 47; Buraku community and, 48
return migration, 91
returnee students from Japan, 27; classroom cooperative strategies of, 40; educational motivations of, 37; effects on schools in Peru, 26; impact on classroom teaching, 40; in Peruvian secondary schools, 30, 33; Japanese popular culture and, 39; personal forms of language expression, 38; relations with teachers, 34, 42; (re)-learning Japanese, 33, 41; reluctance to use Japanese, 37; use of Japanese by (in Peru), 26
Reversing Language Shift, 119
rice, Japanese view regarding, 77
Robertson, Jennifer, 92
root languages (*ruutsu-go*), 51
Ryūkyū Kingdom, 9
Ryūkyū Shobun (Ryūkyū Disposition), 10
Ryūkyūan, 105

Sansei (third generation), 89
sanshin (a stringed musical instrument), 17
Santa Cruz region (Bolivia), 12
schema of cofiguration, 100
scholarships, for study and training in Japan, 39
school-based heritage education philosophy, negative effects of, 41
schooling process, as heritage practice, 84
schools, as legitimizers, 65; as sites of ideological struggles, 65; differentiation of students in, 65
second language education, heritage language and, 85
self-identity, language and, 104
self-presentation, linguistic strategies for, 95

semiotic bundling, 117
settlers, status of in Santa Cruz, Bolivia, 12
shimedaiko drums, 17
Shin-niseis, 91
Sino-Japan War, 4
social relationships and contexts, language use in, 111

sociality, hierarchical, authoritative structuring of, 121
sociolinguistic disjuncture, 117
Spanish, preference for (in Peru) over Japanese, 31
spatialization, language learning and, 122
speakers of minority languages, discrimination against, 105
Special Measures Legislation (1969), 50
Standard Japanese, 4, 38, 110; benefits attached to speaking, 23; imperative to learn, 20
standard national language, imposition of, 105; language ideology and, 4
standardization, student interactions, 81
student interactions, effects and influences, 75
Study Group on Promoting Tabunka Kyōsei, 45
subject positions, schools as nurturers of, 65
subject-position, Okinawans and, 11
subjects, Althusser and, 65; subjects, constitution of, 66
Swardspeak, 101
systems of categories, 65

tabunka kyōsei shakai, 45
Taiwan, 10
textbooks, Japanese government certified, 68
three-generation model, language shift and, 88
Tigner, James L., 12
Tokyo dialect, 71
Tomoni, foundation and goals of, 49
transnational lived histories, 38
transnational political economies, linguistic hierarchies and, 109
transnational subjectivities, as disruptive agents, 86; constitution of, 86

U.S. Civil Administration of the Ryukyu Islands (Uscar), 11
U.S. military bases in Okinawa, expansion of, 12; Okinawans and, 11
Uchināguchi, 8, 17, 23, 109; standard Japanese vs., 21
undokai, 40
Unesco, 1, 2

Volkgeist, 3
von Herder, Johann Gottfried, 3

Weiner, Michael, 92
world heritage designation, 1, 2

youth, ethnographic and analytical perspectives on, 113

zainichi, 107